Collegiate Architecture and Landscape in the West

WILLAMETTE UNIVERSITY, 1842-2012

Collegiate Architecture and Landscape in the West

WILLAMETTE UNIVERSITY, 1842-2012

William F. Willingham, Ph.D.

Hallie Ford Museum of Art
Willamette University
Salem, Oregon

700 State Street
Salem, OR 97301

Front cover: Waller and Eaton Halls from across the quad.
Back cover: Hudson Bay viewed from the West. Both courtesy Frank Miller, Willamette University.

Designed by: Mariane Zenker, Bryan Potter Design, Portland, Oregon.

Printed in Canada by Friesens Corporation.

ISBN: 978-1-93095-781-7

Library of Congress Control Number: 2018964149

Table of Contents

Editorial Note about Building Descriptions

In building descriptions, if an element no longer exists as designed, we use past tense. This results in a few descriptions in which present and past tense are mixed. We feel, however, that this strategy provides for the most accuracy while maintaining brevity.

We have been careful to refer to buildings by the name(s) to which they were referred in the period which is being described. Thus, for example, you might encounter Music School, School of Music, Music Hall, or simply Music, within the same discussion.

Table of Articles and Sidebars

Introduction

The founding of Willamette University in 1842 marked the shift in the educational efforts of the Methodist missionaries in the Oregon Country from focusing on educating and converting Native Americans to Protestant Christianity to providing higher education to Euro-American settlers. In carrying out this new mission, the university ultimately developed a campus of 61 acres containing 46 buildings by 2012. This study describes and evaluates the buildings and landscape that were designed and constructed over time, identifying architects, styles, and purposes. The book also delineates the university's physical expansion by describing and analyzing the landscape elements of the campus. In addition, by examining the development of these buildings and grounds in a regional and national context, we can see how the educational processes in this and similar institutions of higher education have evolved over time. This study demonstrates how the architecture and landscape of Willamette University are more than a reflection of the institution. By understanding what is typical and atypical about Willamette's physical development, we can see how the growth of its physical elements and the architectural and design decisions made over time have helped to shape Willamette's current place in higher education.

A series of key questions guide the research and writing of this study. For example, it is necessary to explain the decision making leading to specific buildings and their construction, their initial purpose, and why and how usage often changed across time. Information on the funding, construction, architectural style, and functions of each building provides a starting point for the discussion of the evolving built environment.

Facing page: Lausanne Hall

The basic background information on buildings and their setting leads to a discussion of how the buildings influenced the educational and social life of the students. The buildings, after all, provide the setting for what the university is all about—shaping young minds toward fulfilling and useful lives.

Other questions to consider include:

» What were the administrators', students', and professors' expectations for the educational facilities, and did their assumptions change over time?

» Did the buildings prove adequate to the university's educational mission?

» How difficult was the fundraising, and what strategies did administrators use to meet the challenges of expanding the campus?

» How systematic and forward-thinking was the planning that went into the development of the campus?

» How do alumni use their recollection of the physical sense of the campus to maintain their ties to the university?

Finally, the study reveals the interplay across time between the individuals who plan, finance, and build the buildings and the students and professors who use them. The buildings and landscape elements of the Willamette campus have an instructive story to tell, and this book attempts to relate it.

Any book about architecture that did not contain appropriate illustrations would be seriously deficient. Accordingly, this study makes generous use of graphic elements such as historic and present-day photographs, drawings, and maps. Archival and pertinent secondary sources form the basis of the research materials used to develop and document the narrative. Where appropriate, the book makes use of oral interviews with the architects and university administrators involved in the recent history of the university's development.

Some explanation is necessary to make clear the criteria used in this work to describe and evaluate the campus architecture of Willamette. In simplest terms, a campus is a collection of buildings, landscapes, and infrastructure arranged to further the purposes of higher education. The idea of campus architecture, therefore, encompasses the purposeful or planned engagement and integration of buildings and landscape to achieve an educational mission. Good planning requires a consistent use of place *making*, which is the articulation of building groups and structures, landscapes, and circulation patterns set in response to site conditions, programmatic and functional relationships, and desired visual sequencing. Carefully considered master plans can help achieve this goal, but much change, for better or worse, also happens serendipitously. So much depends of the decision-making process employed by the key parties involved in planning: trustees, administrators, architects, faculty, donors, and students, and whether the decisions about buildings and landscape were made collaboratively or imposed by a few key players. This study seeks to reveal how that process has played out at Willamette.[1]

In addition, place *marking* is necessary to strengthen and connect the overall design pattern and give it a visual character. For example, place *marking* at Willamette includes the consistent use of materials, such as the red brick applied on most university buildings; the application of a continuity of style, such as variations on the Georgian; the focus on a heritage building as an institutional symbol, such as the treatment of Waller Hall; or attention to a landscape element such as the clock tower and surrounding plaza in front of the Mark O. Hatfield Library. All of these design elements help to reinforce a sense of place and create a readily recognized institutional character.

Finally, campus design has been influenced increasingly by environmental awareness and technology. In fact, these two elements considered together can have a profound impact on how a college or university carries out its mission of transmitting knowledge through teaching, research, and community service. In addition, the proper uses of environmentally-sustainable building and maintenance practices can help to tame or humanize technology-driven learning. Hopefully, students surrounded by carefully crafted and vital campus architecture will come to understand the value of good design and a healthy environment.

It is important to keep in mind that the creation and development of campus architecture is a never-completed process. New methods of teaching, research, and community service may demand altered concepts of what is appropriate in building and landscape design for the ever-evolving educational mission of the university. By understanding Willamette University's experience with creating a campus architecture, we can better identify the fundamental factors that go into creating a built and landscape environment that successfully serves the educational mission.

The research and writing of this book took much longer than I originally anticipated. The process began in 2006 when the then dean of the College of Liberal Arts, Carol Long, asked me to write a book about the architecture of Willamette University. I had just completed a stint as a visiting professor in the Willamette history department and at the time was working on several other book projects. The idea of a book about Willamette's architecture, however, appealed to me. As a Willamette alumnus and an architectural historian, I felt a special attraction to the subject, and I knew that a number of prominent architects had designed campus buildings. I thought it would be of interest to explain how their work was put in the service of higher education at Willamette. So, I agreed to undertake the project and moved it into the queue along with my other book projects at the time.

Fortunately, at the very moment I started researching the Willamette architecture book, the university administration had finally established a university archive and hired a full-time professional archivist to head up the program. In the past, unfortunately, the university had treated its records rather cavalierly and many had become lost or destroyed. For example, when the university refurbished the interior of Eaton Hall in 1983, ledgers containing early Board of Trustees' minutes were inadvertently thrown out and lost. I should mention, on the other hand, that Robert Gatke, long-time Willamette history professor, fortuitously had access to some early records that have subsequently gone missing. He made copies or took notes on such records and, since his files were in the Willamette archives, I was able to use them in my research. As the new archivist, Mary McRobinson, and her staff began gathering and organizing records from across the campus, I was able to participate in the process and have access to a range of materials that would otherwise have been unavailable. Without the unflagging assistance and support of Mary, this book could never have been written.

Other key assistance over the course of the project has come from Kristi Negri and Professor Emeritus Roger Hull of the art history department. As the project editor and a dear friend, Kristi read and suggested many improvements to the text. She wields a sharp editorial pen. In addition, she played a major role in the design and layout of the book. Roger Hull also read early drafts of chapters and made valuable suggestions. His perspective on campus architecture was especially useful, since he observed and at times participated in shaping the design of the buildings added during the 1980s and 1990s.

David McCreery, professor emeritus, took me on an extremely informative campus tour, showing me, among other things, the original position of the Oregon Institute building. Ron Nichols was a wealth of information about the grounds.

During the middle stages of the project, Marlene Moore, Dean of the College of Liberal Arts following Carol Long, continued to provide support and encouragement. Additional assistance came from Jan Gardner, Director of Facilities at Willamette, who gave me access to his records of campus buildings; they contained information not otherwise available. A special thanks to Shelby Radcliffe in the Willamette Development Office for getting behind the project. Serendipitously, near the end of the process, Carol Long returned to Willamette as Senior Vice President for Academic and Student Affairs, thus bringing the endeavor full circle. Finally, to do research on the Willamette University buildings designed by Pietro Belluschi, I received the help of Nicole Dittrich of the Special Collections Research Center, Syracuse University Library. While all of these individuals deserve credit for making this a better book, I alone am responsible for whatever shortcomings remain.

I also want to acknowledge a number of Willamette alumni who, in response to an appeal from Roger Hull, financially contributed to the project in its initial stage. I sincerely thank them for their early confidence that this was a worthwhile project to support. They are Margaret Moreland, Nathan Sonstegard, Ellen Stevens, Daniel and Doreen Hagelin, Carrie Lee Patterson, and Lisa Borok.

Endnotes

1 This and the following paragraph draw on the ideas of Richard P. Dober, *Campus Architecture: Building in the Groves of Academe* (New York, McGraw Hill, Co., 1996), 157-94.

The author wishes to thank the many architects, planners and construction staff who have not only contributed to the historic campus described in this book, but who also gave their time and philanthropic support to help bring the project to fruition. With special gratitude to Peggy Tasker and Bob Packard at ZGF Architects, Tim Eddy and David Wark at Hennebery Eddy, Jon Weiner at SRG Partnership, Dan Danielson at Soderstrom Architects, and the Drinkward family at Hoffman Construction.

All book proceeds will be directed to the Willamette University Archives in recognition of their invaluable partnership, and to support opportunities for Willamette students to learn, preserve and tell the stories that have shaped the university for generations.

1

The Founding of Willamette University

Willamette University emerged in the 1840s as the product of the cultural phenomenon known as the American college movement. College-founding became something of a "cottage industry" in the United States during the first half of the nineteenth century. In 1800, for example, the new nation had 25 degree-granting institutions of higher education. By 1820, the number had increased to 52, while in 1860 the total reached 241. Many of these were church-related colleges, and the founding of Willamette University in 1842 and its subsequent growth was typical of the development of such institutions. During this era, numerous states chartered other colleges, often with a more secular orientation, adding to the opportunities for higher learning in the new nation.[1]

The drive on the part of various Protestant denominations to found colleges or universities in the early years of the new nation was one manifestation of the religious enthusiasm known as the Second Great Awakening. The reinvigorated churches hoped that these newly established colleges would lead the battle against the dark forces of atheism and deism. The magnitude of the effort was apparent from the fact that, of the 78 colleges operating in 1840, fully 35 were denominational institutions created after 1830. In all, the various Protestant denominations initiated 180 colleges between 1820 and 1860.

Methodists, in particular, competed fiercely in the drive to found colleges. As early as 1824, the Methodist General Conference voted to establish at least one college in each of its conferences, with special attention to the needs of western settlements. The success of the Methodists was apparent from the fact that, by 1860, their colleges accounted for 34 (21 percent) of the 160

Facing page: Waller Hall in early days

denominational institutions of higher education in existence. Overcoming an earlier disdain for a learned clergy, the Methodists, by the 1820s, had embraced the notion of an educated ministry and desired to have the colleges providing that training under their control rather than in the hands of competing denominations. This would ensure doctrinal purity. At the same time, they asserted that whatever other religious denominations might do, Methodist colleges would operate on a non-sectarian basis, opening their doors to all comers.[2]

Another aspect of the religious awakening of the early nineteenth century that influenced denominational college-founding was the strong, evangelistic missionary zeal it promoted. Methodists, along with other Protestant churches felt that education and religion would help to bring order to the newly settled West. Eastern religious leaders believed that Protestant higher education was a major tool in establishing culture and godliness among what they perceived as the raw, disorderly conditions of life on the western frontier. Over time, these church-related colleges afforded the youth of a rapidly growing population, widely scattered across an expanding nation, an education fitting them to take advantage of the nascent business and professional opportunities of the new nation.

Finally, college-founding also played a role in another phenomenon of American expansion during the early national period, known as "civic boosterism." As new towns sprang up across Ohio, Michigan, and Illinois, they competed with one another to attract settlers. The ability to claim the cultural and educational opportunities afforded by having a college provided a leg up in the town-building competition. New colleges, moreover, could also benefit in this competition if they had surplus land to sell to the newly arriving settlers in a rising community. Town and college growth proved to be a mutually supportive process and one pursued with great optimism. As one historian of American higher education noted

> *College-founding in the nineteenth century was undertaken in the same spirit as canal-building, cotton-ginning, farming, and gold-mining. In none of these activities did completely rational procedures prevail. All were touched by the American faith in tomorrow, in the unquestionable capacity of Americans to accept a better world. In the founding of colleges reason could not combat the romantic belief in endless progress.*

Establishing colleges was just one more aspect of national ambition in the first half of the nineteenth century.[3]

American collegiate architecture and planning developed to fit the distinctively American ways of higher education that emerged in the eighteenth and nineteenth centuries. Initially rooted in the English university model, where students and teachers lived and studied together in small tightly controlled colleges, American institutions of higher education provided not only classrooms and other academic spaces, but also, whenever possible, dormitories, chapels, dining halls, and recreation facilities. In effect, the physical implementation of the American college or university's goals was as a community unto itself.

In carrying out this ideal, Americans—reflecting the dispersed nature of their new nation—departed from the English tradition by establishing many colleges in separate locations across the land. Often, these new schools were located in a rural setting, distant from cities or towns. Another distinctive aspect of the American college or university was its spaciousness and openness, with buildings set in a broad green, which contrasted with the European tradition of

This depiction of Jefferson's Academical Village in this Tanner engraving from the 1820s shows the rotunda, lawn, professors' housing and classrooms at University of Virginia.

cloistered buildings forming an enclosed quadrangle. American colleges and universities tended to be physically outward looking rather than inward. Over time, the American campus would be shaped more by unique American social, economic, and cultural forces than by English or European precedents.[4]

Thomas Jefferson's plan for the University of Virginia (1817) took the idea of a collegiate community and gave it a uniquely American expression, which would have a lasting influence on American college and university planning. Jefferson's scheme consisted of a series of professors' houses, alternating with clusters of students' rooms, along the colonnaded sides of a mall, terminating at one end in a domed library and flanked on the sides by gardens and outer rows of buildings.

While probably influenced by his own collegiate experience at the College of William and Mary, Jefferson also drew upon his ideas about a democratic educational system fitted to American circumstances and on his European tours, which had given him the opportunity to closely observe examples of Classical architecture. His ideas for an "Academical Village" for the University of Virginia brought all of these sources together, creating educational pavilions set in an expansive green that united professors and students in a familial relationship. As architectural writer Paul Turner has noted, Jefferson's "notion of a collegiate town, composed of independent buildings

The Pre-Euro American Setting

When Jason Lee planted his Methodist mission on the banks of the Willamette River a few miles north of modern-day Salem, he was, according to his lights, going to bring salvation to the native populations and educate their children. Lee's mission was of mixed success at best, but, through the written records of those who accompanied him, we have insights into the Kalapuya people who gathered camas root, fished the streams, and inhabited large swaths of the valley and foothills. Chemeketa Plain, on which Willamette stands, was their home for many thousands of years, nearby Pringle and Mill Creeks being natural sites for encampments and gatherings. The descendants of the Kalapuyan people encountered by Jason Lee are today members of the Confederated Tribes of the Grand Ronde.

Thanks to Professor David McCreery's classes in archaeological methodology, we have tantalizing glimpses into the campus's geological heritage as well. In 2000, his class discovered casts and parts of the trunk of a large preserved tree under Smith Auditorium. The tree was approximately 36 inches across and about 300 years old, and had probably been 180 to 200 feet tall when it fell. The sediment that encased it suggested that it had fallen into a bed of gravel and was quickly covered by several feet of mud and silt. The tree that had been a sapling sometime between 1150 and 1250 AD fell just before, or as a result of, a large flooding event sometime in the sixteenth century, an event much larger than the flood of recent memory that occurred in 1996, that also impacted the campus.

And there the tree rested until 1938, when a Willamette University football stadium was built on the site. That venture and the later construction of Smith Auditorium in the same location in 1955 cut into the tree but did not otherwise disturb a large section and casts which McCreery's class was able to study. (The Summer 2002 issue of *Willamette Journal* contains a detailed description of this dig.)

But of course, prehistory contains many thousands of dramatic geological events on our site. The most notable of these was the Missoula Flood, which occurred in the late Pleistocene, between 15,000 and 12,000 years ago when ice dams east of the present-day Columbia River gorge broke free, carved out the gorge, and created a 400-foot-deep lake that extended from present-day Portland south to Eugene. At the site of the Willamette campus, the silts from this massive body of water accumulated to a depth of over three-and-a-half meters. Beneath that silt is a thick layer of gravel that had been deposited prior to the flood by the North Santiam River, which flowed through the site of today's campus from 15,000 to 35,000 years ago. The Missoula Flood naturally impacted the topography of the valley, and after the lake waters receded, the North Santiam, its course changed, emptied into the Willamette River south of Jefferson, and its old stream bed was taken over by the Mill Stream.

around a village green, with the possibility of growth by extension, suited the American College perfectly ... [and] seems to embody ... the ideal of an intimate and enlightened dialogue between students and teachers."[5]

Regardless of where located, most small denominational colleges and universities began with one all-purpose building. Designed usually in either a Classical or Gothic Revival style, the building housed classrooms, library, chapel, administrative offices, and even lodgings for professors and some students. This arrangement provided the setting for a close-knit relationship between student and teacher and emphasized the home-like, moral character of the school. It also reflected the limited financial resources of most such institutions of higher education in their early years. Some new colleges and universities with stronger financial backing created more lavish campus plans and constructed high-style buildings from designs by architects such as Alexander Jackson Davis and Andrew Jackson Downing, but these were the exceptions. The simple educational demands of the classical liberal arts curriculum did not require elaborate building projects.[6]

When a group of determined Methodist missionaries laid the foundation for Willamette University in 1842, prospects for an institution of higher learning hardly seemed auspicious. Scarcely 200 Euro-Americans resided on the Pacific Slope, and a series of deadly epidemics had decimated the Native American population. Eight years previously, in 1834, Reverend Jason Lee and his ordained nephew, Daniel Lee, with the help of three lay members, had established a mission society 10 miles north of the present site of Salem and begun attempting to convert the Native Americans settled nearby. Although his missionary efforts over the next few years produced few converts, Reverend Lee convinced his East Coast backers, the Missionary Society of the Methodist Episcopal Church, to invest more resources in the undertaking. In 1839, the Missionary Society sent 53 persons (36 adults and 17 children) with sufficient supplies and farming equipment to expand the Willamette Mission and to aid the outlying missionary stations at The Dalles and Astoria. The revitalized Willamette Mission proved more successful at farming than converting and educating the local Native American population. The settlers' children often outnumbered the natives being taught at the mission school.[7]

Between 1842 and 1844, almost 2,000 American immigrants crossed the plains to the Willamette Valley, setting the stage for the mass migrations of the ensuing 18 years. This growing community became concerned for the education of its children. As Reverend Gustavus Hines of the Willamette Mission put it, "Children and youth were becoming somewhat numerous, and were growing up in comparative ignorance, and the general voice seemed to call loudly upon the friends of science to make one united effort in some way to furnish means to supply the pressing educational demands of the infant though rising colony." In response to this concern, and the expectation that the brewing Oregon Fever would soon be bringing thousands of immigrants to the Willamette Valley, Jason Lee called a general meeting of interested settlers and members of the Mission at his home in what is now North Salem on January 12, 1842 to discuss the subject of education in Oregon. The discussion resulted in a committee of three to prepare for a later, widely publicized meeting to be held on February 1, 1842 at the original mission house at Garrison's Landing.[8]

Those friends of education attending the February meeting, after a thorough canvass of the difficulties involved, "unanimously resolved ...," as Gustavus Hines later wrote, "to establish a collegiate institution for the benefit of the rising generation of Oregon." After further discussion, the meeting voted to call the new institution the Oregon Institute and elected the first Board of Trustees to consist of the Reverends Jason Lee, David Leslie, Gustavus Hines, Josiah Parrish, and Lewis Judson; and laymen George Abernathy, Alanson Beers, Hamilton Campbell, and Dr. Ira Babcock. Before breaking up, the meeting also formed a committee to find a suitable location for the educational operation. Initially, the committee selected a site called Wallace Prairie, about 2.5 miles below, or north of, Salem.[9]

Left: Rev. Jason Lee, 1803-1845, the Methodist minister who founded the Willamette Mission, which eventually became the Oregon Institute and then Willamette University. **Right:** Rev. Gustavus Hines, 1809-1873, Methodist minister, founding trustee of Willamette University and author of *Oregon and Its Institutions*.

On March 9, 1842, the Board of Trustees met to establish a committee to draft a constitution, bylaws, and prospectus for the Oregon Institute. One week later, on March 15, the board adopted the work of the committee, announcing the prospectus:

> *Whereas it is believed to be highly important, and indispensably necessary to the future welfare of this rising community, that a permanent literary institution be established in this valley, of such a*

Left: Rev. David Leslie, 1797-1869, influential in the founding of Willamette University and in early Oregon government. **Right:** George Abernathy, 1807-1877, a trustee of the Oregon Institute and the first governor of Oregon's provisional government.

character as fully to meet the present and prospective wants of the children and youth of Oregon, in which they may receive that intellectual and moral training which alone can prepare them for respectability and usefulness; therefore a respectable number of the inhabitants of the Willamette settlement have entered into arrangements for the purpose of raising funds and carrying into operation a respectable boarding school.[10]

Most importantly, the prospectus went on to announce, "It is also contemplated, as soon as the community and the resources of the institution shall justify it, that it will become a university. The contemplated institution is to be called the 'Oregon Institute.'" Twenty-two individuals immediately subscribed almost $4,000. to fund a boarding school. The Institute's constitution stated that the project would not go into effect, nor would the subscriptions be payable, until a Protestant Christian church stepped forward with a pledge to sustain the school. This matter was resolved when both ministers and laymen of the Methodist Episcopal Church of Oregon met at the Willamette Mission on October 26, 1842, and unanimously voted to "pledge ourselves to make every reasonable effort to sustain the Oregon Institute." A subsequent general meeting of the Methodist Episcopal Church and community on May 29, 1843 reaffirmed the previous commitment to assume responsibility for the Oregon Institute.[11]

While members of the Willamette Mission and others addressed the educational needs of the growing community of settlers in the Willamette Valley, Lee returned east in 1843 to answer the concerns raised by the Methodist Missionary Board about conditions at the Willamette Mission. While there, he was replaced as leader of the Mission, and never returned to Oregon.

The board sent a new superintendent, George Gary, in 1844 to evaluate the operation of the Willamette Mission and the continuing viability of its Native American manual labor school. Gary, after a thorough canvass of the situation, decided to close the Mission and the school for Native Americans and sell the property connected with the school. Built in 1842 for a cost of $10,000 at the mission's relocated site in present-day Salem, the Greek Revival styled, three-story school building was the most imposing structure of its kind in the Pacific Northwest. One mission employee referred to it as "the big Castle."

The building was located roughly at the site of present-day Smullin and Walton Halls extending into the sidewalk area and stretching back toward the Lee Pelton Theatre building. A plaque inside Smullen near the West entrance marks the approximate location of the front door of the Oregon Institute building. Additionally, across State Street and to the West of Ford Hall is a narrow strip of sidewalk that crosses the grassy margin. It was in a line with a sidewalk on the campus side of the street that lead straight into the building.

Gary offered the building and 640 acres to the trustees of the Oregon Institute for $4,000. The trustees accepted this offer and sold the Institute's property below Salem for $3,000. By these transactions, the Indian Mission School became the Oregon Institute.[12]

Reverend Hines congratulated his fellow trustees on their fine purchase and in the process revealed a bit of anti-Catholic bias. He wrote,

> *It may be properly observed, that Mr. Gary had an opportunity to sell the Mission School property to the Catholics for double the amount that he was to receive for it from the trustees of the Institute, but in that case it would have been converted into a nunnery; and every evangelical Christian will say, 'Rather destroy it entirely than desecrate it to so impious a purpose.' For the promotion of the interest of the Church of Christ, and for the general welfare of this rising country, a more judicious appropriation of the property could not have been made than to place it in the hands of the trustees of the Oregon Institute.*[13]

Much of the building's interior remained unfinished at the time of purchase, but the Board of Trustees wasted little time initiating a school for white children in the Willamette Valley. They hired Mrs. Chloe Clarke Willson to begin classes on August 13, 1844. Her husband, William Willson, remarked to a friend at the time that "it appears to be the general wish that Mrs. Willson should go into the Institute and if she does you know I must remain somewhere about." She had arrived in Oregon in 1839 as a member of the "Great Reinforcement" of missionaries and others who came aboard the ship *Lausanne*. Willson began her duties with great trepidation, confiding in her diary, "Tuesday morning commence School with five

The Oregon Institute building

The Oregon Institute

The well-proportioned wood-frame, end-gabled structure, sheathed in white painted clapboards measured 75 feet in length and 48 feet in width, including two 24-square-foot wings. Multi-lighted, double-hung windows symmetrically graced the front face of the Greek Revival building. Pilaster corner boards and a plain entablature provided the finishing details of the structure. A centrally-placed short, square bell tower with corner finials surmounted the roof.

Chloe Clark Willson, 1818-1874, the first instructor at the Oregon Institute.

scholars I feel the weight of responsibility which rests upon me in giving character to this infant Institution." By August 21, she wrote, "I have 9 in school now and so far things go on much to my mind." On September 15, she confidently noted that "the number in my school has increased to 13 I feel that I am in the path of duty and the Lord blesses me in it." In April 1845, she began her second term of school, thanking God in her diary "for thy goodness and blessing which crowned my efforts during the first term." Her diary indicated that Willson continued teaching at the Institute for a number of years with great satisfaction.[14]

In order to pay for finishing the interior of the Institute building and financing the school's operations, the trustees developed a plan to lay out a city and sell lots on the land claim that had come with the building purchase. The timing for this scheme seemed appropriate as a large immigration arrived in the Willamette Valley during 1845 and the land around the Institute was soon taken up. After the trustees had the claim surveyed in 1846, they had to deal with the issue of their title to the land. The existing provisional government in Oregon had not provided for the incorporation of public bodies such as the Oregon Institute. This forced the trustees to seek other means to protect the Institute's land holdings, as many recent settlers questioned its right to hold the land and threatened to "jump" the claim. The cloud on the title also made it impossible for the trustees to pass clear ownership to potential purchasers of town lots. Fortunately, a solution to the trustees' dilemma existed, as the Provisional Government had passed a law allowing the holding of land by a partnership of persons. Supporters of the Institute held the land claims that surrounded its land. These four individuals agreed to extend their claims to cover those of the Institute and have the new holding recorded as a partnership claim. The individuals then gave bonds to

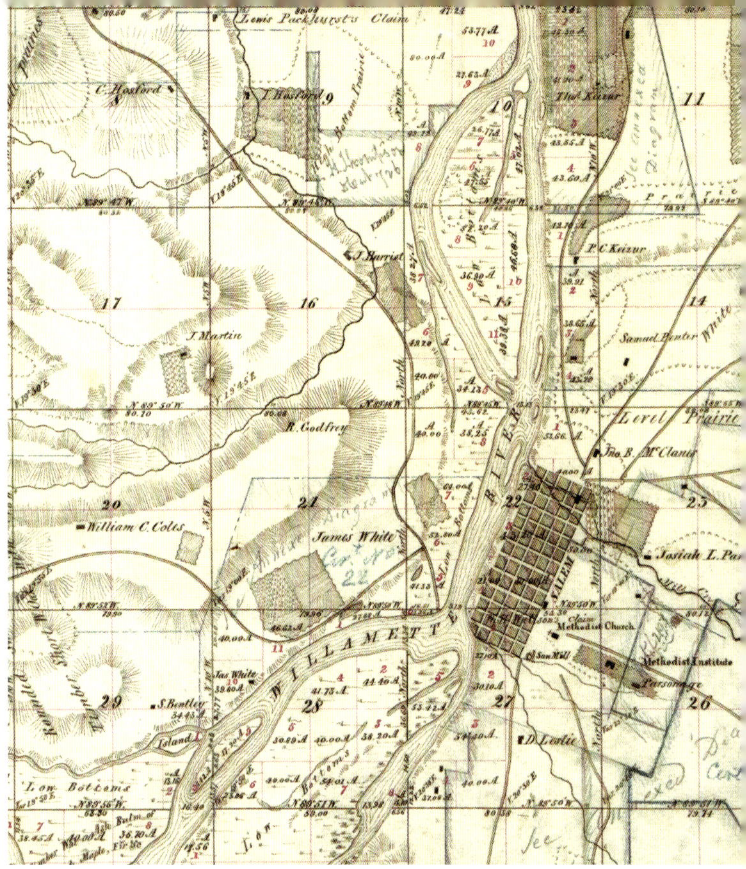

Portion of the of the General Land Office Map of 1853 (T7S, R5W) showing the location of Oregon Institute Lands and the original plat for the city of Salem. Also shown are residences identified by name, many of which were held by Willamette University Trustees.

the trustees, committing to maintain the partnership until the board could incorporate and receive back and legally hold the land. The partnership held the Institute claim for about two years.

In March 1846, the trustees and the partnership agreed that one of the partners, William H. Willson, Chloe Clark Willson's husband, should act as the agent for the parties to the arrangement, with the power to sell lots from the Institute holdings. At that time, the Institute claim covered the entire site of Salem. The trustees instructed Willson to encourage settlement by donating one lot each to 20 individuals and ordered him to sell the remaining lots by public auction and dispose of the Institute's waterpower rights. With the proceeds from the sales, the trustees took steps to finish the Institute building and improve the grounds surrounding it. While promoting the development of Salem, the trustees operated the Oregon Institute to provide the basic level of education sought at that early stage of the settlement of Oregon. The initial effort to assure the financial foundation of the future Willamette University thus depended, in large part, on its role in the process of "civic boosterism," which sought the growth of Salem.

To carry out his duties as the agent of the Institute, Willson disposed of his personal land claim and moved onto the Institute's property. In 1847, the other partners decided to withdraw from the joint ownership agreement, and subsequently Willson obligated himself by a bond in the amount of $100,000 to perfect and hold the Institute claim in trust until such time as the trustees could legally take it back. For his troubles, Willson was to have one third of the 640-acre claim, except for a sixty-acre reserve and the Institute buildings it contained. The lands surrounding the Institute's claim continued to change hands as more settlers poured into the Salem area in the late 1840s and early 1850s. The establishment of a territorial

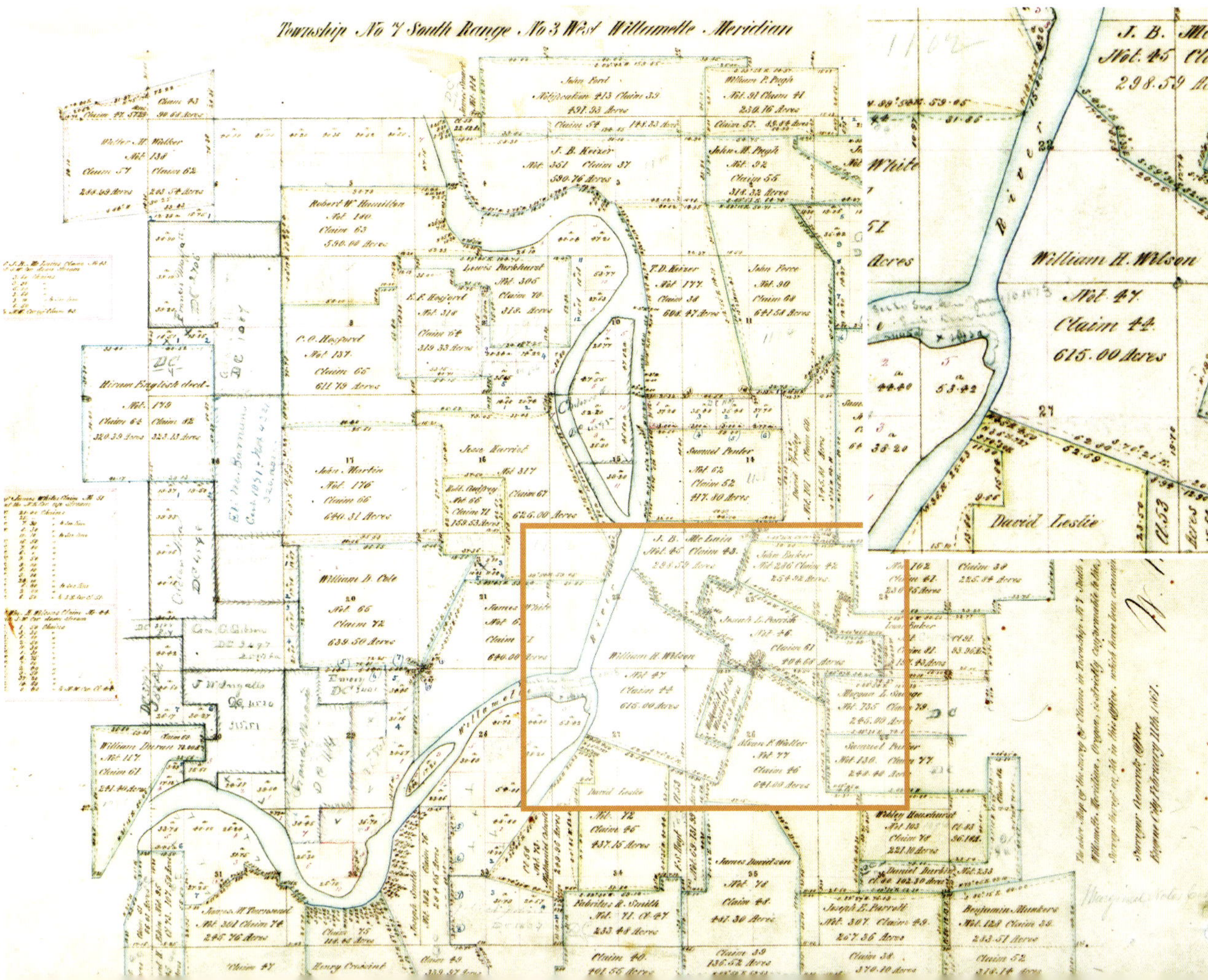

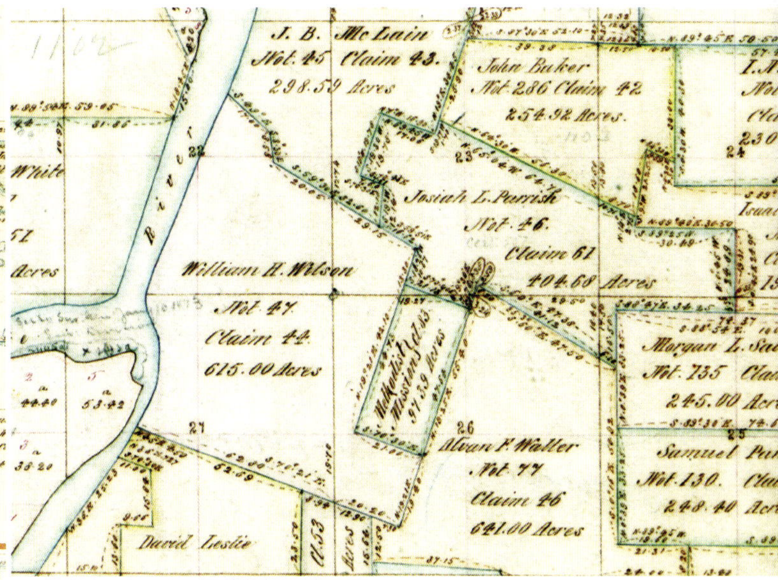

General Land Office Map drawn in 1867 showing the original boundaries of the donation land claims. Notice the trustee land claims surrounding the Methodist Mission (Willamette) claim.

Francis S. Hoyt, 1822-1912, dedicated educator who oversaw the transition of the Oregon Institute into Willamette University.

government for Oregon in 1848 and the passage of the Donation Land Claim Act of 1850 further complicated the ownership and sale of Institute land. The Donation law finally established the means of gaining legal title to land and became the source of controversy between Willson and his wife on one hand and the trustees on the other. Under the Donation Land Claim Act, a husband and wife were each entitled to 320 acres of land. Since Willson's wife, Chloe, was not a party to her husband's bond with the trustees, she could ignore its obligation with regard to her half of the claim. The Willsons apparently threatened to have the line drawn between their two halves of the claim so that the Institute's sixty acres and building were within her land claim and thus not subject to her husband's obligations under his bond to the trustees.[15]

Oregon's changing governmental structure forced the trustees and the Willsons to resolve their differences. The replacement of Oregon's provisional government with territorial status heightened the need to settle the land claim issues between Willson and the trustees, because it became possible for the trustees of the Oregon Institute to establish legal land holding status through incorporation. On January 12, 1853, the territorial legislature incorporated the Oregon Institute as Wallamet University, endowing it, in Gustavus Hines' words, "all the rights and privileges belonging to universities of the first grade in the United States." With the charter in hand, the Board of Trustees immediately took steps to recover from Willson their share of the land claim which he had held in trust for them. Willson, at first, resisted reaching a final settlement with the trustees. Finally, in November 1854, the parties resolved the impasse when the trustees agreed to a proposal from Willson, as Hines put it, "on the principle that a half loaf is better than no bread." Wilson offered to hand over the sixty-acre reserve and Institute building, secure to the trustees two-thirds of the unsold portion of his half of the original claim, and meet the other outstanding financial issues related to his bond. His wife would keep her half of the claim in total.[16]

With its charter of incorporation in hand and its land claim issues resolved, the new Willamette University began strengthening its educational operations. In the first meeting of the Oregon-California Conference of the Methodist Episcopal in 1849, the Oregon Institute had been officially recognized as a Methodist school. This act would provide important financial support over time from the Methodist Church.

From its opening day in 1844, Willamette University was operated as a co-educational school, and continued as such under the new charter. This marked Willamette as one of the oldest universities in the nation admitting both men and women. In recognition of the needs of a frontier society needing basic education as well as adequate preparation for students seeking a college degree, the university consisted of two departments, a preparatory or academic department (K-12) as well as a collegiate department. For many years, the academic department would enroll more students than the collegiate division. During the 1850s, the collegiate department had two or three professors (including the president), while the primary division (K-8) usually had two teachers. The Reverend Francis Hoyt was named principal of the Oregon Institute in 1850, and he continued as the first president of Willamette University until 1860.[17]

As one of their first acts under the new charter, the trustees enacted rules of student conduct. They expressly prohibited "drinking wine or intoxicating liquors, smoking, card-playing, swearing, immorality of any kind, quarreling, rude and unkind treatment of fellow-pupils, the throwing of stone, disobedience, indolence, and any other acts or behavior calculated

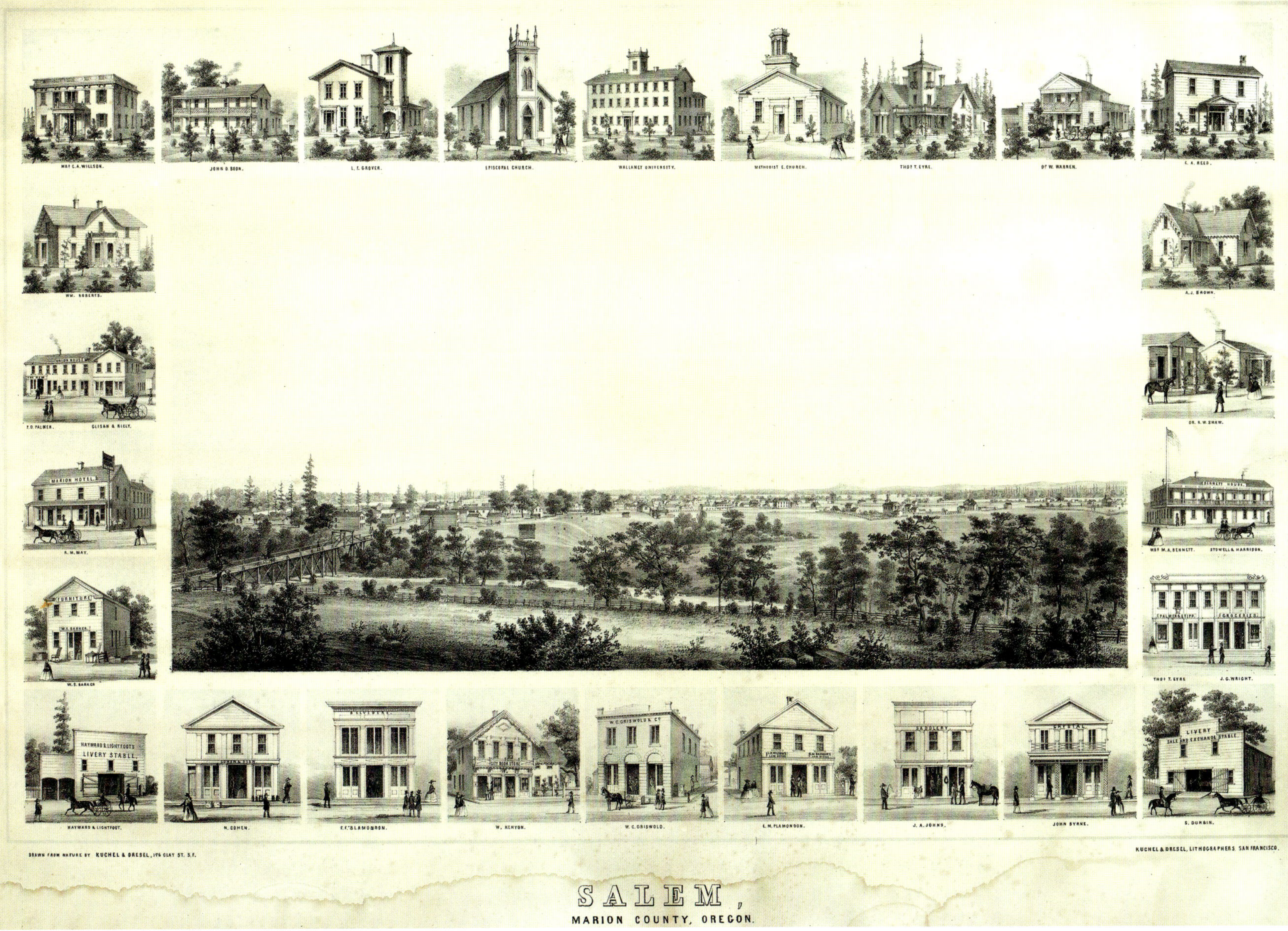

Bird's-eye view of Salem, Oregon, from 1857. The Oregon Institute building is located in a field to the right of the town plat.

to injure the reputation and peace of the university, or moral habits of the students." The rules, applying to students all the way from the elementary grades through young adulthood, were probably hard to enforce during the early years because the university operated only partly as a boarding school. While some male students lived on the third floor of the Institute building, other young men and women lived with family or others in the surrounding community. At times, the trustees allowed for a private boarding house to operate on the campus. The rules of conduct also prescribed study hours and provided for their enforcement by the president and faculty. The student housing and rules of conduct for Willamette students were typical of the collegiate way of life during the nineteenth century, whether at a denominational or publicly supported college.[18]

The grounds of the new university had a rough appearance in their first decade of existence. The Institute building and bell tower sat in an open grain field, surrounded by clusters of locust and cottonwood trees. The ground to the southwest contained an orchard of seedling trees. In 1857, the students made the first attempt at landscaping the campus by planting a double row of trees leading from the entrance to the Institute building to the junction of Capitol and State streets. In the late 1850s, the trustees had a plank fence built to prevent stray cattle from entering the grain field that made up a large portion of the campus. In order to pay for this improvement, the trustees had to sell several town lots—a precedent that was followed for all early additions to the campus buildings and grounds.

President Hoyt reported in the early 1850s that the number of students averaged 65 and the Institute building had been finished to the point that it had four large classrooms, a library, a chapel, and a student dormitory on the top floor. According to Hoyt, the school's greatest needs included scientific equipment, maps, library books, and a piano. He complained privately that the trustees ought to more aggressively raise the needed money, for "it is not possible to make an Institution worthy of the name without a library, apparatus, and funds." Impatiently, he urged that "a good agent ought to be sent into the field. ... Why cannot our Board of Trustees do something? Why not send a man out, why not? Other Institutions do it. ... They seem to think that in the course of time, somehow or in some way, without any action or energy on our part, an Institution will grow up." Although a frustrated Hoyt threatened to resign, he soldiered on for another three years. Meanwhile, with the charter in hand, the university began to offer collegiate classes in the mid-1850s, and by 1859, sufficient instruction allowed Emily York to complete a course of study and receive the degree of Mistress of English Literature. In later years, she remembered her graduation as a rather simple affair: "As I was the only graduate, I was valedictorian. The young men made the chapel a perfect bower of flowers."[19]

The hardest task facing the trustees involved financing the university's operations. Unfortunately, their chief stratagem, relying on the sale of scholarships, proved ruinous over time. The trustees tried many combinations of terms, but typically they offered anyone who promised to pay $500 in cash or land a perpetual scholarship to either the preparatory or collegiate department of the university. For $250, a person could buy a scholarship good for ten years. Since the scholarship purchaser could pay for the right over time (up to five years with interest), the device never produced enough immediate cash and served, with rising tuition fees, as a constant reduction of future income. In 1856, the trustees received an assist from the General Conference of the Methodist Episcopal Church when it agreed to give the Willamette University endowment fund $5,000 from the sale of mission property in Oregon, provided that the trustees secured a matching $15,000. Through the herculean efforts of Willamette's financial agent, Rev. Alvin F. Waller, the trustees raised the matching money in three years, but the Methodist Missionary Board failed to meet its obligation until 1867. At that time, the Missionary Board turned over to the trustees about 80 acres of land in the vicinity of Salem worth $5,000 in lieu of the promised cash. By 1867, the trustees had raised an endowment of $20,000, exclusive of the Missionary Board grant.[20] The annual expenses of $6,700—mostly for faculty salaries—was balanced by about the same amount of income from tuition and interest earnings. Financially, thanks especially to Alvin Waller, the university was on a sounder financial footing.

Willamette University's funding efforts were again typical of the pre-Civil War church-supported colleges. As one historian has observed, denominational "colleges tended to be small in enrollment, lean in operations, and poor in endowments." The students usually came from families of modest means and tuition was kept commensurately low. Each college depended upon its affiliated congregations to continuously raise money for its maintenance. College presidents or their agents spent much time on fundraising or "canvassing trips" throughout the region from which the schools drew students. Willamette's use of a paid financial agent was not unusual among nineteenth-century colleges, either. A college financial agent was not a professional fundraiser as developed in the twentieth century, but simply a dedicated clergyman who canvassed for money, taking a percentage of the proceeds for his efforts. Of course, if private or public philanthropy had been adequate, colleges would not have been compelled to rely on the desperate device of selling perpetual scholarships, which over time universally proved to be a burden rather than a panacea for the financial needs of the institutions.[21]

In 1860, the trustees chose Thomas Gatch to serve as the new president. Gatch, one of the key pioneer educators of the Pacific Northwest, would continue until 1865 and then return to the presidency in 1870 to serve another nine years. His work in higher education also included 11 years as president of the University of Washington and nine years in that capacity at Oregon State College.[22] A central problem Gatch would have to face was the inadequacy of the physical plant to serve the growing student body.

The old Institute building was showing its age and did not provide adequate facilities for the number of students now enrolled. A student at Willamette University in the early 1860s recalled, many years later, the crowded conditions of the old Institute building:

> *We still used the three story wooden building constructed by the early missionaries. On the first floor was our chapel and one schoolroom. In the rear were rooms occupied by the president and family. The second floor had two schoolrooms on the east side of the stairway while on the west side were three small rooms built for a library and laboratory, as yet only a dream to be fulfilled.*
>
> *The third story was divided into small rooms occupied by young men who in the slang of that day "batched," or boarded themselves thus making their small incomes stretch out farther. East of the school building the Methodist parsonage stood surrounded by oak trees. On the south across Mill Creek was eastward from the school's eastern line open pasture land where the cows of the city fed all day. Father Waller's donation claim extended eastward from the school's eastern line.*[23]

In 1912, lawyer and historian Joseph Gaston similarly remembered the early, bucolic conditions of the Oregon Institute and its surroundings:

> *When I went to Salem first to try a law suit before the Supreme Court, 49 years ago, the Willamette University—then generally called the 'Institute'—was housed in a long plain three story frame building, standing about the middle of the Campus, with a few trees, but no fence around the place to relieve the frontier appearance of the scene.*[24]

Writing in 1867, trustee Gustavus Hines described the problems presented by the worn out Institute building for a student body in all departments that had reached 320 students in 1860: "The old building had been constructed with a view to its occupancy for other purposes than that of a college edifice. ... [T]he rooms were low and uncomfortable, and the building was becoming dilapidated, the roof being scarcely a

Rev. Alvin F. Waller, 1808-1872, who literally wore himself out in the service of Willamette University. His house still stands as a private residence in Salem.

Rev. Thomas M. Gatch, 1833-1913, a leading figure in higher education in the Pacific Northwest. In addition to serving as president of Willamette University, he later served as president of Oregon State University and the University of Washington.

protection from the storm, … and the whole building had become so weakened by age and decay that the winter winds would shake it from the cupola to the foundation." Although the straightened finances of the university prevented immediate action by the trustees, Gustavus Hines expressed the thoughts of his fellow trustees when he wrote, "The inability of the community to meet the expenses of such an undertaking [i.e., a new building] restrained the Board for some time from making the attempt to erect a new college edifice; but the increasingly dilapidated condition of the old building and the increase of students rendered it absolutely necessary for them either to build or abandon the whole enterprise. The latter idea, however, did not belong to their vocabulary." [25]

Although the trustees voted to raise funds for the new building in October 1860, nothing was accomplished for two years. At that time, the university agent, Reverend Waller, began to solicit subscriptions for the building fund. Accepting little or no pay for his efforts, Waller crisscrossed the Willamette Valley in search of subscriptions or donations. His long absences from home caused his long-suffering wife to complain that "he loved the university more than his family." His dogged pursuit of money for the building led one observer to humorously write that Waller "seems to have an unwavering faith in the divineness of his call to secure the needful [funds] for the completion of the edifice of the Willamette University. We suggest to all that meet Bro. W., to give him something for the College at once, as it is the cheapest method of getting clear of him."[26]

Initially, the trustees sought to raise $20,000. When almost $13,000 had been promised by May 1863, they appointed a committee to develop a plan for the new collegiate structure. As the building committee, consisting at first of trustees Alvin Waller, J. H. Moores, and E. N. Cook, considered different plans, they soon realized the $20,000 would not be sufficient to complete the project. Resolving to press ahead regardless of the cost, the committee finally settled on a plan proposed by Waller. As Hines described it,

> *The plan of the building is that of a Greek cross, and was recommended to the agent [Waller] by Bishop Janes when he last visited the Oregon conference. The two parts of the cross are each eighty-four feet long and forty-four feet wide. These cross each other exactly in the center, so that the building presents about the same appearance from which ever side you take your observation. The height of the building from the basement to the top of the dome is one hundred feet, and from the base to the eaves fifty feet. The basement story is twelve feet, the first story above is sixteen feet, the second twelve feet, and the third twelve feet. There are three entrances to the building, the main entrance into the chapel being in the end of the north wing, and the other entrances being in the east and west wings. … The chapel is very commodious, occupying the entire story of the cross above the basement, running north and south. … It is nicely finished, with a broad platform at the south end finely and comfortably seated throughout.*[27]

In February 1864, the trustees broke ground for the building's foundation. Following the trustees' decision to construct the building of brick, the contractor found that the earth dug for the basement consisted of clay of sufficient quality to make the needed bricks. The trustees hired a professional brickmaker who proceeded to manufacture 500,000 bricks at the building site. Before laying the brick walls, the contractor built a three-foot high stone foundation, costing $655, to protect the bricks from the dampness of the earth. The brick mason's bill came to approximately $5,443. Reverend Waller served as the

University Hall (Waller) from the State Street side, soon after its dedication in 1868. The Oregon Institute building is shown behind it to the east.

University Hall

University Hall, our present day Waller Hall, presented a handsome yet restrained interpretation of the Greek or Classical Revival style. Each facade of the four wings held three bays with Doric-capped pilasters. Full pediments with simple entablatures accentuated each end of the cross, and within the pediments sat paired, roundheaded windows. Brick-denticulated lintels surmounted the tall, multi-paned windows. Three simple porticoed entrances allowed ingress and egress and expressed, on a smaller scale, the appearance of the gabled pediments. A well-proportioned multi-paned cupola adorned the top of the building.

general contractor, and by the time the trustees held the cornerstone ceremony in July 1864, he also had raised $25,000 toward completion of the building. The solidity of the building is attested to by the fact that over time, the outer walls survived two fires that each time severely damaged the interior.[28]

The use of Greek Revival for Willamette's new academic building was in keeping with the dominant architectural style of the early decades of the nineteenth century, especially for public structures. Willamette's trustees simply followed the fashion of the times. As one historian of college architecture noted, "More than any other institution, the college had good reasons for embracing the Greek style—or generally, any architecture suggesting classical antiquity—since it fortified the ideal of the classical curriculum and its nobility. The college claimed preeminently to embody the wisdom of the Greco-Roman tradition, and in the early nineteenth century it reminded the public of this in every way possible."[29]

The difficulty of turning subscriptions to cash on hand delayed completion of the building until the late summer of 1867, and students did not begin attending classes in the new University Hall until October of that year. Again, Hines describes the simple events leading to the occupation of the building:

> *At 9 o'clock of the 21st day of October, 1867, the school was marched, by the acting president, to the sound of martial music, from the old house to the new, where some of the members of the Board of Trustees, and friends of the institution, were assembled to receive them. There was no formal dedication of the house, as is usual on such occasions; but the venerable president of the Board of Trustees, Rev. David Leslie, by an appropriate address to the faculty and students, opened so much of the house as had been finished for the occupancy, and the other members of the Board present, gave the school a most cordial and hearty welcome and greeting to the neat and commodious halls of the new college edifice.*[30]

The editor of the *Salem Daily Record* captured the multi-purpose nature of the building:

> *On Saturday afternoon we went over the new edifice, to obtain a correct idea of its departments. The basement remains as yet unfinished. On the first floor is the largest hall in this city, occupying the main portion of that floor, the chapel, which is handsomely finished, and capable of seating five hundred persons. This can be entered by the main portal on the north, or by side entrances from the east and west halls. The east entrance is intended for the use of males, the west for females. At the west wing is a handsome parlor and ladies reception room, carpeted, and to be neatly furnished to contain a piano; a library room well stocked with volumes, is behind the circular stairway in a room in the same wing. In the east wing is a recitation room, with an apparatus room similarly located to the library room in the west wing.*
>
> *Ascending handsome circular flights of stairs, we arrive at the second floor which is devoted to the primary, academical, and classical departments. There are four very convenient school rooms, capable of containing from 50 to 75 pupils each. Very handsome and convenient desks are arranged, and in most of the rooms the walls are spanned with blackboards. At the head of the respective stairways are dressing rooms, with multitudes of hooks and accommodations for hats and coats. … .*
>
> *On the third floor are two elegant halls for the use of College societies, two rooms for the medical and surgical departments, and a school room for the Collegiate Classes. The attic is still above this, where abundant room remains unemployed for callisthenic and gymnastic purposes, and intended to be so applied.*
>
> *One more flight—it may almost be called a flight of fancy—and the views of the beautiful town, with the circling landscapes of varied and unrivaled beauty, repay you for ascending to the cupola, and making, at leisure, the circuit of the railing that guards one from incautious steps. … Our sketch would be incomplete did it fail to say that the work is most substantial, and even elegantly done. The whole building is very handsomely finished and most conveniently arranged.*[31]

By 1870, the new building's cost had risen to almost $40,000 and an estimated $5,000 remained to be raised to cover the final expenses to complete the furnishing. The debt caused by University Hall added a heavy burden to the already financially struggling college located in a pioneer society with limited monetary resources. Still, the educational mission now had adequate quarters for an expanding curriculum and student body.

Although most university activity centered on the new

University Hall after 1867, the old Institute building remained in use until it burned in 1872. In particular, the third floor continued to house male students. Total enrollment during the 1860s averaged about 270 (roughly 60 percent male and 40 percent female) –up substantially from the average of 65 just a decade before. As previously, the majority of students were in the pre-collegiate preparatory and academic programs. The collegiate level attracted about 40 students each year. At the end of the decade, the trustees discontinued the primary department when basic, tax-supported public education became available.

Most of the younger students attending the preparatory program, now called the Academy, came from the Salem area and lived at home. Older students in the Academy or collegiate departments made other living arrangements. Women students typically boarded in private homes in Salem. The men who lived on the third floor of the old Institute did their own cooking and supplemented the food supplies that they received from home by hunting and fishing in the forests and open areas surrounding the campus. Some of the male students also built small shacks along Mill Creek at the southern border of the campus. This collection of cottages became known as "String Town," reflecting their linear layout.

Conduct at Willamette in the 1870s continued to be strictly regulated under the patronage of the Methodist Episcopal Church. The university took pride in pointing out that while the school was denominational in support, it was not sectarian in operation, yet many of the founding Methodist missionaries continued to play an active role on the Board of Trustees and to interact with the student body, influencing the moral and spiritual life of the institution. The published university rules of conduct required, among other things, that

> *Due respect must be observed towards all officers of the Institution. A gentlemanly and ladylike deportment is at all times expected. … Profanity, rude and indecent language, smoking in any of the rooms or halls of the Institution, or upon the premises, drinking intoxicating liquors, playing at games of chance, the use of fire-arms on or about the premises, loitering or idling away time, protracted visiting in each other's rooms, and all other practices calculated to injure the morals or disturb the good order of the school, are totally forbidden. Special attention must be paid to cleanliness.*[32]

Willamette's collegiate department instruction focused heavily on classical Latin and Greek literature, composition, and philosophy. Higher mathematics, science, rhetoric, political economy, and modern history received due attention, as did Christian theology. Electives included French, German, and Hebrew. A scientific course of study could be substituted for the classical instruction, the difference being the omission of classical languages and the addition of French and more English language courses. Music and art were available at extra cost outside of the regular tuition. Following the practice of liberal arts colleges of the day, term examination exercises were oral and public. The Willamette faculty marched their students onto the Chapel stage and conducted the examinations with active participation from official visitors and an audience drawn from the general populace. The faculty at the time consisted of the president and one or two full-time professors, supplemented by other staff members teaching in the preparatory department.

Much of the broader intellectual and social life of Willamette revolved around the school's two, and sometimes four, literary societies. The students had founded the oldest, Concordia, in 1861 for women, while the men established the Hesperian Society in

University Hall (Waller) in 1869 or 1870, prior to the burning of the Oregon Institute building. (shown just beyond University Hall.) The people in their best dress could be attending a graduation ceremony or other special event.

1865. Subsequently, two other societies emerged: Alka for men (1866) and Atheneum for women (1870). These organizations became of such interest that even non-students in Salem joined them. The new University Hall provided the setting for society meetings.

This structure was typical of college liberal arts studies across the nation. Some Antebellum era educational critics proposed reforms that would have expanded the subjects taught, in recognition of the explosion of knowledge during the eighteenth and nineteenth centuries and of the diffusion of learning necessary to meet the needs of a more democratic society. The educational traditionalists, led by the example of Yale's rejection of reform in 1828, however, won the day, and the standard classical curriculum prevailed. Methods of instruction in America's small colleges also changed little during the period. Students learned by recitation based on textbook materials; the classroom did not provide a place for discussion. Written examinations slowly gained acceptance during the nineteenth century, but primarily, examination was by disputation of a thesis presented in public. The limitations of the classical liberal arts curriculum and the need to engage in the world of ideas outside of those explored in the classroom made the debating and literary societies an important part of the university experience nationwide. In all of these educational procedures, Willamette adhered to the prevailing traditional model.[33]

Even without broad reform, the trustees at Willamette were dedicated to the educational mission of the school. They even sought to expand it. During the time they struggled to finance and build University Hall, they responded to a widespread recognition that the Pacific Northwest needed a school to train physicians. Most doctors of that day had gained their medical knowledge from apprenticeships with practicing physicians rather than from medical schools. The quality of doctors, especially in the early West, varied greatly, and the numbers of those available was limited. As an established university with the legal right to create colleges, Willamette was the logical entity to start a medical school. Accordingly, the Board of Trustees in 1867, the year University Hall was completed, responded to the request of Oregon Governor A. C. Gibbs (also a Willamette University trustee) by establishing a medical department at Willamette University. The trustees probably had encouragement in this endeavor from the university's new president, Joseph Wythe, who was himself a well-trained and highly-regarded practicing physician. Wythe had become president in 1865. The graduation requirements in medicine entailed three years of study, satisfactory passage of an examination, and submittal of a thesis on a medical topic. Willamette's medical school was the first in the Pacific Northwest and only the third in the West—the other two being in California.[34]

Willamette's Board of Trustees had grand ambitions for the university in the late 1860s and early 1870s. In addition to the medical school, they sought to start colleges of law and theology. Alas, the trustees overestimated the number of paying students for such professional education, and these additions to the university would have to wait until the 1880s to be realized. The trustees, moreover, had other pressing matters requiring their attention – keeping the post of president filled. Apparently unhappy that President Wythe smoked in public, the trustees replaced him in 1867 with a strict churchman from the East, Nelson Rounds. Ill health, however, forced Rounds' retirement in 1870. Over the coming years, Willamette would face new challenges to finance, house, and advance its academic mission.

Endnotes

1 For background on the development of the American college movement in the early nineteenth century, see Frederick Rudolph, *The American College and University: A History* (Athens, Georgia: The University of Georgia Press, 1990), 3-68; John R. Thelin, *A History of American Higher Education*, 2nd ed. (Baltimore: The Johns Hopkins University Press, 2011), 1-41; Roger L. Geiger, *The History of American Higher Education* (Princeton: Princeton University Press, 2015), 1-267; Russel Blaine Nye, *Society and Culture in America, 1830-1860* (New York: Harper and Row, 1974), 385-99.

2 The next two most active college-building denominations, the Presbyterians and Baptists, accounted for 46 percent of the religious colleges. Nye, *Society and Culture*, 386.

3 Quote in Rudolph, *The American College*, 48.

4 Paul Venable Turner, *Campus: An American Planning Tradition* (Cambridge, Mass.: MIT Press, 1987), 3-51.

5 Ibid., 87.

6 Ibid., 89-140.

7 Much of the following narrative on the founding of Willamette University is based on Robert Moulton Gatke, *Chronicles of Willamette: The Pioneer University of the West* (Portland, Oregon: Binfords and Mort, 1943); Gustavus Hines, *Oregon and Its Institutions; Comprising a Full History of the Willamette University* (Carlton and Porter, 1868); Charles Henry Carey, ed., "Diary of Rev. George Gary," *Oregon Historical Quarterly*, vol. XXIV (Mar.-Dec., 1923), 68-105, 153-85, 269-333, and 386-433.

8 Quote in Hines, *Oregon and Its Institutions*, 138.

9 Ibid., 141.

10 Ibid., 142-43.

11 Ibid., 143, 153.

12 Quote in William Willson to Josiah Parrish, July 2, 1844, Willamette University Archives.

13 Hines, *Oregon and Its Institutions*, 161-62.

14 Quotes in Diary of Chloe Willson, MS, Willamette University Archives, 45-48; William Willson to Josiah Parrish, July 2, 1844, Willamette University Archives.

15 The discussion of the Willson controversy is based in part on Hines, *Oregon and Its Institutions*, Gatke, *Chronicles of Willamette*, and Earle K. Stewart, "Some Aspects of the So-Called Willson Land Dispute and Willamette University" (master's theses, Willamette University, 1938); see also, Sybil Westenhouse, "The Willsons in Salem," *Marion County History*, vol. XV (Salem, Oregon, Marion County Historical Society, 1998), 13-49; Abstract of Title for Lot 3, Block 9, University Addition (Reiggelman, Chain of Title, 1864-1912), Willamette University Archives.

16 Quotes in Hines, *Oregon and Its Institutions*, 172, 183. Apparently, Mrs. Willson also promised to make future gifts of land from her share of the settlement to the university for scientific equipment and other purposes. M. Simpson to Robert Thornton, Apr. 12, 1854, Willamette University Archives.

17 Oberlin College began coeducational higher education in 1836. Willamette University and about five other institutions adopted coeducation prior to 1860. Willamette was probably the second one. Geiger, *The History of Higher Education*, 204.

18 Quote in Hines, *Oregon and Its Institutions*, 190-91; Thelin, *History of Higher Education*, 63-67; Rudolph, *The American College*, 87-89, 104-09; Geiger, *The History of Higher Education*, 129, 138, 215-17.

19 Francis Hoyt to Alvin Waller, May 19, 1857, Willamette University Archives; Judy Goard, "Emily York: A Face in the Shadows," *Willamette Scene* (Spring 1994), 28.

20 Transcription of Board of Trustees Minutes, Vol. I, 9, 48, 63, 104, Gatke Papers, Box 4, Willamette University Archives; Methodist Missionary Board to Board of Trustees, Oct. 17, 1866, File 13, Box 1, Willamette University Records, 1855-1900, Willamette University Archives.

21 Quote in Thelin, *History of Higher Education*, 61; Rudolph, *The American College*, 177-200; Geiger, *The History of Higher Education*, 203-06.

22 For more on Gatch, see Chapter II, endnote 6.

23 Quote in Gatke, *Chronicles of Willamette*, 214

24 Joseph Gaston to Prof. Gaylord Patterson, Apr. 11, 1912, Smith Papers, Box 100/101, Willamette University Archives.

25 Hines, *Oregon and Its Institutions,* 261-62.

26 Quote in Gatke, *Chronicles of Willamette*, 216; Transcription of Board of Trustees Minutes, Vol. I, 90, 122, 147, 152, Gatke Papers, Box 4, Willamette University Archives.

27 Hines, *Oregon and Its Institutions*, 266; see also *The Oregonian*, May 3, 1912; Transcription of Board of Trustees Minutes, Vol. I, 160, 162, 164, 168, Gatke Papers, Box 4, Willamette University Archives.

28 Various receipts for the materials and construction of Waller Hall, 1864-67, can be found in Willamette University Records, 1855-1900, Box 1, Willamette University Archives; Transcription of Board of Trustees Minutes, Vol. I, 169, 172, 181, Gatke Papers, Box 4, Willamette University Archives.

29 Robert K. Sutton, *Americans Interpret the Parthenon: The Progression of Greek Revival Architecture from the East Coast to Oregon, 1800-1860* (Niwot, Colo.: The University Press of Colorado, 1992), 158-61; Turner, *Campus*, 90-109, quote on page 90.

30 Hines, *Oregon and its Institutions*, 268.

31 Quote in Gatke, *Chronicles of Willamette*, 221-22; see also *The Oregonian*, Oct. 23, 1867; Transcription of Board of Trustees Minutes, Vol. II, 7, 27, 50, 51.

32 Gatke, *Chronicles of Willamette*, 228-29.

33 Rudolph, *The American College,* 110-55; Thelin, *History of Higher Education,* 64-65, 68, 69; Geiger, *The History of Higher Education,* 187-93.

34 O. Larsell, *The Doctor in Oregon: A Medical History* (Portland, OR: Binfords and Mort, 1947), 343-50.

2 Times of Change and Turbulence

In the last third of the century, higher education faced challenging times. Traditional liberal arts colleges, already familiar with the debates over curriculum reform, encountered new questions about the utility of their approach to teaching and learning. New institutional structures, and even types of colleges or universities, appeared. With the adoption of the Morrill Act in 1862, Congress had gotten into the act of financing institutions of higher education, which, while slow in starting, over time resulted in colleges and universities that emphasized a broader, more utilitarian curriculum than that offered by schools focused on the liberal arts. As part of the new diversity in higher education offerings, state-supported normal schools arose to train public school teachers.

Most importantly, out of the ferment in educational thinking, a fresh concept of the role of universities arose, focusing on scholarly inquiry at the graduate level. Yale, the most traditional of the liberal arts colleges, awarded the first earned Ph.D. in 1861. Cornell, established in 1865 pointed the way to an expanded curriculum that combined classical studies with more practical and modern scientific courses at the undergraduate level, while emphasizing scholarly inquiry and research at the graduate level. Johns Hopkins established a major graduate university on the German model in 1867, while operating a traditional undergraduate program based on the classics. By 1876, 25 institutions of higher education awarded the Ph.D. degree.

In the same period, President Charles Eliot, of Harvard, led a movement to substitute an elective course of study for the old prescribed classical curriculum. Support for reform swept higher education. This movement sought a more utilitarian,

Facing page: Waller Hall after the first fire

scientific set of courses to satisfy individual needs and preferences. The elective system also strengthened the spirit of inquiry and scholarship at the heart of the new, graduate-level-focused university and brought vitality to higher education as a whole. In short, many educators and commentators believed that the traditional liberal arts curriculum had an air of narrowness and superficiality about it that required major reforms.

The reformers' approach to learning sat clearly in opposition to the traditional prescribed curriculum, which relied on a belief in the underlying unity of knowledge, compulsory class attendance, religious instruction, and strict supervision and discipline to cultivate the essential faculties of the mind. As one traditionalist put it, "Education is essentially the training of the mind. … The powers of mind are numerous and varied, the senses, the memory, the fancy, judgment, reasoning, conscience, the feelings, the will, the mathematical, the metaphysical, the mechanical, the poetical, the prosaic … ; and all these should be cultivated." The traditionalists betrayed a distrust of a student's ability to wisely choose a course of study and instead simply ordained what should be taught to create a well-educated person. On a more practical level, colleges wishing to adopt the elective curriculum often found it difficult to do because of the expense involved in adding the faculty, laboratories, and libraries necessary to carry out the reform. Nevertheless, the movement in higher education toward an elective curriculum proved irresistible over time.[1]

One final, dramatic change in higher education in the late nineteenth century involved the advent of the model university created through the philanthropy of captains of industry. In the 1890s, for example, John D. Rockefeller established the University of Chicago and Leland Stanford endowed Stanford University. These institutions amalgamated the wealth of benefactors with the ambitions of prominent educators to create the so-called "great American universities." They offered expanded undergraduate curriculums and, in time, graduate schools. As this diversity in higher education developed, educators sought to define more clearly what constituted a university. The discussions about curriculum reform and what constituted higher learning were not going to fade away and would result in a more demanding and academically selective college and university environment. [2]

Despite the reform fervor, and the addition of new departments and professional programs, Willamette University and many other institutions of higher learning continued to exemplify the older, traditional approach. The Willamette catalogue for 1889, for example, listed course offerings in the traditional liberal arts and professional programs in law, medicine, pharmacy, and theology. The curriculum also offered business and normal school courses.

Ultimately, there would be no single type of American university. As one historian of higher education noted, "The United States in its universities was to reveal a remarkable diversity, an unwillingness to be categorized, a variety that would encompass differences in wealth, leadership, public influence, regional needs." In other words, the university concept could cover just about any educational program that occurred within an American institution of higher education.[3]

Regardless of how one defined a university, the problem of preparing students for college continued to be an issue in the late nineteenth century. Public, tax-supported secondary education was not widely available outside of large urban centers. Most college-preparatory schools were private academies, usually affiliated with or attached to existing colleges.

Willamette University, for example, operated an academy on its campus from the 1850s until 1917. It also drew students from several other Methodist-sponsored private academies in the Willamette Valley and beyond. As late as 1895, 57 percent of students admitted to American colleges and universities came from college preparatory departments or separate private preparatory schools. Only when public high schools became commonplace in the early twentieth century could institutions of higher education drop their own academies or reliance on private prep academies.

With the luxury of hindsight, there is much to recognize in the last thirty years of the nineteenth century, both at Willamette and in the region, as laying the foundation for the new world that would emerge in the early twentieth century. Even though Willamette was bent toward the traditional in some ways, looking at the 30 years from roughly 1870 to 1900, we can see the forces at play, both physical and otherwise, that would propel it into the future. Despite the debt and financial struggles of the 1860s, at the beginning of the 1870s, Willamette University appeared well-positioned to prosper.

Oregon now had a population of about 91,000, and Willamette's location in Salem—the state capital—and the Willamette Valley provided ample access to potential students and funding. The arrival of the railroad in the valley in the 1870s did much to boost its agricultural economy and to gradually eliminate the valley's reliance on limited-capacity steamboats for shipping produce and moving passengers. After a tour of Oregon in the mid-1870s, one observant traveler wrote, "I would say that no visitor to Oregon who had any opportunity of observing the condition of the people would fail to be impressed by their great general prosperity." During the 1880s, Oregon would continue to experience economic growth as the population

The Morrill Act

The land grant colleges created by the Morrill Act (1862), which offered land from the public domain to states for financing such institutions, established a new network of universities with a practical focus on meeting the needs of a society still resting on a large agrarian base. These schools sought to provide education and training founded on the emerging advances occurring in scientific agriculture. Many farmers, though, remained skeptical of the value of scientific agriculture and were slow to take up reforms proposed by the new agricultural schools. The Morrill Act led to a variety of arrangements for accomplishing its goal. Some states created agricultural and mechanical colleges out of previously chartered agricultural colleges. Other states turned over to existing state universities the responsibility and endowment for serving the agricultural and mechanical interests. Still others set up entirely new colleges, which over time competed with existing state universities for public support. Finally, a few states even arranged for private colleges to provide the new educational program called for in the Morrill Act, and some of these schools eventually became state universities. This is what happened in Oregon with Corvallis College.

It took some time to develop the scientific and technical curriculums for these land grant schools, and for many years most such institutions simply offered the traditional college courses. Agricultural education drew increased student enrollments only after university-based experiment stations—which emerged in the 1890s—found ways to increase crop output and thereby demonstrated the value of applying scientific methods to agriculture. Until then, the land grant schools offered little competition to the state's private colleges and universities.

An 1876 bird's-eye view of Salem. The inset shows Willamette University – essentially a large field with University Hall (Waller). The landscaping is probably artistic license.

expanded to about 175,000, an increase of 92 percent over the course of the decade. By 1890, the economy was no longer so dependent on agriculture, as other industries such as lumbering and salmon canning began to emerge. Portland had developed into a major center of trade and transportation with a population of over 46,000. Salem, in addition to housing the state capitol and various governmental departments, took advantage of the many streams within its boundaries to establish several water-powered industries, including woolen and flour mills. At the beginning of the 1890s, Willamette University President Van Scoy boasted that "all circumstances combine to make Salem the best University town on the Coast. It is not too large, so as to absorb the interest of a University in its business affairs, and it is not so small as to be unable to accommodate all its interests."[4]

Willamette University's chief competitors in Oregon in the field of higher education consisted of Pacific University, founded at Forest Grove in 1848, and Albany College, established at Albany in 1867. These small institutions operated on the same educational basis as Willamette: they had a liberal arts curriculum, were co-educational, and enrolled most students in their preparatory divisions. During the 1870s and 1880s, both colleges struggled with small numbers of students and limited funding. Although Linfield College (called McMinnville College until 1922) began operating at McMinnville in 1857, it did not award its first B. A. degree until 1884. It functioned chiefly as a preparatory school until the 1890s. The University of Oregon opened its doors in 1876, and Oregon State College, originally tiny private Corvallis College, received the initial state land grant from the Morrill Act in 1868 and became a full-fledged state institution in 1886. The state institutions of higher education developed slowly, offering little competition to the state's private colleges and universities during the last decades of the nineteenth century. Two deeper rivalries, both of which threatened Willamette's very existence, arose in the later years of the century, but those stories are still to come. [5]

The physical setting of the Willamette campus in the 1870s and 1880s retained its open, rural look, even though the grounds were surrounded by residential and state government buildings. An 1876 bird's-eye lithograph of Salem showed the campus as a pasture-like setting with the four-story brick University Hall on the northwestern edge dominating the landscape. Rows of trees marked the perimeter of the grounds and a mill stream meandered along the southern boundary, while the state capitol grounds across State Street marked the northern edge of the campus. In its early years, Willamette's campus was typical of many small denominational colleges and universities that started in the nineteenth century. One main building and a few subsidiary structures set in an open field in either a rural or small town setting represented the beginnings of most such institutions. They had neither the financial resources nor the educational need to establish anything more complicated than this kind of physical layout.[6]

The trustees had voted in November 1872 to have the dilapidated old Institute structure removed, but before college officials could carry out the order, someone torched it in December of that year. At the time, the editor of the *Oregonian* nostalgically noted the old Institute's passing: "Since 1867 it had been but little used, as the new brick [University Hall] was completed about that time. The old frame was left standing as a land-mark in the history of Oregon, until the ruthless hand of an incendiary, as is supposed, applied to it the torch, and whence so much mental illumination had erewhile gone forth, there sprang out material flames which soon laid the venerable pile in ruins." Once the Institute building was gone, male students' housing had to depend mostly on quarters in the attic of University Hall or on the student-built shacks situated south of Mill Creek on the border of the campus (String Town).[7]

From 1870 to 1900, Willamette University had five presidents – three arguably successful, and two terms very short-lived. The presidencies of all five men were marked by conflict and turmoil, often generated by events outside their control. The first, Thomas Gatch, was a popular president who had returned to the presidency after Nelson Rounds, who was appointed in 1868, had resigned due to poor health after only two years in office. Gatch had previously been president from 1860 to 1865 and left again in 1879, when he and the faculty resigned en masse in the middle of the financial crisis at the time. His successor, Reverend Charles Lambert, while modernizing the administration and the office of the presidency in some ways, was in office for only one year. The next president, Thomas Van Scoy, was replaced in 1891. His was a noteworthy presidency that also ended in turmoil. He was replaced by George Whitaker, who did not sit well with the students nor the board. As will be seen, his two years dealt him some major challenges. The next president, Willis Hawley, inherited many problems and even larger and more dramatic ones came his way. But he was well-suited to the job and finally retired from Willamette in 1902, when he was elected to the U.S. House of Representatives. The story of Willamette University as the nineteenth century drew to a close is well-illustrated by the contentious, tumultuous, and one could say even drama-filled, terms of these five men. As we look at the student body, the curriculum, and, of course, the physical structures of the university during these thirty years, we can see the imprint of their work and of the times in which they lived. The larger battles that engaged Willamette at the close of the century had lasting impacts, not just for the university, but regionally as well.

During the 1870s, Willamette operated with three professors at the collegiate level, two in the preparatory division, and one in the music department. All carried a heavy teaching load. The university continued the preparatory department and the Medical School, while also offering courses leading to degrees in three specialized departments: normal (public school teaching certification), commercial (business skills), and music and art. In 1870-71, 82 students enrolled in the College of Liberal Arts, while 14 attended the Medical School and another 188 studied in the preparatory program. Average attendance for all departments during the 1870s stood at 279, with 81 being the average number of college students in the various programs. During the decade, 96 students graduated with a liberal arts degree, 6 earned degrees in music, and 72 received diplomas from the Medical School. Typical of most higher education institutions of the period, large numbers attended Willamette without completing degrees. Of those who did graduate, most entered the teaching profession, while lesser numbers became lawyers or ministers. Many simply engaged in farming or business after graduating.[8]

Thomas Gatch began his term in 1870 facing a $10,000 debt left from the construction of University Hall. Despite ample enrollment, tuition income and earnings from the small endowment failed to cover essential expenditures. As a result of the annual shortfall, the debt load grew and with it the mounting annual interest payments. To make ends meet, the trustees tried two methods. They slowly sold off the lands owned by the university—but this was never sufficient—and they increasingly relied on the ruinous policy, which had been problematic in earlier decades, of selling perpetual scholarships for $500 each. These obligations entitled the owner (or transferee) the right to send a student to the school tuition free for as long as the university existed. Over time, the interest earned on the $500 (often not collected for many years) failed to cover the university's expenses for educating the scholarship student.

Assets, consisting of the campus, University Hall, endowment, and land in Salem, amounted to roughly $140,000. Annual income, chiefly from tuition and interest on the endowment (about $7,500), failed to cover current expenses (about $9,000). For most of the 1870s, Willamette seemed unable to reduce a cumulative debt load of almost $20,000. Supporters of Willamette tried to rescue the university. Methodist ministers of the Oregon conference pledged $20,000 in 1872 to pay off the debt, but the effects of a national financial Depression in 1873 cut the sum realized to half the amount pledged. The heavy debt load led the Board of Trustees to ever more desperate measures. The university took out two short-term loans of $10,000 each. The first, taken out in 1874 for a term of three years, came from the Ladd and Bush Bank in Salem; the second, for a term of five years, followed from Edward Bennett, a New York capitalist. In each case, a mortgage on the university campus served as collateral for the loans. By 1876, the total indebtedness of the university, unfortunately, had risen back to $20,000.[9]

The financial plight reached a crisis point in 1879. President Gatch and the entire faculty resigned, and Gatch accepted a teaching position at the new University of Oregon. In desperation and—as one observer noted—after "a long and stormy debate," the trustees offered to give Gatch complete financial and educational control over the institution if he could get released from his obligation to the University of

Oregon and return to Willamette. The University of Oregon Regents refused to release Gatch, and some discouraged Willamette trustees proposed closing the university for the coming academic year. Cooler heads prevailed, and the Willamette University board instead hired a new faculty and a new president, the Reverend Charles Lambert.

Up to this point, the trustees had played a very active role in governing the university; the president focused on teaching and supervising the faculty. The university agent, who answered directly to the board, carried out most of the administrative and financial duties related to the operation of the institution and served as the chief fundraiser. While during the 1870s the board had met on an average of 13 times a year, the attendance at most meetings averaged only 10 members (less than a third of the total) due to the difficulties of travel. For this reason, when President Lambert took office, and perhaps in response to the turmoil with Gatch, the board realized that it could not handle the administration of the institution effectively and enabled the new president to take on more administrative authority. President Lambert remained only a year, but in his short term he instituted a number of reforms that modernized the office of the president and streamlined the administration of the university.

In 1880, the trustees, in seeking a replacement for President Lambert, turned to Reverend Thomas Van Scoy. He had joined the faculty the previous year as a professor of ancient languages and now assumed the position he would successfully carry out for the rest of the decade. Van Scoy, an earnest and respected scholar of theology, made a favorable impression on the students because of his teaching style, open and affable manner, and kindness toward students of meager circumstances. One observer also noted his concern for the physical appearance of the university: "We have often seen him with his coat off and hammer and nails in his hand repairing the University fences, engaged in setting out shrubbery, or in some way adding to the beauty of the campus, thus evincing an interest in the general appearance of the surroundings, in appreciation of the fact that all tended toward making the students more interested in their studies." In fact, it was under Van Scoy that the old board fences that had previously surrounded the campus to keep out grazing cows were removed. The campus, now reduced to about 18 acres, was now in the center of a more urban context. The *Salem Statesman* approvingly wrote of the fence removal and urged "It would be a good thing if many of the citizens [of Salem] ... would do likewise with their old fences and thus give to the city, as well as the campus, the appearance of a park rather than that of a pound." An inspirational teacher and able administrator, Van Scoy made a strong mark on Willamette during his tenure as president.[10]

Van Scoy presided over a considerable amount of change in the 1880s. To accomplish all of this, however, he had first to address the issues of finances and student housing. A generally robust national and state economy for much of the decade would eventually help the university to prosper financially, but the inherited financial crisis that existed when Van Scoy took office demanded that he immediately take measures to rectify the problem.

Careful administration by President Van Scoy did much, but heroic fundraising by the university agent, Reverend F. P. Tower, accounted for much of the improvement in Willamette's balance sheet in the 1880s. The effort had been jump-started in 1879 when the Portland Academy, no longer able to compete with the Portland public high school, decided to close and offered to donate to the university the proceeds from the sale of its property. The Academy trustees stipulated that Willamette must raise $12,000 in new

Thomas VanScoy, 1848-1901, served as president of Willamette University from 1880-1891.

endowment money and reduce the existing debt to less than $5,000 to receive the gift. Agent Tower struggled mightily to meet the terms of the offer, and, while he succeeded in reducing the existing indebtedness, found it difficult to raise the additional $12,000.

In search of new donors, agent Tower made a fundraising foray to the East Coast from September 1881 to February 1883. When Tower canvassed in the East, however, he found competition from agents attempting to raise money for other institutions of higher education and a multitude of additional benevolent causes. As a result of his fundraising efforts in the East, he managed to raise $10,561, but his salary during that time amounted to $2,200 and his expenses came to $1,361. Finally, however, the university met the conditions of the Portland Academy gift in August 1882, and by the time Willamette actually realized the proceeds from the sale of the Academy's property, the amount brought in stood at $15,000. As a result of Agent Tower's fundraising and the Academy's gift, Willamette increased its endowment to $27,000 and reduced the floating debt to $4,000.[11]

F.P. Tower, financial agent for the University and a member of the Methodist Conference.

As noted previously, Willamette tended to the conservative side in issues of curriculum reform. Van Scoy began his presidential term in 1880, however, by establishing a Women's College within the university structure. His wholehearted commitment to this new department was evidenced by the purchase with his own funds of the home of Mrs. Chloe Clark Willson for use as a living hall and classroom space for the women enrolled in the new college. To furnish and finance the new college hall, the board formed the Woman's Guild made up of trustees' wives, women graduates of Willamette, and other female supporters of the university. The main purpose of the Women's College, as announced in the university catalogue, was to provide housing and supervision for the increasing numbers of women students attending Willamette from a distance and to house new course offerings in the decorative arts and design and music.

This is the original Italianate configuration of Chloe Clark Willson's house when it was moved to the Willamette Campus to house the Women's College in 1880.

The university catalogue hastened to assure its readers that the Women's College was "in no sense a surrender of co-education." The new college was simply a residence hall with space to offer instruction in music and art. Men and women still attended all of the regular liberal arts courses together and a few men even ventured to take the occasional art or music course in the Women's College. A new, third course of study in the College of Liberal Arts, Modern Literature and Art, allowed the substitution of other foreign languages and music and art courses for Greek and advanced Latin, while requiring the standard courses in mathematics and sciences.[12]

The advent of the Women's College ultimately led to the admission of women to the university's Board of Trustees. In 1883, in recognition of the help women had provided in establishing the Women's College – and in hopes that they would actively help in raising funds from other women to sustain it – six women were elected to the board. The Willamette *College Journal* proudly announced at the time that "Willamette University is among the very first institutions of its grade to admit ladies into the board of trustees."

Other changes made under Van Scoy included reorganization of the Academy to contain the business and Normal School courses as well as liberal arts preparatory subjects. In 1883, after many years of consideration, Willamette University finally launched a law school. In announcing the start of the law school, the Willamette *College Journal* noted that Salem offered a "most suitable location in Oregon for a law school. Here are held all grades of courts, and a greater variety and complexity of law questions are discussed than at any other place in the State." The course of study consisted of two years of study, and entrance required a college degree or evidence presented to the faculty that the person seeking admittance possessed the equivalent of such an education. The school was slow to gain its footing, however. In its first year of operation, only three students enrolled in the law course—one less than the number of faculty—and even at the end of the decade, the number of law students had never exceeded seven in a given year.

While Willamette added new departments during the 1880s, the enrollment numbers in the older programs did not deviate substantially from those of the earlier decade. Average attendance for all departments during the 1880s averaged 330. Once again, the preparatory academy accounted for the largest numbers, running about 200 yearly. The College of Liberal Arts had about 25 each year, while the Medical School enrolled approximately 28 and the Music School numbered 100. The number of liberal arts graduates declined during the 1880s: 59 received a diploma. The Music School graduated 34; the Medical School, 87; and the new Law School, 6. During the 1880s, the total faculty grew to number 44, with the College of Liberal Arts faculty fluctuating between 7 and 10, some serving only part-time. Willamette made further adjustments in board membership in the mid-1880s. While typically

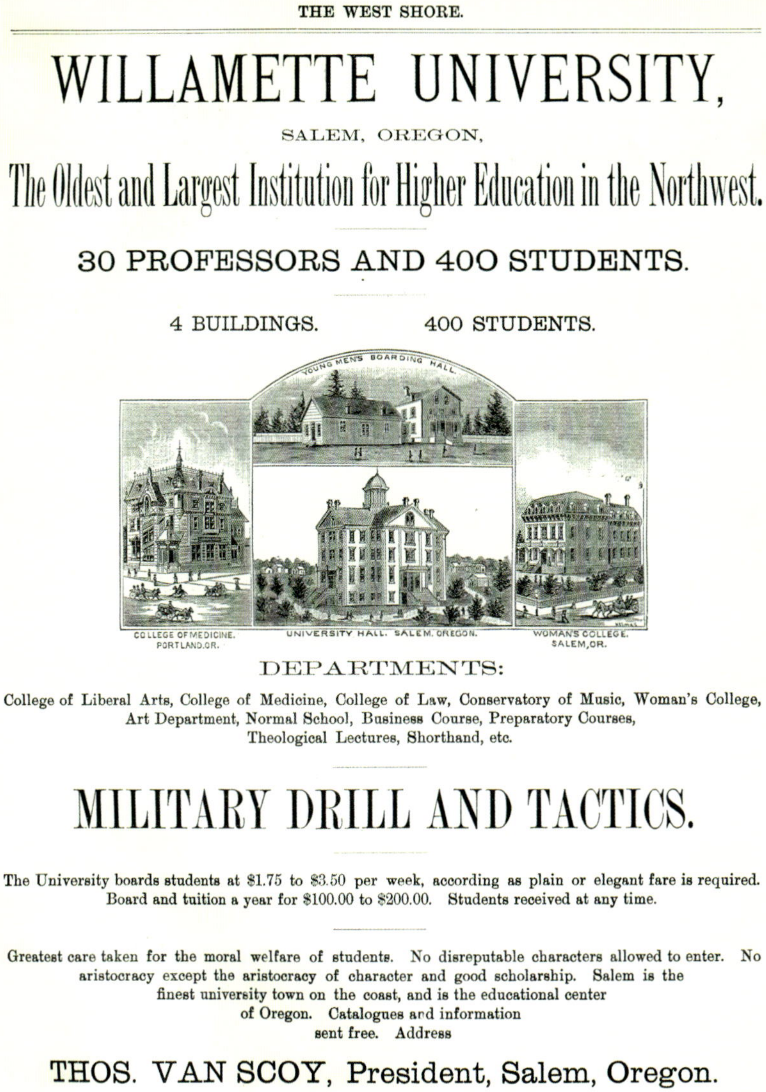
THE WEST SHORE.

WILLAMETTE UNIVERSITY,

SALEM, OREGON,

The Oldest and Largest Institution for Higher Education in the Northwest.

30 PROFESSORS AND 400 STUDENTS.

4 BUILDINGS. 400 STUDENTS.

DEPARTMENTS:

College of Liberal Arts, College of Medicine, College of Law, Conservatory of Music, Woman's College, Art Department, Normal School, Business Course, Preparatory Courses, Theological Lectures, Shorthand, etc.

MILITARY DRILL AND TACTICS.

The University boards students at $1.75 to $3.50 per week, according as plain or elegant fare is required. Board and tuition a year for $100.00 to $200.00. Students received at any time.

Greatest care taken for the moral welfare of students. No disreputable characters allowed to enter. No aristocracy except the aristocracy of character and good scholarship. Salem is the finest university town on the coast, and is the educational center of Oregon. Catalogues and information sent free. Address

THOS. VAN SCOY, President, Salem, Oregon.

Advertisement from the 1880s in *West Shore* magazine, which was circulated throughout the Pacific Northwest.

University Hall (Waller) in the late 1870s.

choosing the men proposed by the board, the Oregon Conference of the Methodist Episcopal Church nominally elected the members of the board until 1885. That year, however, the university amended its charter to allow the trustees to elect 9; the alumni, 3; the Oregon Conference, 12; and the Washington and Idaho Conferences, 6. By spreading board membership throughout the Pacific Northwest, Willamette's leaders hoped that the university would strengthen and broaden its support across the region.

With all of these substantive changes in structure, even seemingly solid traditions at Willamette University came under scrutiny. In the 1870s, much of the social and extra-curricular life of the college students had continued to focus on the literary societies established in the previous decade. Each organization had its own meeting rooms in University Hall, and rivalry among the societies remained keen. During the 1880s, however, the literary societies underwent considerable turmoil as the faculty and board sought to assert greater control over these extra-curricular organizations. The faculty objected, in particular, to allowing non-Willamette students to become members and to the often late closing hours of the male societies. After much discussion and initial student resistance to the faculty's assertion of control, the board settled matters by prohibiting non-student membership and placing the University Hall rooms and furniture of the societies under the direct control of the faculty and agents of the board. Finally, when the societies demonstrated continued defiance of the faculty, the board, in 1883, abolished the four existing societies and constituted two new ones—the Philodorian for men and the Philodosian for women. These new groups continued to play a major role in the educational and social life of the university into the early twentieth century.

This action illustrates that while advances were being made, those in power still wished to exert a certain amount of social control over the student body. In the 1870s, under the well-liked President Gatch, the faculty attempted to maintain student discipline and decorum through an elaborate system of demerits that punished misbehavior, absences, tardiness, and failure to attend chapel. Penalties for demerits ranged from reprimand to expulsion and had to take into account a broad age-range among students, which extended from teenagers in the preparatory department to young adults in the liberal arts and other academic courses. These policies were apparently an improvement in the eyes of the student body, as Gatch's advent as president in 1870 generated sighs of relief from the students after the strict discipline imposed by his predecessor, Nelson Rounds.

During the 1880s, under President Van Scoy, the university administration continued emphasizing to prospective students through its catalogue that "the government of the university aims to be mild, but firm in what few regulations it has. Constant thought is exercised to cultivate qualities of manhood and womanhood discoverable in nearly every student. Whenever a student aims to do right, and be diligent and successful in his daily work, he scarcely realizes that he is under government. While the general oversight has especial care to Christian training, yet the school is non-sectarian in its teaching and government. Its courses of study are little different from any other Institution of equal grade."

University rules specified attendance at daily chapel services and at church on Sunday. The rules mandated study during recitation hours and from 7 to 9 pm. They prohibited profanity and tobacco in the school. The rules also required the faculty to hold examinations every term in the college and every five weeks in the academy. No student was allowed to board at a hotel or public boarding house. Other regulations concerned fees and withdrawal for illness or other reasons. In addition, the faculty, from time to time, enacted and enforced specific rules of student conduct, reflecting the mores of the period concerning acceptable deportment between the sexes.[13]

Expectations for student conduct were not the only carryover from earlier times, of course. Leaders of Willamette University in the 1880s would also struggle to find ways to deal with the two ever-present needs for the growing university: operating funds and buildings.

The Women's College housing concept instigated when Van Scoy took office in 1880 proved so popular that the Willson house soon needed enlargement. As the Willamette *College Journal* announced in June 1882, "The growth and work of the Woman's College has thus far been very satisfactory. ... With these satisfactory results before them, those most interested in the work have decided to very much enlarge and improve the building during the summer." Van Scoy's plan called for expanding the two-story house by adding another story and replacing the hip-roof with

Over time, Chloe Clark Willson's Italianate cottage was enlarged and stylistically altered. The first enlargement reflected the then-popular Empire Style with a mansard roof, and later a raised foundation and Victorian tower was added to transform it into the Queen Anne style.

WOMANS' COLLEGE.

the then fashionable mansard roof and the erection of a two-story wing, forty feet long by thirty feet wide. When completed in 1882, the remodeled building measured 80 feet in length and 43 feet in width. Contemporary prints reveal the transition of Willson's house from a vernacular version of an Italianate cottage style to a somewhat awkward Empire style of architecture. Later, in 1887, the Women's College building (the original Lausanne Hall) would be moved from the corner of Court and Capitol streets to the southwest portion of the campus. Van Scoy had the house placed on a high foundation, adding yet another story and a tower to the modified house. Each new addition only increased the architectural muddle that the Willson house had become and so would remain until replaced in 1920 by Lausanne Hall.[14]

While the Women's College provided adequate housing for women on campus, the university struggled to accommodate the male students. The board had aggravated the situation in 1879 when it ordered the owners of the String Town shanties to tear them down. Unfortunately, the university had only the attic and basement of University Hall to offer as alternative dormitory space. At most, University Hall could house only about 30 students. To remedy the situation, the university, in 1885, purchased and remodeled a building two blocks from campus to accommodate 40 young men. The university charged $1.00 a month for room, and board cost another $1.50 per week.

While all of this new housing capacity boded well for an expanding physical plant at Willamette, the university desperately needed new buildings to house a library, science labs, and a gymnasium. It also sought to establish endowed faculty chairs. Thus, no sooner had Tower reached his initial fundraising goal than, at the board's direction, he started seeking more money. Unfortunately, the travails of the Medical School and a serious threat to the existence of the Salem campus would dominate the attention of all concerned over the remainder of the decade.

While the Willamette University Medical School had gotten off to a rocky start in the late 1860s, the medical department soon gained its footing and seemed to thrive over the next 20 years. Starting with a faculty of nine Salem-area physicians under the leadership of Dr. Horace Carpenter as dean, the medical school initially held its lectures in University Hall and used a shed on campus for dissections. The small population of Salem limited the clinical facilities available for instruction, but as one medical historian noted in retrospect, "Compared with many other medical schools, even in the older settlements of the East, the new Department at Salem does not suffer too much."[15]

Nominally under the authority of the Willamette University Board of Trustees, the medical school largely governed itself. This degree of freedom occasioned many misunderstandings and almost constant dissension within the faculty, especially over which doctors could hold certain professorships. Until he resigned as dean in 1875, Dr. Carpenter seemed to be the focus of much of the dissention within the faculty. In 1873, after outgrowing the space available in University Hall, the medical school moved to quarters on the second floor of a building in downtown Salem. Regardless of where it was located, the school financed its operations solely from student tuition fees. During the first decade of operation (1867-77), 77 students received medical degrees after attending the prescribed two courses (20 weeks each) of lectures. Three of the graduates in the first decade of operation were women.[16]

Although the Willamette Medical School was advanced for the times in allowing women to receive a medical education, the example of Mary Sawtelle indicated that it was not an easy undertaking. Sawtelle protested to the Willamette Board of Trustees in August 1871 that she had completed all of the requirements for graduation and all but one professor, who had joined the faculty only a few weeks before the end of her final term, had voted to grant her a diploma. She charged that the holdout professor had "informed me that I had made a blunder in the choice of a profession. That he was opposed to females being physicians and I of all women was unfit for the high position." With great exasperation, she claimed that "each time that I came into his august presence for an examination he has vouched safe the information before asking me a question that I could not pass his chair." She further claimed that the "Dean assured me that my being a woman should make no difference and promised me again that in July I should graduate." The offending professor denied that he was prejudiced against Sawtelle "either personally or because you are a woman." He, however, would not reconsider his refusal to grant her another examination, bluntly stating, "Simply your request is preposterous and I cannot do anything for you." Even though the offending professor resigned from the medical school in November 1872, the trustees failed to act on Sawtelle's grievance. In the meantime, she went East to the New York Medical College and graduated in 1872. Her husband completed his medical degree at Willamette in 1873, and they both subsequently practiced medicine in Portland and San Francisco.[17]

In 1878, the Willamette board decided to relocate the medical school to Portland. Several factors influenced this decision. Continued dissension within the Salem medical faculty, the more abundant clinical facilities available in Portland—a city with a population almost ten times the size of Salem—and the fear that a rival medical school might organize in Portland led to the move. Initially, the relocated medical school had to operate in rented quarters, with dissecting carried out in the loft of a livery stable. Anxious to better establish its credibility, the Willamette Medical School joined the Association of American Medical Colleges in 1880. By 1884, it began raising funds for a new building dedicated to medical instruction. Friends and supporters of the medical school raised $25,000 by 1886 and construction began on the new building. When completed, the three-story brick building boasted state-of-the-art medical facilities. The first floor contained a dispensary, infirmary, and two lecture rooms while the second floor housed an auditorium with seating for 150 and rooms for the chemical laboratory, library, and faculty offices. The third floor featured a dissecting room with 20 tables and a refrigerating plant capable of accommodating 30 bodies. The new medical school building cost about $35,000 when complete.[18]

The medical school building, designed by Portland architect William Stokes, was quite an imposing structure. The brick and masonry building, located at NW 14th and Couch Street, was crowned with a mansard roof upon which, as Robert Gatke noted, "had been exercised all the decorative arts loved in that day of ornate building." Designed in the high Victorian manner, the Medical College combined both Renaissance and Gothic stylistic elements. The building's abundant application of sheet-metal trim on multiple towers, pinnacles, and gables, and metal cresting on the roof—coupled with the heavy use of stone belt courses, window molding, and corner trim on the exterior—exhibited all the hallmarks of the high Empire Style of architecture. The end result of Stokes' architectural confection justified a reporter for the *Oregonian* in observing that "the [medical] college was the most ornamental brick building in the city."[19]

During its years in Portland, the medical school attempted to increase its instructional standards by

Mary Sawtelle in 1891.

requiring a longer course of study to obtain a medical degree. In 1883, it tried to require three courses of lectures for graduation, but by1886, it retreated and the requirement became a strong recommendation only. The school did manage to increase each course of lectures and clinical studies to six months instead of five. In 1891, the school once again instituted a three-year program and recommended a fourth year of additional study. During the 1880s, with a faculty typically numbering 14, attendance averaged 28 students. Between 1877 and 1887, 85 graduated with medical degrees. From 1888 to 1900, the medical school graduated another 70.[20]

As the medical school settled into its new modern facilities, disaster struck on two fronts. On December 16, 1886, workmen left untended a portable stove that was drying the newly plastered walls and it caught the wood trim on fire. The ensuing conflagration gutted much of the interior of the new building. Fortunately, insurance covered the damage, and the building contractor quickly carried out the necessary repairs. Then, just as the new building was ready for occupancy, serious divisions once again engulfed the faculty. The deep divisions within the medical faculty appeared very starkly in a lengthy letter from one of the dissident members—purporting to represent a majority of the aggrieved faculty—to the Board of Trustees. After averring that "my colleagues and myself have always hewed with solicitude for the welfare of the College," the angry doctor immediately got to the point of the grievance:

> *the appointment immediate and continued of Dr. Frasier as Dean of the Faculty. This factor is and has been always the 'casus Belli'—Why? Because the majority of them believe that he is not possessed of the stability and character and*

Cover of the Medical Department Annual Announcement 1892-93

> *standing in this community which are necessary in one occupying the position of Dean to give solidity and support and consequence to the institution over which he presides.*

The doctor continued his criticism of the dean by charging that "his conduct in the administration of the affairs of the institution—the appointment of professors—his decisions in the chair—his treatment, unjust and unfair of his fellow doctors and the faculty—have at different times laid him liable to the charges of unfitness and incapacity." The doctor then turned his attention to the actions of the board, which, he lamented,

> *impowers this doubtful character [i.e. the Dean] to eliminate from all connection with a school, for whose welfare they have toiled and suffered and sacrificed time and opportunities—men—honorable men, whose reputations have never been assailed. Who have never even laid themselves open to misconstruction—and forsooth to elect in their places men who are aliens and unknown—Oh! Justice thou are fled to Brutish beasts and men have lost their reason!*

The angry doctor concluded by stating that "as a matter of necessity and with belief and confidence in the Board of Trustees, as an important tribunal—one and all tender their resignations and the result is awaited with anxious anticipation."[21]

In the face of the mass resignation of the medical faculty, the board continued to support the dean. After an independent investigation, the trustees stated that the "characterization you (i.e. the dissidents) make concerning him is not justified by any facts ... [and that] all agree, yourselves included, that Doctor Frasier is eminently fitted to perform the business duties of the office of Dean, and has performed them in the past in an manner preeminently satisfactory to all concerned." The trustees also felt that Dr. Frasier's administrative and financial skills were essential in raising funds for equipping and furnishing the newly completed medical school building. Finally, the trustees admonished the dissident doctors that "some considerations urged in the latter part of your communication [to the board], the Trustees believe you will yourselves on reflection consider as not dictated by a judicial spirit and that in calmer moments you would not have brought them forward." The medical students even felt it necessary to weigh in on the controversy. In a letter to the trustees, some of the students urged that if keeping the current dean meant the loss of the dissident faculty and with them vital clinical privileges, then the students "would much prefer to keep the clinical advantages." A continuing controversy between the Board of Trustees and the medical faculty over paying off the remaining debt from building the new medical building in Portland also embroiled the relationship between the two bodies in the late 1880s.[22]

A revamped faculty left out some of the irreconcilable members, who then joined with other Portland physicians to found a second medical school in Portland during the fall of 1887. The new medical school had the backing of the University of Oregon and soon had enough clout to deny the Willamette Medical School doctors clinical privileges at Portland's two existing hospitals. To overcome this potentially devastating hurdle, supporters of the Willamette Medical School started a Methodist hospital to provide the crucial clinical facilities and, in 1889, added a College of Pharmacy. Unfortunately, the hospital struggled financially and suffered from internal dissension among the medical staff. When the Methodist hospital failed financially in 1895 and subsequently was sold to homeopathic physicians, the Willamette medical faculty again lacked hospital privileges. Nothing more could be done in Portland, so the Willamette Board of Trustees moved the medical

Charles Stratton, 1833-1910.

department back to Salem. Until Willamette University built a new medical school building on campus in 1905, the medical school once again operated out of rented quarters in Salem's downtown.[23]

During the 1890s, while struggling to maintain its medical school, Willamette University also fought a major battle for its very existence. The university's troubles began when some erstwhile friends thought that Willamette might have a brighter future in the rapidly growing, more cosmopolitan city of Portland than in much smaller, out-of-the-way Salem. Members of the Willamette Board of Trustees and the Methodist Conference split over the matter. One group wanted either to move Willamette or, failing that, organize a rival Methodist college in Portland, while others fought to keep Willamette alive in Salem and prevent the creation of a rival school.

The impetus for the move seems to have come from Charles Stratton, who became chancellor (a newly created but short-lived position) of Willamette University in 1890. Stratton and his supporters among the Methodist Conference had a vision of a grander Methodist university than currently existed in the form of Willamette. They wanted more buildings and better equipment and facilities to carry out the school's educational mission. This faction felt that a move to Portland, with its greater financial and cultural advantages, could better secure their goal. Powerful civic interests in Portland seemed receptive to the move. The *Oregonian*, Portland's leading newspaper, editorialized that the city would benefit both economically and culturally from having a "high grade" institution of learning, and a relocated Willamette seemed to meet that requirement: "The advantages to Portland of an institution of this grade are beyond computation … . Portland has no institution of this grade; it may now secure the best and it cannot afford to neglect the opportunity."[24]

Willamette soon received offers of free land from Portland real estate speculators who wanted to use the presence of a university to market their undeveloped land holdings on the east side of the city. Not to be outdone and fearing the effects of losing one of their prime cultural institutions, Salem citizens offered financial inducements, also based on a real estate speculation, to remain in their city. Opponents of the move secured a legal opinion that Willamette's charter prohibited a move from Salem without the approval of the state legislature. In response to the threat of legal action to keep Willamette in Salem, the Board of Trustees voted in December 1890 to remain in Salem, coupled with an urgent request for better support of the school. But the matter did not end there.[25]

The Methodist ministers and laymen wanting a university in Portland decided that if they could not move Willamette, they would start one of their own. After the new institution incorporated in early 1891, Chancellor Stratton accepted the presidency of the new university—named Portland University—even before he resigned his position at Willamette. The promoters of Portland University sought to finance it by developing and selling home sites from a 600-acre tract of land along the Willamette River in north Portland. The campus would sit on a high bluff overlooking the river on land platted and marketed as the University Park addition to Portland. Developers hoped that the presence of the university would be a major selling point for land sales. As the new speculative development got underway, a surprising defection from Willamette to the fledgling university seemed to give the undertaking added strength. Thomas Van Scoy, Willamette's president under Chancellor Stratton, agreed to become dean of Portland University and brought with him a number of Willamette students. Angry friends of Willamette considered Stratton and Van Scoy "turncoats."[26]

The new Portland University (later to become the Catholic-run University of Portland) announced in its initial catalogue that it did not intend "to come into collision or competition with any other educational institution, present or prospective." An intense struggle, however, soon arose between the two universities for the sole support of the Methodist Church. Willamette keenly felt the loss of President Van Scoy and other defecting faculty, trustees, and students. Many in Salem accused Van Scoy of engaging in improper recruiting practices and of spreading unfounded rumors that the Willamette campus did not maintain proper sanitation, supposedly creating an unhealthy environment for students. Most unsettling of all was the fact that Willamette could ill afford to lose the financial support of the Methodist Conference. When that happened in the early 1890s, it set in motion events culminating in a deep financial crisis later in the decade. To deal with the crisis initially, the board, in July 1891, selected Reverend George Whitaker as the tenth president of Willamette. His tenure was brief, however. Whitaker, while a good administrator, apparently created much disgruntlement among the students for his attempts to limit association between the sexes and upset the board with his demands to control all aspects of administration and finance. One student present during Whitaker's presidency later described him as "a straight laced old hard shell [from the east] who … couldn't understand why the western boys and girls resented his tyranny." He resigned in the fall of 1893.[27]

At the start of Whitaker's brief tenure, Willamette experienced another potentially devastating setback. On September 16, 1891, University Hall caught fire.

Above: University Hall (now Waller Hall) immediately after the fire as smoke is still coming off the roof. Lausanne is in the left background. **Below:** University Hall, now in Empire Style, as it was rebuilt after the first fire in 1891. Note the Mansard roof and Victorian tower.

James Matthews, 1864-1942, beloved long-time mathematics professor, for whom Matthews Hall is named.

The ensuing conflagration destroyed the roof and caused extensive fire and water damage to the rest of the building. Much of the library was burned, and students living in the attic lost most of their personal possessions. President Whitaker noted in his annual report to the board that the fire had caused "much inconvenience to our pupils and teachers which has been uncomplainingly endured without any real injury to any." With insurance proceeds and gifts from friends, Willamette soon repaired the damage to the building. Unfortunately, to gain more space, the original Greek Revival-styled cross-gabled roof was replaced with a mansard roof sporting a heavy tower atop it. Old University Hall had gained another floor of much needed space at the expense of architectural integrity and symmetry.[28]

The board replaced Whitaker with Willis Hawley, a Willamette graduate (1884) who was then serving as a mathematics and history professor at the university. Hawley continued to serve Willamette as president until 1902 and remained on the faculty until 1907, when he resigned after his election to the United States Congress. Hawley proved to be just the right leader to carry Willamette through the dark years of the 1890s. According to Professor James T. Matthews, longtime member of the Willamette faculty, Hawley possessed "imagination, and enthusiasm and tireless physical energy." Matthews went on to state that Hawley "held up our scholastic standards, conciliated the students, held together an excellent faculty, and made every dollar do the work of two." The latter quality was especially needed given the financially precarious state of the university at the time.[29]

There existed among faculty, students, and trustees alike a strong sentiment that Willamette needed to add buildings and acquire better equipment to achieve its academic goals. As historian Robert Gatke so succinctly put it, "All of the great dreams of enlarged campus, new buildings, and fine equipment, which had been associated with the attempted move of the school to Portland, naturally caused all the students and friends of Willamette to dream of better housing for the pioneer university." The school catalogue for 1891-92 even contained a drawing of the proposed new academic building, which President Whitaker suggested should be named Waller Hall. (The then-named University Hall would be renamed Waller Hall at a later date.) It was estimated to cost $25,000, and would house classrooms, science laboratories, offices, and a 1,300-seat auditorium. Amid the onset of a national economic depression and the competition from the new Portland University, which had won the full financial support of the Methodist Conference, however, the funds were not to be found.[30] Subsequent catalogues for the rest of the decade dropped the picture and any mention of a new academic building.

Budgets during the early 1890s give some idea of the university's straightened financial condition. Willamette had a long-term debt of about $25,000, mostly stemming from the cost of erecting the Medical College building in Portland and repairing and remodeling University Hall after the fire of 1891. Typical yearly budgets ranged between $9,000 and $11,000, including roughly $1,500 in interest on the existing debt. Income from tuition, endowment, and gifts usually brought in about $8,000 to $9,000, leaving yearly deficits in excess of $2,000. The faculty felt the brunt of the diminished resources. At the beginning of the decade, the president earned $1,500 a year and the full-time College of Liberal Arts faculty received $1,000 each. By the middle of the 1890s, the president's salary had been reduced to $1,000 and the professors received only $800. Salaries were often in arrears. To meet the ever-rising debt and some current expenses, the trustees resorted to borrowing as they had in the 1870s. They took out a $16,000 five-year mortgage on the university campus in May 1892, and the following year secured a loan for $8,000 with the medical college property in Portland as collateral. The situation became so dire in 1899 that to avoid foreclosure on the mortgages, the trustees had to borrow from the endowment fund and foreclose on its own bankrupt debtors in order to raise the money necessary to pay the accrued interest on the loans. Throughout the decade of the 1890s, President Hawley complained to the trustees that the university buildings were sorely in need of repairs.[31]

Willamette's financial problems largely stemmed from the loss of the yearly contributions from the Methodist Church of the Pacific Northwest. The education commission of the Methodist Conference stubbornly remained committed to the notion of united church support for one great Methodist university in the region, located in Portland. This institution was to be strengthened by consolidating the Portland and Puget Sound universities. The latter school was an equally struggling Methodist college in Tacoma, Washington. Both of these institutions had been promoted originally as elements of larger speculative real estate ventures. When these speculations toppled into bankruptcy during the economic depression of the 1890s, the effort to combine the Portland and Puget Sound universities failed because neither institution had any actual assets.

The Methodist Conference finally recognized the inevitable in 1899 and adopted the following resolution at its annual meeting:

> *Whereas, the consolidation of the Universities [Portland and Puget Sound] failed through the inability of the two universities to meet these conditions of consolidation; and whereas, University Park and West Hall have been surrendered to the creditors of Portland University, said surrender being caused by the great financial degradation of values, and the University Corporation is without endowment or land; therefore Resolved, ... That we recommend the consolidation of Willamette University and Portland University; that we request Portland University to close up its work as a separate school by the end of the present year; and that we recommend ... the Willamette University to adopt the alumni of Portland University and publish their names in its catalogue.*

The proposed building for the College of Liberal Arts.

The proposed College of Liberal Arts building. If built, it would have been stylistically ahead of its time.

The Willamette catalogue for 1899-1900, in fact, noted that "the Executive Boards of the two institutions have made and accepted with utmost good will a liberal and its hoped acceptable and permanent union of the two institutions." It was ironic, perhaps, that the last president of Portland University and the person responsible for winding up its affairs as it closed its doors was none other than Reverend George Whitaker—the same person who had presided over

Willis Hawley, 1864-1941, who served as president of Willamette during the 1890s when the future of Willamette University was in question.

Willamette University at the beginning of the decade of struggle between the two universities. President Hawley noted to the Board of Trustees that Whitaker's "loyalty to the church and her educational interests, and his hearty cooperation with us to ensure the future success of Willamette University are worthy of the highest commendation."[32]

While the core administrative and academic structure of Willamette remained intact during the stressful nineties, the university was not immune to the reforms sweeping higher education during the period. The basic curriculum of the College of Liberal Arts during the troubled 1890s showed little change from that of prior years, but nevertheless, there were additions. A College of Theology – long sought by the Methodist Church – was established in 1889, but was slow starting due to a chronic lack of funds and an insufficient number of students interested in the ministry. In addition, a College of Pharmacy operated until 1896. An awareness of the new trends in higher education was evident at Willamette University throughout the 1890s. The Academy continued normal school and business divisions within its structure. New elective courses in history, social sciences, science, and literature appeared in the college offerings. Already in 1891, Professor Willis Hawley argued for the teaching of contemporary history:

> *There is room for a wide reform in college curricula which [at present] do not include a systematic study of current history as required work. … It requires a wider knowledge for a man to be abreast with his times to-day, than to know the lores of antiquity. … They [i.e. students] get credits for amassing ancient lore and they amass it. It seems to me a chair of current history is an imperative necessity in every college. The study of ancient times furnishes a key to much history of our times. That study is important and cannot be omitted. If that study is so valuable as a key to current history, of how much greater importance is the understanding of the events of to-day. … The college which requires a systematic study of current history as required work, is deserving of hearty public support.*

In 1896, President Hawley reported that Willamette had adopted a credit system for graduation requirements, based on the plan developed by Northwestern University. Limitations in the size of the faculty governed the speed with which curriculum change occurred. Willamette's institutional peers, such as Pacific University, McMinnville College (Linfield), and Albany College (Lewis and Clark) also began to adopt curricular changes such as Willamette was undertaking.[33]

Defections to Portland University in the early 1890s affected enrollment in the College of Liberal Arts; for several years it averaged only 20 college-level students. By the later years of the decade, when the survival of Portland University appeared less certain, the Liberal Arts' student body as a whole averaged 164. Throughout the 1890s, the College of Music continued to attract large numbers, averaging close to 200 students. The Academy, as in earlier years, accounted for a high percentage of all students registered at Willamette.[34]

Until the 1890s, Willamette undergraduates lived a somewhat isolated educational existence. Gradually, they began to engage with other colleges and university students in the region through religious associations, such as the YMCA and YWCA; oratorical and debate contests; and athletic meets. In 1894, the editor of the *Collegian* noted this student awakening and intercollegiate engagement:

> *Until a few years ago the average college student of Oregon knew little if anything, about the other schools of the state. Neither was any desire felt to know more, and the exchange journals which*

> *were few, could do little to disturb this complacent ignorance. Now, the exchange editor is not the only one in school who is aware that there are other colleges in the state; but all have a keen interest in their affairs. … This mutual interest has resulted from the intercourse of the students brought about primarily by the Christian Association convention. Through this the Oratorical Association was formed, and now the Football Association has been instituted. Now, the students of the Oregon Colleges are not strangers but meet as friends and acquaintances on a plane of spiritual, mental and physical activity.*[35]

The early 1890s also marked the beginning of Willamette students' interest in athletics. There is evidence of baseball clubs in earlier decades, but as a *Collegian* writer noted in October 1893, "Willamette is undoubtedly behind other Oregon colleges in athletics." The *Collegian* writer went on to plea, "Cannot some of the students arouse an interest in this direction? They will deserve the gratitude of all if successful." At first, the student athletes operated without a coach and achieved indifferent results, especially in football. The *Collegian* editorialized in 1896:

> *The season is over and foot ball has been a farce in Willamette this year. Nor does the blame for our failure to make a creditable showing fall upon the manager. It is true that he put forth the most strenuous efforts to place a good team in the field. The result only serves to emphasize two or three facts. First, we must have a coach, if we expect to accomplish much. … Again the team itself must be formed from persons who are regular and permanent students in the university. The man who enters only for the benefit of football has no interest in the University and cares little for its success. A team selected from regular students and association in the class rooms with the other students will inevitably awaken a deeper interest and arouse a greater enthusiasm for this particular kind of athletics.*[36]

In the early years of college athletics, the Willamette students generally took the initiative in organizing and funding the effort. They hired trainers and coaches to guide their football, basketball, and track teams. As one historian of higher education in the 1890s has noted, this was typical of colleges at the time: "Intercollegiate sports shared with other extracurricular activities that characteristic of originally having been run by and for students. Attempts by faculty and administration to gain control were usually derailed by determined undergraduates. Logistics of travel, scheduling, and maintenance of facilities and equipment were coordinated by student managers." Given Willamette's financial difficulties, it was probably the only way intercollegiate sports could have worked. In time, trustees, as well as students and even townspeople, contributed money to support athletics at Willamette. Track and field events also attracted student interest. As many as eight colleges competed in intercollegiate track meets held annually at Willamette during the 1890s. Women students also showed an interest in organized sports, starting a tennis club and giving gymnastic exhibitions.[37]

The new role of athletics in campus life culminated in a drive for a stand-alone gymnasium at Willamette. Initially, a room for weights and other physical education training equipment was set aside in University Hall, but this quickly proved insufficient. In 1894, the board authorized its financial agent to begin raising funds for a gym, and by 1895 the university had such a building. The new two-story gymnasium building was constructed of wood and measured 60 by 80 feet and contained, according the university catalogue of 1894-95, "offices, lockers, shower and tub baths, wash rooms, and all the usual apparatus." It exhibited the Victorian Stick-Style of architecture, in which a stick-work of boards intersecting at right angles was applied over the clapboard sheathing to

The gymnasium and the adjacent bell tower, which housed the victory bell rung after each winning game.

suggest interior framing. The steep, hipped roof had large intersecting gables. The building cost about $2,500.[38]

Typical of the era, Willamette students' increasing contacts with other colleges and universities in the Willamette Valley led the collegians to adopt university colors, yells, and songs. This was a way to establish loyalty to one's own campus and distinguish it from other institutions. The *Collegian* of January 1892 reported "the several committees, after close consultation, decided that cardinal red and gold shall be the representative." The impact of increasing intercollegiate contacts through athletics, oratorical, and debate competitions; the adoption of school colors; and the freer association between male and female students all reflected a new sense of student self-awareness. Student life in the 1890s was becoming more rounded as athletics and new social activities joined academics and the existing literary societies in defining collegiate existence. A *Collegian* editor writing in December 1896 tried to capture this new student dynamic:

> *There is a vague something which binds together the students of our higher school known as 'College Spirit.' It is that sense of sympathy and brotherhood which grows out of a community of interests and a similarity of aspirations and difficulties. The stronger this feeling of brotherhood the more perfect the union of student effort, and the more surely will success attend all student understandings. But let this spirit languish and die out and there is no union of effort. Student enterprises are at best but desultory under such circumstances. Each person puts forth his solitary effort and those students who have sufficient spirit to undertake college enterprises find themselves unsupported. We believe that Willamette has much room for improvement in these lines.*[39]

The *Collegian* itself played a major role in student life, reporting on all aspects of student and faculty activities and offering considerable space for student-produced literary material. (In fact, there is some evidence that a student newspaper named the *Willamette Collegian* existed as early as 1875, but no copies survived to indicate its contents or how long it continued publication.)

Through the determined efforts of the trustees, faculty, students, and friends, Willamette University managed to survive the turbulent decade of the nineties intact. In spite of the turmoil over finances and competition from Portland University, the College of Liberal Arts graduated 79 students. Even the need to uproot the medical school from Portland and reestablish it in Salem did not prevent the college from graduating 54 doctors during the decade. From its founding in 1884 until 1899, the College of Law matriculated 47 students, with 41 of that number graduating in the latter decade. The liberal arts curriculum broadened, and student life took on a new spirit that reflected a more diverse array of activities and levels of involvement. As Willamette looked at the new century with renewed vigor, it still faced some old problems that would soon need solutions. It desperately required new buildings and better equipment and library facilities for educating undergraduates. It needed to grow the small endowment to insure the institution's future viability after the near-death experience of the 1890s. Still, with a committed faculty, a dedicated Board of Trustees, a band of enthusiastic students, and loyal alumni, Willamette seemed ready to meet the challenges ahead.[40]

After seeing Willamette through some of its darkest days and skillfully reuniting Willamette with its wayward offspring in Portland, President Hawley felt optimistic about Willamette's future. In his report to the Board of Trustees in June 1900, he noted the "happy solution of the educational problem which has disturbed the Methodist Northwest for several years. … Our field is now undivided, our patrons not disturbed in mind by the conflicting claims of two institutions under the patronage of the same church. … Under such favorable conditions it is to be hoped that the coming years may prove prosperous." On such an auspicious note, Hawley asked to be relieved of his presidency. He felt that an ordained minister could more effectively raise money from individual Methodist churches throughout the Pacific Northwest. The board, however, did not replace Hawley until 1902, when they elected Reverend John Coleman as the new President of Willamette.[41]

A hand-colored photograph postcard from 1907 of Willamette University showing University Hall, the Gymnasium and Lausanne.

Endnotes

1 Quote in Rudolph, *The American College*, 298.

2 For background on the development of the American college movement in the late nineteenth century, see Rudolph, *The American College*, 241-354, and Thelin, *History of Higher Education*, 74-180; Geiger, *American Higher Education*, 269-421. See also, William G. Robbins, "From Church to State: The Sectarian Roots Of Oregon State University, 1868-1888," *Oregon Historical Quarterly* (Spring, 2016), 76-99.

3 Rudolph, *The American College*, 332.

4 Quote in Gatke, *Chronicles of Willamette*, 276; quote in, *Collegian*, Sep. 1893, 11.

5 James H. Hitchman, *Liberal Arts Colleges in Oregon and Washington, 1842-1980* (Bellingham, Washington: Center for Pacific Northwest Studies, 1981), 37-40, 59-60, 79-82; Howard McKinley Corning, ed., *Dictionary of Oregon History* (Portland, OR: Binfords and Mort, 1956), 185, 253.

6 Turner, *Campus*, 53-167.

7 *Oregonian*, Dec. 30, 1872.

8 The Willamette University Alumni Register (Jan. 1920).

9 Cancelled $10,000 note for loan from Land and Bush Bank, 1874-77, Willamette University Records, 1855-1900, Box 1, Willamette University Archives; Satisfaction of $10,000 loan guaranteed by mortgage (1877) for 5 years, release, Jul. 1882, by William Bennett of New York, ibid.

10 Quote in Gatke, *Chronicles of Willamette*, 354.

11 Report of the Endowment Agent, Feb. 17, 1883, Willamette University Records, 1855-1900, Box 1, Willamette University Archives.

12 *Willamette University Catalogue 1880-81*, 29-33.

13 *Willamette University Catalogue 1885-86*, 33-34.

14 *Willamette College Journal*, June 1882, 5.

15 Quote in O. Larsell, "Willamette University Medical School," *Surgery, Gynecology and Obstetrics*, LIV (May, 1932): 852-855. For background on the Willamette University Medical School, see also Larsell, "Joseph Henry Wythe 1822-1904," *Oregon Historical Quarterly* XXVI (1925): 435-38; Larsell, "The Development of Medical Education in the Pacific Northwest," *Oregon Historical Quarterly*, XXVII, No. 1 (1926): 65-112; Thelma Wilson, "A Century of Medical Education in Oregon," *Northwest Medicine* (1967): 3-12; John N. Ramage, "History of Willamette University Medical School," (paper presented at a meeting of the Medical History Club of the University of Oregon Medical School, March 26, 1936); O. Larsell, *The Doctor in Oregon: A Medical History* (Portland, OR: Binfords and Mort, 1947), 343-61.

16 On Dr. Carpenter's resignation, see H. Carpenter to Board of Trustees, Dec. 3, 1875, WU 2006/14, Box 100/01, Willamette University Archives; The Willamette University Alumni Register (Jan. 1920), 42-44.

17 Mary Sawtelle to Board of Trustees, Aug. 28, 1871, WU 2006/14, Box 100/01, Willamette University Archives; E. Chase, M.D. to Mary Sawtelle, Aug. 22, 1871, ibid.; H. Carpenter to C. N. Terry, Nov. 30, 1872, 2006/14, Box 100/01, Willamette University Archives; The Willamette University Alumni Register (Jan. 1920), 43; Jean Ward, "Mary Priscilla Avery Sawtelle (1833-1894), *The Oregon Encyclopedia*, www.oregonencyclopedia.org/articles/sawtelle_mary_priscilla_avery_1835_1894, accessed Jul. 20, 2017.

18 On the move to Portland, see T. L. Rowland to Board of Trustees, Jun. 10, 1878, Medical School and Gatke Papers, Willamette University Archives; *Oregonian*, Jan. 1, 1887, 4.

19 Quote in Gatke, *Chronicles of Willamette*, 372; quote in *Oregonian*, Dec. 16, 1886, see also *Oregonian*, Dec. 24, 1886; for identification of Stokes as architect, see also *Oregonian*, Jan. 1, 1887, 4.

20 The Willamette University Alumni Register (Jan. 1920), 44-47.

21 *Oregonian*, Dec. 16, 1886; Kenneth A. J. MacKenzie to Mr. Moores, Apr. 23, 1887, Willamette Records, 1855-1900, Box 1, Willamette University Archives.

22 Board of Trustees to Otto S. Binswanger, M.D., et al., Apr. 21, 1887, WU 2006/14, Box 100/01, Willamette University Archives; Junior Class, Medical Department to Board of Trustees, Apr. 2, 1887, ibid; Dean E. P. Fraser to C. B. Moores, Jun. 6, 1887, ibid.; Petition of Medical Faculty to Board of Trustees, Jun. 11, 1888, ibid.; F. P. Tower to George Hughes, Nov. 27, 1889, ibid.

23 The travails of the Willamette University Medical School in Portland generated much press coverage. See for example *Oregonian*, Sep. 24, 1887, 8; Sep. 19, 1895, 10; Sep. 21, 1895, 8; Sep. 24, 1895, 5; Sep. 25, 1895, 6; Sep. 26, 1895; Oct. 1, 1895, 8; Oct. 8, 1895, 3. *Collegian*, Dec. 1895, 10; Mar. 9, 1911; see also Larsell, *The Doctor in Oregon*, 360-62.

24 *Oregonian*, Sep. 7, 1890; Feb. 28, 1891, 8. Charles Stratton had graduated from Willamette in 1869 and went on to achieve distinction as an educator. Before being named Willamette's chancellor—at the instigation of Van Scoy—he served as president of the College of the Pacific and Mills College, both in California; Gatke, *Chronicles of Willamette*, 408-09.

25 For the arguments against giving Methodist support to the speculative venture to move Willamette University to Portland, see "Minority Report of the Committee on Education to the Oregon Conference, 1891," Willamette University Archives; Proposal from Citizens of Salem to the Board of Trustees, 1890, WU 2006/14, Box 100/01, Willamette University Archives; see also, Wright Cowger, "Two Difficult Decades for Willamette," *Willamette Scene* (Summer 1981), 4-5.

26 *Oregonian*, Feb. 8, 1891, 8; Cowger, "Two Difficult Decades for Willamette."

27 Quote in Gatke, *Chronicles of Willamette*, 414; John Dennison to Rev. George Whitaker, Nov. 25, 1892 and Dec. 14, 1892, Jun. 8, 1893, Whitaker Papers, Willamette University Archives; F. P. Tower to George Whitaker, Jan. 20, 1892, Whitaker Papers, Willamette University Archives; Report of Committee Reviewing the Complaints of President Whitaker, Sep. 4, 1893, Willamette University Records, 1890-1948, Box 2, Willamette University Archives; the *Collegian*, Oct. 1893, 11, described Whitaker as "a man of high culture, tireless activity, and rare eloquence." Last quote from Burt Brown Barker to Robert Gatke, Apr. 21, 1942, Gatke Papers, Folder 21, Box 1, Willamette University Archives; see also, Cowger, "Two Difficult Decades for Willamette."

28 On the fire damage, see "Editorial," *Pacific Christian Advocate* (Sept. 23, 1891), 4; quote in George Whitaker, Annual Report of President to Board of Trustees, Jun. 14, 1892, Whitaker Papers, Willamette University Archives. The fire cost about $9,600 in damages, while the insurance proceeds came to a little over $6,600, Willamette University Records, 1855-1900, Box 2, Willamette University Archives.

29 Quote in Gatke, *Chronicles of Willamette*, 421-22.

30 Quote in ibid., 465. George Whitaker, Annual Report of President to Board of Trustees, June 14, 1892, Whitaker Papers, Willamette University Archives. The *Collegian* reported in May 1896, 4-5, an effort led by the students to raise funds for a new college building. At a student-called meeting after a regular chapel session, the assembled body pledged $1,551, and the faculty committed $875 to a building fund for the university.

31 On Willamette's indebtedness, see *Collegian*, Sept. 1893, 2-3. See also Financial Report, Willamette University, 1895-96, Willamette Archives 2006/14, Box 100-01, Willamette University Archives; Annual Reports of the President, 1896, 1897, 1899, Office of the President Records, ibid.; Miscellaneous Annual Financial Records, 1891-1897, Willamette University Records, 1855-1900, Box 2, Willamette University Archives.

32 Quote in Gatke, *Chronicles of Willamette*, 472, and see also "Report on Consolidation of Puget Sound University and Portland University, Sep. 12, 1898, Willamette University Archives; Minutes of the 47th Session of the Oregon Annual Conference of the Methodist Episcopal Church, Report on Education, Sep. 20-25, Gatke Papers, Box 4, Willamette University Archives; quote in *Willamette University Catalogue 1899-1900*, 80-81; *Oregonian*, Sep. 27, 1899, 12; Apr. 8, 1900. Portland University tried to maintain its independence until the very last. See for example Thomas Van Scoy to Bishop Cranston, Feb. 9, 1898, Early Oregon Methodist Church Records, Willamette University Archives; Annual Report of the President, 1900, Office of the President Records, Willamette University Archives.

33 Quote in *Collegian*, Oct. 1891, 4-5; Annual Reports of the President, 1896, 1897, 1899, Office of the President Records, Willamette University Archives; Hitchman, *Liberal Arts Colleges*, 37-40, 59-60, 79-82.

34 Annual Reports of the President, 1896, 1897, 1899, Office of the President Records, Willamette University Archives.

35 *Collegian*, Jan. 1894, 2-3.

36 Quotes in *Collegian*, Oct. 1893, 2; Dec. 1896, 26.

37 Quote in Thelin, *History of Higher Education*, 178.

38 *Willamette University Catalogue 1894-95*. Board of Trustee Records, Oct. 31, 1894, Willamette University Records, Box 2, Willamette University Archives.

39 Quote in *Collegian*, Jan. 1892; Dec. 1896.

40 The Willamette Alumni Register (Jan. 1920).

41 Annual Reports of the President, 1900, Office of the President Records, Willamette University Archives.

3

Development of the Modern University

From the turn of the twentieth century to the eve of World War II, higher education witnessed the consolidation of the modern university ideals and practices in curriculum, organization, and campus life. Willamette University generally adopted many of the new trends in higher education, but at a slower pace than the larger public and private colleges and universities. The manifold demands of the modern university caused the old-time college professor—a classically trained generalist and something of a character—to be edged out by the Ph.D. specialists organized into ranks within academic departments. The rise of departments teaching specific academic subjects, such as history or economics, reflected the increasing fragmentation and specialization of knowledge with its emphasis on research and publication. The focus on faculty research in turn led to learned journals, professional societies, university presses, and sabbatical leaves.[1]

The professionalization of higher education was matched by the secularization and professionalization of university and college presidents. The complexities of leading the modern institution of higher education demanded managerial, fundraising, and people skills that most old-fashioned clergyman-presidents lacked. As a historian of higher education put it, "The clergyman president went into discard because he lacked skill in the ways of the world, because his commitment to the classical curriculum stood in the way of the more practical and popular emphasis which commended itself to the trustees, and because the world in which the colleges and universities now moved was more secular, less subject to religious influences." Willamette University, however—with one brief exception—did not give in to this trend

Facing page: Eaton Hall under construction

until almost mid-century. The exception involved the presidency of Willis Hawley during Willamette's struggle for survival in the late 1890s. The university finally joined the era of secular presidents when the Board of Trustees elected G. Herbert Smith to the presidency of Willamette in 1942. Whoever held a university presidency in the modern era had to be a skilled organizer, purposeful administrator, and a reconciler of diverse publics. That person had to bring together students, faculty, alumni, and trustees—groups often at cross purposes—to embrace a common goal. While the modern university presidency often was awash in ambiguities, at a minimum it required patience and resourceful leadership.[2]

The financing of the modern university and college became more complex for a college or university president than it had been in earlier times. In addition to the individual donor, often a trustee, the president now had to deal with new givers, such as the philanthropic foundation and the generous alumnus. The wealthy benefactor was still assiduously courted, but now the large philanthropic foundation appeared on the scene as a game changer. The philanthropic foundations had goals of their own in this exchange, which usually involved imposing standards and standardization to the field of American higher education in return for large sums of money. The largest foundations focusing on education included the Rockefeller General Education Board (founded in 1903) with initial resources of $46 million, the Rockefeller Foundation (1913) established with $154 million, the Carnegie Foundation for the Advancement of Teaching (1906) set up with $31 million, and the Carnegie Corporation (1911) possessing $135 million. These philanthropic agencies worked with the U.S. Bureau of Education to gather and analyze data with the goal of reforming colleges and universities into an effective higher education system. The foundations gave their money not to found new campuses, but to shape the administration of a single institution or an entire state system of higher education. Most of their funds were distributed on a matching gift basis. The foundations also believed that the goals of efficiency and accountability could be achieved best by drawing from the corporate model of management; hence their push to fill boards of trustees with corporate executives.

In the process of accomplishing their higher education goals, the foundations sometimes overreached. One example of such excess involved the attempt by the Carnegie Foundation to provide every college and university professor with a pension. Actuaries miscalculated the expense of this effort and almost bankrupted the foundation. Another controversy arose over the Carnegie Foundation's position that denominational colleges were not eligible to join the pension program. Many colleges dropped their denominational connections, only to discover that the original Carnegie-financed pension program had collapsed. Despite the difficulties over providing faculty pensions, on balance the Carnegie and other foundations had a strong influence on university presidents and trustees. As a higher education specialist noted, "National growth and collegiate and university growth, both public and private, demanded something more than the chaos that had been traditional in American higher education. The foundations, using money as a lever, became one of many agencies for bringing order into American higher education, for standardizing, for organizing the academic community along chosen, rational lines."[3]

Universities and colleges also attempted their own internal reorganization and reforms. The outcome was a proliferation of administrative actions, partly a response to growth in enrollments and demands for increased services. Before the era of the modern university, most small or medium-sized institutions of higher education got along with a president, business manager/agent, and a faculty secretary. With the growth of functions and scope on the college campus, a roster of deans arose: deans or directors of women and men, academic divisions, admissions, and athletics. A registrar and a business manager became common positions. According to one study, the median number of college administrative officers in 1860 was four; by 1933 it stood at 30.5. These new administrators soon established patterns of standard procedures, reinforcing the general push to rationalize the operations of American universities and colleges.

The drive for standardization also affected college admissions. The great variety in college preparation among high schools and academies cried out for standardization, and into this void stepped the College Entrance Examination Board, founded in 1901 by a consortium of higher education institutions. By 1910, 25 Eastern colleges and universities were using the standard examination of the College Board. This process of standardizing admissions advanced further when the Carnegie Foundation helped define a unit of admission credit, which gained gradual acceptance prior to World War I.

The organization and diversity of educational offerings of the modern university and college led to remarkable increases in enrollments and physical plants. Between 1890 and 1925, the numbers attending institutions of higher education increased 4.7 times as fast as the population. This growth was undoubtedly a response to the affordability of higher education at the time. From 1880 to 1920, tuition held steady at a relatively reasonable level. This situation changed as college pricing began to jump upward after 1920. Whereas tuition averaged $70 a year in 1920, by 1940 it hit $133. This increase in tuition, especially during the 1930s, came at a time when general prices were declining because of the Great Depression. Rising ever higher, educational costs hit middle and lower income students hard, as most colleges and universities provided little in the way of scholarships or financial aid.

In spite of the seeming triumph of the attributes of the modern university, the old collegiate ideals of a core classical curriculum, class loyalties, social and living organizations, athletics, and undergraduate entertainments still flourished on many campuses. While lecture courses and seminars had replaced recitations, the goal of developing students with enlightened and critical minds, capable of self-reflection and independent thought, still prevailed. Between the World Wars, the ideal of the liberal education found renewed strength through the establishment of core courses, honors programs, concentrations of courses leading to a subject matter major, and the requirement for a senior theses.

The apparent impersonalization of the modern university did change the relationship between administration and student in one important way. The old idea of a college or university providing *in loco parentis* for its students often faded in the face of the daunting size and diversity of the modern schools. To overcome the sense of student disorientation and loss, institutions of higher education established an apparatus of counseling, especially for freshmen. Harvard, with its house system, and Yale, with its collection of colleges—both adopted in the 1930s—reflected the most systematic and expensive effort to recapture the collegiate values of the past within the structure of the modern university. This commitment to educating young men and women for the demands of twentieth-century American society and economy through small, intimate living arrangements was a solution that most universities and colleges could not afford.

As the modern American university developed in the late nineteenth and early twentieth century, it used architecture to assert its new form and function. At first, German-inspired schools, such as Johns Hopkins and Clark, erected plain, utilitarian buildings that merged with the urban setting in which they were located. The initial buildings were simply structures on the city streets with no special plan to set them apart from the city around them. Critics complained that most traditional campuses simply consisted of a group of architecturally unrelated buildings. The complexity of the modern university cried out for a master plan that would organize a multiplicity of academic departments, programs, administrative offices, laboratories, and student housing facilities into a coherent whole.[4] The goal of the new campus planning esthetic was to create unity and harmony out of diversity. The Beaux-Arts system of architectural planning became popular for campuses following the 1893 Columbian Exposition in Chicago. It worked well for the new institutions of higher education because, as one historian noted, "Its principles of monumental organization facilitated orderly planning on a grand scale and were capable of including many disparate buildings or parts within a unified overall pattern." Ambitious growth would require wealthy donors to provide large sums of money; Beaux-Arts architecture provided the grandeur needed to make such donations attractive to benefactors. Although not fully Beaux-Arts in character, Rockefeller's University of Chicago and Leland Stanford's Stanford University generally exemplified this new direction in campus planning and design.[5]

By the beginning of the twentieth century, a number of schools, such as the University of California (Berkeley), Washington University (St. Louis), Carnegie Tech., the University of Minnesota, and the University of Pittsburgh held architectural competitions that produced Beaux-Arts influenced designs. Existing institutions as well as new ones, moreover, were expanding, and the emerging vogue for planning proved popular at these schools as well. Of course, even if a university had a plan, there was no assurance that it would be faithfully carried out.

Whichever variation on the Beaux-Arts overall scheme was applied to a campus plan, the actual architectural style of the buildings could vary widely. Early twentieth-century architects typically employed classical or medieval (Gothic) styles most often. Prominent architectural critics such as Ralph Adams Cram promoted the Georgian Style for collegiate buildings as well.

The Beaux-Arts plan worked best, of course, for new schools or new sites developed as a result of an institution moving to a different location. Existing campuses, such as Willamette's, usually were comprised of a haphazard collection of buildings of different ages and styles. Still, campus planners attempted to transform existing campuses as well, by employing such Beaux-Arts techniques as symmetry, axality, and overall clarity. The Olmsted Brothers architectural landscape firm (Frederick Law Olmsted, senior, and his partner had been the designers of the Columbian Exhibition) specialized in this type of campus planning, with more than 300 college consultations completed before 1920. In particular, their work at Harvard, Guilford College, and Lake Forest University in the early 1900s demonstrated the kind of orderly transformation that could be accomplished in expert hands. Typically, planners such as the Olmsteds recommended demolishing "obsolete" buildings to open up vistas and add new buildings in an ordered, geometric pattern. They paid close attention to the existing topography and usually tried to work with it rather than radically change it.[6]

As the leading landscape architecture firm advising American college and university presidents in the early twentieth century, it is not surprising that several schools in the Pacific Northwest would turn to the Olmsteds for advice on campus planning. John Charles Olmsted made several trips to Oregon and Washington between 1903 and 1911 to prepare landscape plans for many public and private clients, including institutions of higher education. This work began in 1903 when Olmsted travelled to Portland to provide a plan for the Lewis and Clark Exposition and to advise on the development of the Portland Parks system. He returned again several times over the next seven years to consult further on Portland parks development and to advise various private clients about landscape projects. He also went to Seattle in 1903, 1906, and 1911 to consult on that city's park system and planning for the Alaska-Yukon-Pacific Exposition held in 1909.

Presidents and trustees of two small Oregon colleges and the rapidly expanding, larger Oregon State College of Agriculture hoped that the prestige associated with having a campus plan designed by the Olmsted firm would raise their schools' profile and aid in fundraising. After consulting on campus plans for the University of Washington in Seattle (1903), Whitman College in Walla Walla (1906), and the University of Idaho (1906), Olmsted became involved in preparing a campus layout for McMinnville College (later Linfield College) between 1907 and 1909. McMinnville College, at the time Olmsted began his work, was a small, financially struggling institution, so he couched his guidance in terms of the school's future growth. Olmsted recommended "a formal general plan with as much symmetry in the location and design of buildings as possible." He recognized that over time different architects would use different styles, so he urged that buildings be grouped in three quadrangles, "somewhat openly spaced." Although Olmsted visited Pacific University in Forest Grove in 1908, the Board of Trustees never requested a written report or plan. Instead, Olmsted delivered verbal advice to the college president regarding the general layout of the campus for future development. He encouraged the Pacific president to make the best use of the terrain and existing vegetation in the placement of future buildings.[7]

Olmsted's campus planning for the Oregon State College of Agriculture (later Oregon State University) in 1909 produced more personally satisfying results than his work for Oregon's financially strapped private schools. Olmsted prepared a detailed, 60-page report for the future development of the State College campus. This plan, generally following Beaux-Arts principles, was well received by college administrators and guided campus design until 1926. Olmsted's work for schools in Washington had mixed results. The University of Washington campus plan, again showing Beaux-Arts principles, became greatly modified by university officials over time. Olmsted's plan for Whitman College, on the other hand, was more closely adhered to by the college administrators. His plan stressed an open area in the center of the campus and the symmetrical orientation of buildings as they were added in the future. Overall, Olmsted's campus planning for schools in the Pacific Northwest applied generalized Beaux-Arts architectural principles in a manner consistent with each institution's financial resources and stage of development.

By the 1920s and 1930s, campus planning began to be dominated by the reaction against the increasingly complex and impersonal life of undergraduates and graduate students at the large, modern university. In these decades, the revival of traditional collegiate values stressed the educational importance of creating an intimate community of undergraduates

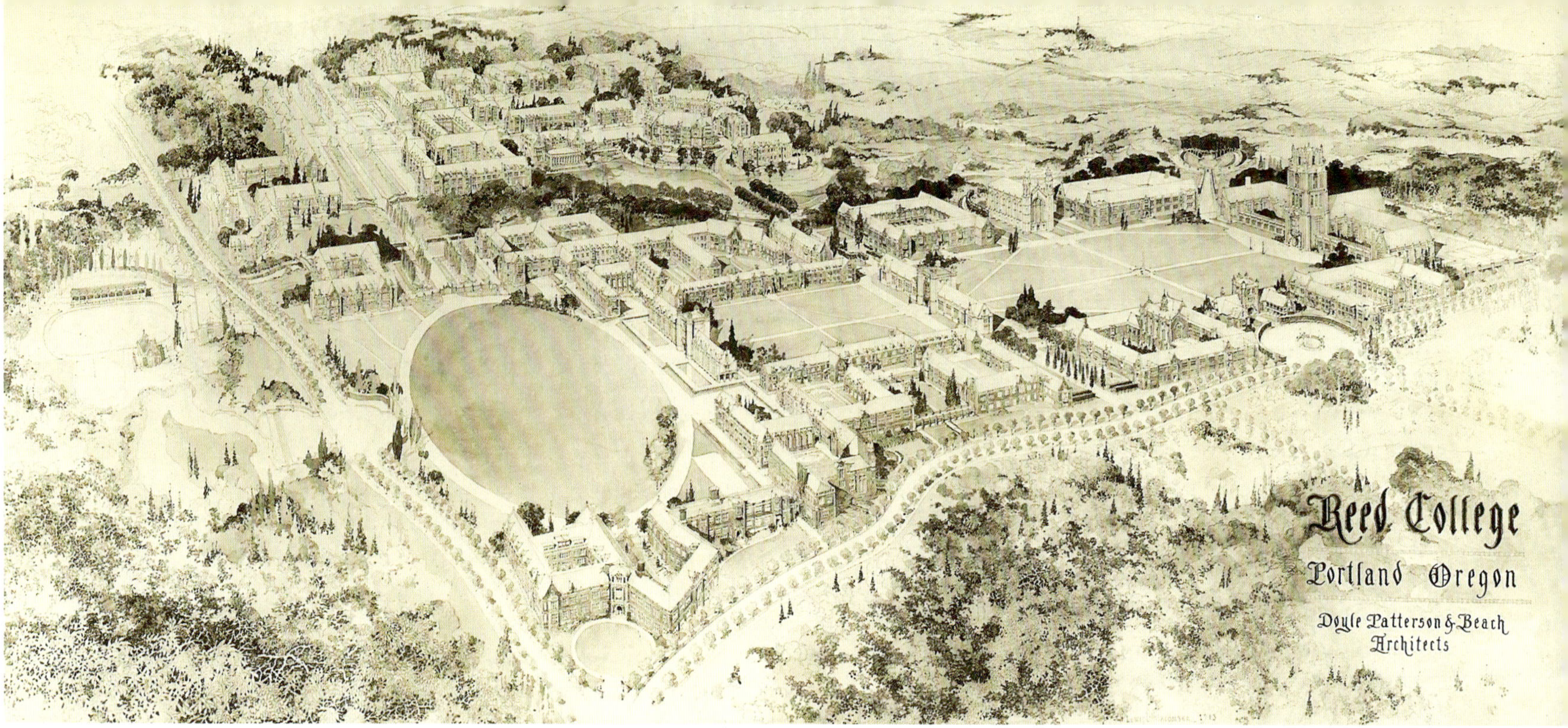

The master plan for Reed College by architect by A.E. Doyle, who designed the gymnasium at Willamette. His company designed most of the major buildings in downtown Portland between 1907 and 1927.

and professors. Many colleges experimented with less costly variations on Harvard's "house system" and Yale's "college system," where undergraduates were divided into smaller groups that lived and dined together in the hopes of developing a shared sense of social and intellectual community. This recognition of the traditional collegiate principle of living and learning together also reaffirmed the university or college's need to provide dormitories on campus. The emphasis on small-scale housing arrangements recalled the English system of collegiate education where students lived and learned in separate colleges within a larger university.

Portland architect A. E. Doyle's master plan for Reed College, prepared in 1911-12, exemplified the symmetrical, ordered quadrangle designed in the Tudor-Gothic style of the traditional English college. Based loosely on St. Johns College at Oxford, Doyle's Beaux-Arts- inflected campus plan deployed open and closed spaces arranged along axes and cross-axes, culminating in various visual focal points. At certain places around the edges of the plan, order gave way to informal irregularity. This latter element demonstrated that American architects were not enslaved to an idealized form of the English Gothic quadrangle.

Unfortunately for Willamette, finances would prohibit seeking such a master plan during this time. Nevertheless, when Willamette University finally did undertake to construct new, badly needed buildings and beautify its campus, it would have this rich tradition of American campus planning to draw upon.[8]

Before then, however, it would have to overcome several decades of financial disaster. In the 1890s, divided allegiance within the Methodist Church in the Pacific Northwest and a national depression almost sank the school. After 1900, however, Willamette began to count again on renewed church support. It would also benefit from the return of economic prosperity extending throughout the Pacific Northwest. Oregon, in particular, enjoyed boom times as businessmen, lumbermen, farmers, and miners exploited the state's vast natural resources of timber, agriculture, and minerals. Population, both rural and urban, exploded as settlers flocked to Oregon to take advantage of the new opportunities. Oregon's numbers grew by 62.7 percent from 1900 to 1910, while Portland doubled in population, increasing from 90,426 to 207,214. The success of the 1905 Lewis and Clark Exposition in Portland, which advertised the natural beauty and economic opportunities of Oregon to people in the East, stimulated much of the growth that the state experienced during the first decade of the twentieth century.[9]

But before Willamette could take advantage of the possibilities offered by an improved economy and renewed church ties, it first had to get its financial house in order. It operated under a debt load that threatened bankruptcy. Interest payments on its debt of $35,000 accounted for a large proportion of current expenses. As President Willis Hawley noted to the Board of Trustees in June 1900, "Under existing [financial] conditions the problem is one of great difficulty. It walks in the night and drives away sleep." To deal with this desperate situation, Hawley recommended that he step aside in favor of a Methodist minister who could more effectively tap church support. The new president was to be relieved of teaching and most administrative duties so that he could concentrate on fundraising. To make that action feasible, the board created the new position of Vice President of the University and Dean of the College of Liberal Arts to oversee the faculty and carry out day-to-day administration. The board offered Hawley this new position, which he accepted. In February 1902, the board selected Dr. John Hamline Coleman as president. Coleman was a nationally respected Methodist church leader with a commanding presence and great eloquence as a public speaker.[10]

The board charged Coleman with getting rid of Willamette's crushing debt and establishing an adequate endowment to support the educational mission. Coleman and the board immediately set in motion a campaign not only to erase the university's debt but also to increase the endowment from $40,000 to $100,000. By May 1903, the indomitable Coleman had raised the needed $35,000 to retire the debt. In recognition of this feat, the *Collegian* shouted out "all hail Him who has made this possible through His servant, the President of Willamette University." More modestly, the *Statesman* noted simply that Coleman's successful fundraising "was a herculean task. It took grit and patience to overcome the obstacles." Of course, it took several years to collect all of the pledges, and when thorough accounting took place, Coleman ultimately needed $45,000 to cover all the debts.[11]

PRESIDENT JOHN H. COLEMAN.

John Coleman, 1847-1914, served as the president of Willamette University from 1902-1908.

Even with the old debt removed, Willamette's basic financial problems remained. The university simply did not realize enough income from tuition, annual gifts, and the interest on the small endowment to meet expenses. Yearly deficits soon began the vicious cycle of debt and heavy interest payments on loans all over again. An increased endowment was clearly the only long-term solution, and President Coleman with board support tackled the matter. They would not achieve the full amount of $100,000 until early in the administration of Coleman's successor.[12]

The debt and insufficient endowment were only part of the problems Willamette faced. The university also required new buildings to keep up with rising national education standards. The Medical College operated in rented rooms off campus and the Music College classes took place in the women's dormitory building. All of the classes of the College of Liberal Arts, law, and the academy were crowded into University Hall. A new

The Medical College

Located on the northwestern corner of the campus, the 52- by 72-foot Classical Revival-styled brick building stood two and one-half stories tall with a daylight basement. The attic housed a large dissecting room and laboratory which were lighted by fluted glass mounted in the top of the hipped roof. Each facade held six large, symmetrically grouped, double-hung windows. On the front elevation, three windows sat on either side of the entry porch, which was supported by two large round columns with ionic capitals. A stone belt course separated the first and second floors, while the top floor window heads had decorative stone caps. In the interior, the first two floors contained laboratories and lecture rooms, while the attic housed the dissecting chamber. An elevator operated from the basement to the top floor.[15]

The Medical College in 1907. Classes in the new building began January 22, 1906.

academic and administration building was sorely needed. Desperate to raise the approximately $40,000 necessary, and realizing that he had tapped out local sources of money by his other fundraising, President Coleman sought money from eastern educational philanthropists and foundations. The discouraging response from Andrew Carnegie's private secretary revealed the skepticism Coleman faced in pleading Willamette's case for a new building: "You state that the University consists of … five colleges. … As these are all carried on in a brick building costing Forty-seven Thousand Dollars, it may be a university in embryo, but it certainly does not seem to be yet a university." Carnegie's secretary concluded his response by curtly observing that "we cannot but think [you] have not made the necessary investigation to enable you to determine what it is you really need. Having only an endowment of Forty-three Thousand Dollars and spending only Twelve Thousand Dollars a year on running the institution, it is not feasible to add large buildings to your existing plant." Undaunted by the secretary's response, Coleman optimistically wrote in his annual report to the board, "The effort made to interest Mr. Carnegie is as yet without result. … Two of the leading men in New York City were very emphatic in their belief that he would finally assist us."[13]

While Coleman struggled to raise funds for the large new academic building, the supporters of Willamette's Medical School set out in 1905 to build a new home specifically for it. Led by the Salem medical community and businessmen, the Medical School campaign sought $10,000 for a building to be erected on Willamette's campus. The backers of the new building pointed out that ever since the Medical School had returned to Salem in 1895, it had been forced to function in rented quarters in Salem's downtown or in the odd room in an already overcrowded University Hall. Dissections occurred in a shack on the southeastern edge of the campus. In spite of the imperfect quarters, the Medical School had increased its enrollment from

16 to 53 students, but needed modern facilities if it were to continue. The Salem community response was immediate and sufficient to raise the money and complete the medical building, which was designed by Salem architects Walter Pugh and Fred Legg, in January 1906.[14]

The College of Music also got a new home early in the first decade of the twentieth century. Until 1906, it had been located in the Women's College [or dormitory], but growth in the music program required expanded facilities. With a gift from a long-time supporter of the university, the board purchased a large Salem residence, moved it to the campus, and remodeled it into 18 rooms housing lecture halls, studios, practice rooms, and offices. With the music classes removed from the women's dormitory, the board remodeled it to house more women students.[16]

After failing in his efforts to get funds from eastern philanthropic interests for the new academic building, Coleman managed to secure a gift of $50,000 from A. E. Eaton in 1907. As a prominent Methodist layman and the prosperous owner of a woolen mill in Union, Oregon, the 74-year-old Eaton wished to leave a lasting legacy to support Christian higher education.[17]

President Coleman's extraordinary efforts to free the university from debt, build its endowment, and find money for the much-needed academic building came at a cost. Friction developed between Coleman and some members of the board and faculty; because of his focus on fundraising, he had paid only nominal attention to oversight of the administration and faculty. In November 1907, shortly after he announced the Eaton gift for a new College of Liberal Arts building, Coleman tendered his resignation.

Since Coleman's resignation was to be effective February 1908, it unfortunately came in the midst of a school year. The board had to act quickly to find a new president to avoid any loss in the university's forward momentum. Coleman's popularity with the general public and high standing with Methodist Church members made the board worry that his leaving would cast the university in an unfavorable light. As the editor of the *Pacific Christian Advocate* wrote, "The going of the president and the incidents connected therewith cast a somber shadow over the institution and those associated with it." In response to this concern, the board acted quickly to find Coleman's successor.[18]

Their choice, Fletcher Homan, came well prepared to aggressively continue Coleman's efforts to put Willamette on a sound financial footing and strengthen its educational mission. He had been the financial vice president of Simpson College when he got the call to come to Willamette University. He had the necessary religious background as well, since he was an ordained Methodist minister. He soon made a positive impression as Willamette's president. The Salem *Daily Oregon Statesman* noted, "President Fletcher Homan, who is comparatively a recent comer

A hand-colored postcard image from the period, circa 1908. Buildings from left to right: The state capitol building, the College of Music building, University Hall (now Waller Hall), the first Lausanne Hall.

Fletcher Homan, president of Willamette University 1908-1914.

to Salem, has made the effect of his coming known and the university has been thriving since his arrival here."[19] Homan arrived on campus in May 1908, and, as tasked by the board, immediately plunged into the endowment campaign while moving the building project forward.

Since Eaton's original commitment to fund a building for Willamette was made to President Coleman, Homan felt it necessary to reassure Eaton that he also understood the pressing need for the gift so that the university could carry out a solid liberal arts program. He wrote Eaton on April 14, 1908, "If we attempt to do everything and do nothing very well, the reputation of the institution will not have a sure and abiding existence as it would should we devote our greatest energy to the building up of the College of Liberal Arts." A few months later, Homan reiterated his belief in Willamette's liberal arts program by stating to Eaton: "Our aim will be to have a faculty that has ability and which is congenial to the students, and to have in Willamette University a first-class course of study, so that we shall not be ashamed when we are compared with any other similar institution of learning." Thus reassured, Eaton moved forward with his gift to the university.[20]

The terms of Eaton's gift to Willamette were somewhat unusual. He did not just give the trustees money to construct a building but, rather, received the right to erect a building on the Willamette campus "for the use of the College of Liberal Arts." He controlled every step of the process, including site designation, selection of the architect, choice of the building's style, and general oversight of the actual construction. Eaton agreed that when the building was finished, he would turn it over "to Willamette University, free from all encumbrances; provided, that no indebtedness incurred in conducting the business of the University shall be existing or unpaid at that time." The latter stipulation necessitated that the trustees raise $15,000 by the summer of 1909—no small feat.[21]

While the trustees apparently had wanted Salem architect Fred Legg to design the new building, Eaton instead selected J. E. Tourtellotte of Boise, Idaho, as his architect. Tourtellotte's firm designed many commercial and public buildings throughout Idaho, Oregon, and Washington, including college and school buildings and hotels. At the time of his commission from Eaton, Tourtellotte was also completing the Idaho State Capitol. At this stage of his career, Tourtellotte preferred designing public buildings in the massive Richardsonian Romanesque style, and so it was in the case of Willamette's Eaton Hall. This choice of style represented a slightly dated design preference, since most commercial or public buildings in the first decade of the twentieth century were being constructed in the Classical Revival style made popular by the 1893 Columbian Exposition.[22]

Burdened by other projects in the summer of 1908, Tourtellotte fell behind schedule in preparing the plans for Eaton Hall. When Homan finally received the plans in late August 1908, he half-humorously wrote Tourtellotte that "we are very glad to get the same, as now we can begin to see something coming. Before we have been living by faith; now we begin to live by sight." Eaton and a committee of the board completed the bidding and contracting phases by the end of August, and in mid-September, workers began excavating the basement. Finally, on December 16, 1908, with much fanfare and about 1,000 onlookers present, the Willamette University community and supporters laid the cornerstone. Eaton spoke at the ceremony, idealistically stating that he wanted to give the building to Willamette University not for "the applause … from his fellowmen, but … for the

Top left: Eaton Hall under construction, 1909, from the State Street side.
Left: Dedication of Eaton Hall, September, 1909.
Above: Architect's rendering showing the front facade and a side view of Eaton Hall.

A hand-colored postcard image from circa 1910.

Eaton Hall

When completed, the red brick, Richardsonian Romanesque-styled Eaton Hall cut an imposing presence on the Willamette University campus. It measured 150 feet wide, 65 feet deep, and stood three-and-a-half stories tall. The architect took great care with each element of the structure. To carry the weight of the massive stone and brick building, he used reinforced concrete beams and floors. The light gray sandstone, used extensively as trim and for the ground-level base of the building, was dressed with irregular hammer marks to give the appearance of broken ashlar. Stone masons used cement mortar colored to match the stone color, and workers fastened each stone in place with iron anchors. Western Clay Manufacturing of Portland, owned by Willamette Trustee Amadee Smith, supplied the deep red, repressed facing brick. The contract specified that the bricks be laid up in a red mortar, slightly darker than the bricks. The bricks used in the circular turrets or towers on each front corner had to be specially molded on a curve consistent with the tower radius. The contractor was instructed to use great care in building the towers in order to make them "absolutely water tight."
The building's imposing main entry section of the front facade projected slightly forward and contained a recessed porch accessed by three semi-circular, slightly-pointed arched openings supported by short, thick Tuscan columns. Tennessee marble panels graced either side of the main entrance doors. A steep, cedar shake hipped roof covered the main body of the building, while the narrower wings at either end of the main volume and at the front entry section had gabled roofs of cedar shake. A cupola surmounted the center at the top of the main roof. The large, double-hung windows were all symmetrically located on each floor. Originally, the window sash was painted black and the frames light gray.

promotion and development of a higher Christian education, that there will go out from its rooms and from beneath its roof many noble young men and women not only of this present generation, but of generations yet unborn, who will be thoroughly prepared and equipped to grapple with the great problems of life for the uplifting of humanity everywhere."[23]

Over the next few months, Eaton showed great interest in the progress of construction, exhorting Homan to keep him well informed and make sure that all work was done "according to plans and specifications." Homan assured Eaton that "I like the way the contractor goes about it [i.e., his work]. He seems to understand his business. I am watching the building day by day and spending a little time around the building every day, and feel satisfied that everything is going all right." By July 1909, Homan could report to Eaton that "the roof is all on and is about ready for the flag pole which is about the last thing to be put up." By early September, the contractor had completed the building and Homan, calling it "a very grand structure," promised to make the dedication of Eaton Hall "a great time."[24]

President Homan, the assembled state officials, and a Methodist bishop conducted the dedication with suitable pomp and celebration. The governor of Oregon introduced the donor as a man of "noble generosity" and Eaton gave a speech praising the value of Christian education. He stated that his gift to Willamette "gave him more satisfaction than anything he had ever done in his life." The newspaper reporter present observed that his "address teemed with the homely good sense and quaint philosophy of a successful business man." At the conclusion of the dedication, President Homan made an appeal for funds to furnish the new building.[25]

In all, Eaton Hall represented a solid, dignified, if slightly dated, presence among the campus's small ensemble of buildings. At any rate, President Homan expressed his satisfaction with the completed Eaton Hall, writing Tourtellotte that "your work is eminently satisfactory, and I have never known a building, every portion of which could be utilized as well as Eaton Hall."[26]

With the opening of Eaton Hall, the Board of Trustees turned its attention to the physical condition of the Willamette campus. Homan reported to the board that with the completion of Eaton Hall, "The grounds ought to be beautified ... and the whole campus made to accord in beauty and taste to the buildings that are now standing thereon." New trustee and wealthy lumberman, Robert A. Booth, in particular, pressed to improve the grounds and to hire an architect to produce a comprehensive plan for future development "at as early a date as practical." In the short term, Homan and the trustees all agreed that funds for laying cement sidewalks and grounds beautification should be solicited. Agreeing on the scope and the right architect to prepare a campus plan for long-term growth proved more difficult.[27]

In October, the Portland architectural firm of MacNaughton, Raymond and Lawrence submitted two proposals "for laying out the future scheme of improvement of the University campus." For $1,000 the architects would provide a plat of all existing landscape worth saving, preliminary drawings and locations for future permanent buildings and landscape, and a bird's-eye perspective of the entire campus showing present and future development. Lawrence indicated that the format of the planning would be similar to that which his firm had prepared for Whitman College. If this proposal was more than the trustees wanted, the firm could simply prepare a block plan and preliminary sketches for $350.[28]

Apparently having second thoughts, President Homan questioned spending precious funds on a campus plan. He wrote Booth, "It seems to me that the plans mentioned are a luxury at the present moment. If we can get people started so that we can have several thousand dollars to fix up this campus, then it may pay, perhaps, to get a set of plans such as are mentioned, but I do not care to run into debt for such a luxury." After some further searching, Homan wrote Booth that he found a Salem architect, a Mr. Hazeltine, "to develop plans for us at simply the cost of the labor of his draughtsmen, giving his own time in investigating and helping us to plan the work." While a committee of the board approved hiring Hazeltine, it is unclear what he proposed, for his campus plan has not survived.[29]

Aside from Eaton Hall, completed early in his term, Homan also worked quickly to close the existing gap in the endowment fight, (Coleman had secured pledges of $78,650 before leaving office). He soon reached the goal of $100,000, but he decided not to stop there. As Homan put it, "In order to make this institution self-supporting, we ought to have on the present basis at least $250,000 interest bearing endowment." To jumpstart Homan's plans for a new endowment drive, Robert A. Booth offered a challenge gift of $100,000—provided that the total endowment be raised to $500,000. To build momentum for his endowment plan, Homan sought other large gifts before beginning the public drive for the innumerable small sums needed to reach the ultimate goal. Homan aggressively courted the railroad magnate James J. Hill, as he had previously given substantial gifts to other colleges. Hill responded to Homan's entreaties in January 1911 by promising $50,000, if within two years Willamette raised an additional $250,000 for its endowment. Hill made similar challenge grants to other Pacific Northwest colleges.[30]

Robert Booth, 1858-1944, long-serving trustee and major benefactor of Willamette University.

The editor of Willamette's *Collegian*, while commenting on Booth's conditional gift of $100,000 in April of 1910, noted that Willamette's financial struggles were not unusual for Oregon's small private colleges: "None of the smaller colleges in Oregon has an adequate endowment. Some of them only meet their current expenses with extreme difficulty. Naturally the instruction which they impart suffers from the lack of means." Pacific University, Linfield College, and Albany College (Lewis and Clark College) all experienced fundraising failures, had trouble meeting current expenses, and had smaller endowments than Willamette prior to World War I.[31]

With the commitment from a man of Hill's financial stature, the board bent every effort to push the endowment campaign. They expected Homan to lead the endowment drive, but authorized him to hire a full-time financial assistant. This man's task was to scout the Methodist churches of the Northwest and their members for every penny that could be had from that source and to raise funds to meet the university's current expenses. What put the fundraising drive over the top, though, was yet another large gift of $100,000 from an elderly retired Portland businessman who wished to remain anonymous. By June 1913, just five years after President Homan took office, the board announced the successful conclusion of the campaign. Willamette now had a $500,000 endowment and a financially secure future.[32]

In addition to new buildings, updated curriculum, and a professional administration and board, there were other ways in which the campus was evolving into a more modern form. In the first decade of the twentieth century, the undergraduates began several popular student traditions that endured for several decades. In 1903, the students started a college yearbook called the *Wallulah*. May Weekend, with a May Queen, May pole, athletic competitions, and a theater production, began in 1909. Perhaps the most singular tradition, also started in 1909, was the institution of Freshman Glee, with the freshman class challenging the other three classes to a song contest. In the spring, freshmen challenged the other classes to compose songs and marching formations according to one of four themes: novelty, serenade, alma mater, or fight song. Over time, the event contributed greatly to school spirit and solidarity. By the eve of World War I, and perhaps due to the evolving curriculum, students began to express a declining interest in intercollegiate debate and the old campus literary societies.[33]

With a small student body, Willamette struggled consistently to field football and basketball teams in the first decade of the twentieth century; coaching was only what the students could pay for themselves. This situation changed in 1909 when President Homan hired George Sweetland, M.D. as the university Physical Director. In hiring Sweetland, Homan made it clear what kind of coach the university wanted: "We want a coach ... who is a Christian gentleman, who will absolutely refuse to play ringers, and who will stand by the faculty and the authorities in maintaining a high standard of clear, wholesome athletics." Homan went on to note that "the general purpose of having an athletic director here is to keep our students physically in the best of health." Homan also told Sweetland that he wanted him to teach some "in order to give you a better standing among the students and faculty." Sweetland proved to be a popular and successful hire, producing many winning teams for the university until he left in 1914.[34]

During this time, the total faculty averaged 44, with the College of Liberal Arts usually having 13 professors; the Medical School, 17; Law and Music, 4 each; and Art and Oratory, 1 each. The remainder taught in the Academy, which now included a normal school offering courses leading to a public school teaching credential, and a business course. Typically, about ten professors held the Ph.D degree during this period. The average enrollment in the College of Liberal Arts between 1900 and 1915 stood at 100, while the Academy had 125 students. Although the endowment and annual gifts supported the College of Liberal Arts, the other educational units such as the Academy and the Colleges of Theology, Medicine, and Law depended on tuition fees for operating funds.

The College of Liberal Arts continued its traditional emphasis on the classics; by 1909, the Bachelor of Arts became the standard degree as the less rigorous Bachelors of Philosophy and Literature degrees were phased out. As early as 1907, a modified elective system allowed a student-selected major and minor concentration of courses grouped in three categories: language and literature, science, and social science. Recognizing that most institutions of higher education were yielding to standards established by outside authorities, the Willamette catalogue announced in 1911 that the university met the standards of regional educational accrediting agencies.

With its new medical facilities built in 1905 and a strong enrollment, Willamette's Medical School also appeared to thrive. In 1908, for example, the school had 34 students; by 1911, enrollment had increased to 60. Between 1900 and 1916, the Medical College graduated 135 doctors. But with its limited finances, equipment, and clinical facilities, the Medical School soon faced insurmountable obstacles to its long-term viability. The rapid strides in modern medicine required costly equipment and extensive clinical facilities for proper medical training. The American Medical Association, in an effort to establish improved standards of medical education, inspected each of the 161 medical colleges in the United States and found that only 80 could be listed as satisfactorily equipped to teach modern medicine. At the conclusion of the study, the Secretary of the American Medical Association wrote President Coleman, "We regret that we could not include the Medical Department of Willamette University in our list of satisfactory colleges because of their serious lack of clinical material."[35]

In 1910, the Flexner Report on Medical Education in the United States, sponsored by the Carnegie Foundation, exposed the continuing low quality of medical schools in the nation and pushed for reforms. The Flexner study ranked the Willamette Medical School as severely deficient (Class C school), and it became clear to the Board of Trustees that without an endowment and better clinical facilities the Medical School could not continue. Accordingly, the board voted in 1913 to merge with the publicly-funded medical school of the University of Oregon located in Portland. This action ended the oldest, continuously operating medical college on the West Coast. The suspension of the Willamette Medical College was not unprecedented: Fully 30 percent of the medical schools in the United States closed within two years of the Flexner Report's critical findings. After the Willamette Medical School stopped operating, its building housed the Academy classes from 1913 until it, too, ceased to operate in 1916. At that time, the science department moved into the old medical college building and stayed until 1941, when it was again renovated, this time to contain the music school.[36]

Another academic building added to the Willamette campus prior to World War I housed the College of Theology. Although the theology department had existed since the late 1880s, the program had never thrived. When President Coleman announced in 1905 his aim to build up the College of Theology, it had only

Kimball School of Theology. The imposing Colonial Revival structure was located just to the north of current-day Smullin Hall and the west of Ford Hall. Both buildings likely encroach on the original Kimball Hall footprint. A scrap of sidewalk crossing the grass strip on the capitol side of State Street and a now-gone corresponding piece on the Willamette side were in line with the front door of the school.

two theological students. In January 1906, Coleman persuaded Reverend Henry D. Kimball, D.D., a highly respected Methodist minister, and his wife to construct and donate a building on campus for the theology program. In return for this gift, the trustees named the institution Kimball College of Theology and elected Kimball as its dean. Dr. Kimball remained at the head of the college until 1914. The College of Theology operated under a separate board of trustees, who were responsible for the financial management of the school. It never became financially stable, however, and the Kimball trustees decided to close the school in 1930. The wooden building was razed in 1942.

Unfortunately, the same confluence of events that brought Coleman's presidency to an end also plagued Homan and caused his abrupt departure from Willamette. Finances were a constant concern, for in spite of President Homan's best efforts, the university had run annual deficits during his tenure and by 1911 the accumulated shortfall came to $12,000. The unrelenting pressures of fundraising coupled with a desire to control every aspect of internal administration led to the seemingly inevitable conflicts between the president, faculty, and students. The board resolved the matter by accepting Homan's resignation and, in recognition of his service, awarded him a full year's salary as severance for "the long and toilsome campaign of raising half a million dollars endowment." In August 1914, the board appointed George Alden, Dean of the College of Liberal Arts as acting president while they searched for a new university leader.[37]

As Willamette University emerged into the twentieth century, it, like most small private colleges, had faced serious financial pressures as it struggled to accommodate changing expectations and models

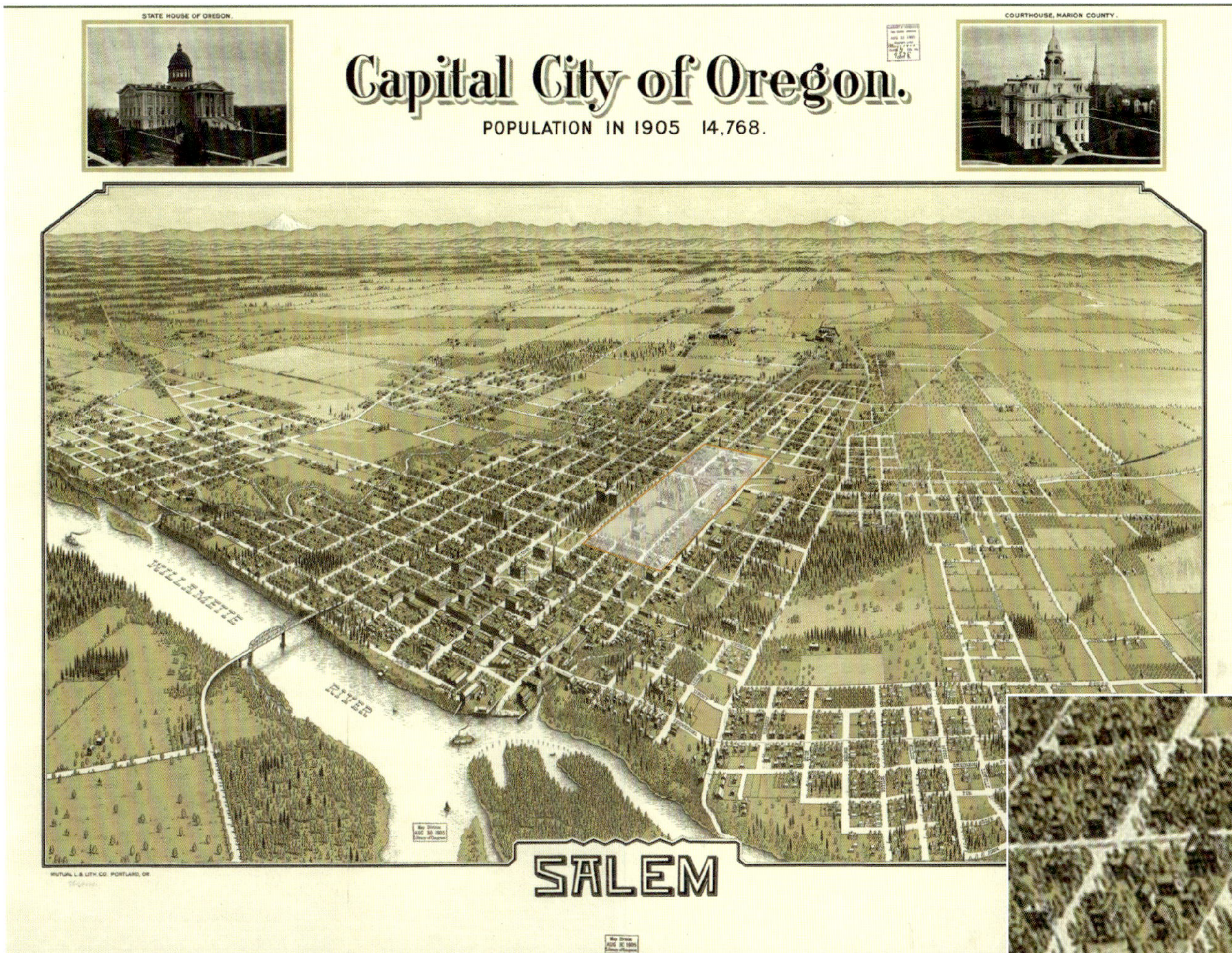

1905 Bird's-eye of Salem and an inset showing the Willamette University campus. The drawing pre-dates the completion of the Medical School building in December 1905.

for higher education. Willamette was no longer a small haven of education and culture in a rugged frontier. National standards and educational trends, such as the movement toward specialization and research, were changing the university drastically. These realities and increasing enrollment would continue to challenge the university in years to come and would require dramatic changes to the campus physical plant. Willamette University was on its way to becoming a modern university and would require much of its next president.

Endnotes

1 For background on the development of the American college and university movement between 1900 and 1940, see Rudolph, *The American College,* 329-482; Thelin, *A History of Higher Education,* 155-259; Hitchman, *Liberal Arts Colleges*, 1-9, 211-36.

2 Quote in Rudolph, *The American College*, 419.

3 Ibid., 434.

4 The following discussion of campus architecture and planning is based on Turner, *Campus*, and Fredrick Jens Larson and Archie Mac Innes Palmer, *Architectural Planning of the American College* (New York: McGraw-Hill Book Company, 1933).

5 Quote in Turner, *Campus*, 167.

6 The following discussion of the Olmsted firm's campus planning work in the Pacific Northwest is based on Joan Hockaday, *Greenscapes: Olmsted's Pacific Northwest* (Pullman, WA: Washington State University Press, 2009), 13-36, 83-100, 117-23 and Hockaday, "John Charles Olmsted and Campus Design in Oregon," *Oregon Historical Quarterly* (Summer 2007), 278-93.

7 Quotes in Hockaday, *Greenscapes*, 30.

8 Philip Niles, *Beauty of the City: A. E. Doyle, Portland's Architect* (Corvallis, OR: Oregon State University Press, 2008), 85-90.

9 Background on Oregon's growth during the first decade of the 20th century can be found in many sources. The following are particularly helpful: Dorothy O. Johansen, *Empire of the Columbia*, 2nd ed. (New York: Harper and Row, 1967), 369-383; Carlos A. Schwantes, *The Pacific Northwest*, 2nd ed. (Lincoln, NE: University of Nebraska Press, 1996), 179-362; William Robbins and Katrine Barber, *Nature's Northwest* (Tucson, AZ: University of Arizona Press, 2012), 1-56; Carl Abbott, *Portland in Three Centuries* (Corvallis, OR: Oregon State University Press, 2011), 71-96; Carl Abbott, *Portland: Planning, Politics, and Growth in a Twentieth-Century City* (Lincoln, NE: University of Nebraska Press, 1983), 1-70.

10 Annual Report of the President, 1900, 1902, Office of President Papers, Willamette University Archives.

11 Fundraising Appeal, Aug. 14, 1902, Homan Papers, Box 1, Willamette University Archives; *Collegian* (May 1903); Secretary of the Board Report, 1904, Board of Trustees Records, Box 1, Willamette University Archives; *Statesman*, Jan. 27, 1906; see also, voluminous correspondence related to financial matters in the Board of Trustees Records, Box 1, Willamette University Archives.

12 Ibid.; *Oregon Statesman*, Apr. 1, 1908.

13 James Batiam to John H. Coleman, Mar. 21, 1905, Willamette University, 2006/14, Box 107A, Willamette University Archives; President John Coleman, Annual Report to the Board of Trustees, 1905, Homan Papers, Willamette University Archives; Willamette University Announcement, Nov. 16, 1905, Smith Papers, Box 9, ibid.

14 *Oregonian*, Dec. 22, 1905; Fundraising Appeal for Medical College Building, Apr. 8, 1905, Homan Papers, Box 2, Willamette University Archives; *Oregonian*, Mar. 7, May 1, Aug. 25, 1904; architects for medical college also noted in *Willamette University Catalogue, 1905*, 81.

15 *Statesman*, Jan. 2, 1906; *Daily Capitol Journal*, Jan. 23, 1906.

16 For a survey of the condition of the music program at Willamette during the administrations of Coleman and Homan, see President Homan to F. S. Mendenhall, Aug. 14, 1908, Homan Papers, Box 1, Willamette University Archives.

17 John Coleman, Willamette University Announcement, Nov. 16, 1905, Homan Papers, Box 1, Willamette University Archives; M. B. Rankin to C. O. Boyer, Nov. 22, 1907, Homan Papers, Box 2, Willamette University Archives; *The Daily Capital Journal*, Dec. 17, 1908; *Oregon Statesman*, Oct. 24, 1907.

18 A. J. Prideaux, Minutes of Faculty Meetings, Jan. 8 and 9, 1908, Miscellaneous Papers, Willamette University Archives; *Collegian*, Mar. 13, 1907; quote in Gatke, *Chronicles*, 497; John Coleman, Telegram of Resignation, Nov. 9, 1907, Homan Papers, Box 2, Willamette University Archives; Minutes of the Trustees, Jan. 30, 1908, ibid.; Charles Boyer to T. S. McDaniel, Feb. 25, 1908, Office of the President Papers, ibid.; T. S. McDaniel to Charles Boyer, Feb. 26, 1908, Office Of the President Papers, ibid.

19 *Daily Oregon Statesman*, May 11, 1909; Minutes of the Trustees, May 16, 1908, Office of the President Papers, Willamette University Archives.

20 Fletcher Homan to A. E. Eaton, Apr. 14, 1908 and Jul. 16, 1908, Homan Papers, Box 1, Willamette University Archives.

21 Agreement between the Board of Trustees of Willamette University and A. E. Eaton, August, 1908, Homan Papers, Box 1, Willamette University Archives; John Homan to Amedee Smith, Nov. 11, 1908, Homan Papers, Box 2, ibid.; Fletcher Homan to T. S. McDaniel, Oct. 20, 1908, Office of the President Papers, Willamette University Archives.

22 Richard E. Ritz, *Architects of Oregon* (Portland, OR: Lair Hill Publishing Co., 2002), 391-92.

23 Quotes in Fletcher Homan to J. E. Tourtellotte, Aug. 12, 1908, Homan Papers, Box 2, Willamette University Archives; *The Daily Capitol Journal*, Dec. 17, 1908. See also Homan to Tourtellotte, Aug. 7, 12, Sep. 14, Oct. 8, 1908; Tourtellottee to Fletcher Homan, Aug. 5, 10, Nov. 5, 1908, Homan Papers, Box 2, Willamette University Archives; A. E. Eaton to Fletcher Homan, Aug. 11, Sep. 12, 22, 1908, Homan Papers, Box 1, ibid.; Fletcher Homan to A. E. Eaton, Aug. 14, Sep. 14, Oct 24, Dec. 3, 1908, ibid.

24 Quotes in A. E. Eaton to Fletcher Homan, Sep. 22, 1908, Homan Papers, Box 1, Willamette University Archives; Fletcher Homan to A. E. Eaton, Oct. 24, 1908, Jul. 3, 1909, ibid.

25 *The Daily Capitol Journal*, Sep. 22, 1909.

26 Fletcher Homan to J. E. Tourtellotte, Oct. 9, 1909, Homan Papers, Box 2, Willamette University Archives; "Plans and Specifications for Eaton Hall," ibid. The original design called for administrative offices on the first floor, with classrooms and a library on the second floor. The third floor held a large lecture hall, drawing room, museum, and more classrooms. The fourth floor yielded more classrooms and science laboratories; see *The Daily Capitol Journal*, Jun. 16, 1908.

27 Quotes in Annual Report of President Homan, Jun. 16, 1909, Homan Papers, Box 2, Willamette University Archives and R. A. Booth to Fletcher Homan, Oct. 11, 1909, Homan Papers, Box 1, ibid.; Homan to Booth, Sep. 30, Dec. 22, 1909, ibid.; Booth to C. P. Bishop, Sep. 24, 1909, ibid.; Booth to Homan, Sep. 24, Oct. 9, 1909, ibid.

28 E. A. Lawrence to Booth, Oct. 4, 1909, Homan Papers, Box 1, Willamette University Archives; Lawrence to Homan, Oct. 4, 1909, ibid.

29 Quote in Homan to Booth, Oct. 11, 1909, Homan Papers, Box 1, Willamette University Archives; Homan to Booth, Dec. 22, 1909, ibid.

30 Quote in Fletcher Homan to T. S. McDaniel, Sep. 18, 1908, Office of the President Papers, Willamette University Archives; Fletcher Homan to Florian Von Eschen, July 4, 1908, Homan Papers, Box 2, Willamette University Archives; John Homan to R. A. Booth, Nov. 10, 1908, Apr. 21, 1909, Homan Papers, Box 1, ibid.; Fletcher Homan to A. E. Eaton, June 15, 1910, ibid.; Homan to Dr. Nicholson, Mar. 19, Apr. 9, 1910, Feb. 3, 1911, Homan Papers, Box 2, ibid.; Dr. Nicholson to Homan, Feb. 11, Apr. 18, May 10, Aug, 8, 1910, ibid.; *Collegian*, Apr. 7, 1910 and Jan. 26, 1911; *Oregonian Statesman*, Apr. 1, 1908; *The Daily Capitol Journal*, Mar. 31, 1910; Hitchman, *Liberal Arts Colleges*, 15, 41, 61, 84, and 146.

31 *Collegian*, Apr. 7, 1910; Hitchman, *Liberal Arts Colleges*, 15, 41-42, 61-62, and 83-84.

32 Annual Report of President Homan, Jun. 14, 1910, Homan Papers, Box 2, Willamette University Archives; Fletcher Homan to A. E. Eaton, June 15, 1910, Homan Papers, Box 1, ibid.; see also Homan to Booth, Mar. 2, 1911, ibid. The retired businessman was P. W. Severson; Fletcher Homan to Trustees, Mar. 29, 1912, ibid.; *Oregonian*, Mar. 24, 1912.

33 For the early history of debate at Willamette, see *Collegian*, Jan. 20, 1910; for a brief history of Freshman Glee, see ibid., Mar. 3, 1939.

34 Fletcher Homan to G. J. Sweetland, Mar. 9, 1909, Homan Papers, Box 2, Willamette University Archives; *Wallulah*, 1915.

35 N. P. Coldwell to John Coleman, Mar. 19, 1908, Homan Papers, Box 1, Willamette University Archives; see also *Collegian*, Mar. 9, 1911.

36 Thelin, *A History of Higher Education*, 148-49; O. Larsell, "Willamette University Medical School," *Surgery, Gynecology and Obstetrics*, vol. LIV (May 1932), 855; John Ramage, "History of Willamette University Medical School (unpublished paper, Mar. 26, 1936), Willamette University Archives.

37 Quote in Gatke, *Chronicles*, 502; Financial Statement, Jun. 15, 1911, Homan Papers, Box 2, Willamette University Archives.

4

Growing Into the New Century

When Dr. Carl Gregg Doney took over the presidency of Willamette in the fall of 1915, the university began a remarkable 19 years of growth. Unlike the presidents before Coleman, Doney was not a teacher and, unlike his immediate predecessors, Coleman and Homan, he was not primarily a field agent out raising money. While not entirely escaping the burden of personally seeking funds, the president now relied on professional fundraisers to build up the endowment. Doney's career was that of a college chief executive. While at Willamette, he devoted his time and talent to the day-to-day administration of the university. Doney was the first Willamette University president to hold an earned doctorate degree. From 1907 to 1915 he had served as president of West Virginia Wesleyan. Previous to that post he had been a Methodist minister and lawyer.[1]

When he arrived at Willamette, Doney had a fully formed philosophy of education. He believed that a technically or vocationally focused education was insufficient to the full development of a person's potential. Rather, Doney maintained that exposure to a carefully constructed liberal arts curriculum enabled students to fully realize their true talents. Doney, however, had come to realize that while the overly-rigid liberal arts programs of the past could deaden learning, an indiscriminate elective system could be equally bad, encouraging indolence and superficiality. A limited elective system, on the other hand, would provide a balanced approach to mental and moral growth. As he succinctly put it, "A college course is to provide a student with a foundation of body, mind, and character upon which he later is to build that structure which his unfolded ability, wisdom, and desires cause him to select."[2]

Facing page: Waller Hall

Carl Doney, 1867-1955, was president of Willamette from 1915 to 1934. His book, *Cheerful Yesterdays and Confident Tomorrows*, includes reminiscences of his time at Willamette.

As he summed the matter up in his book, *Cheerful Yesterdays and Confident Tomorrows*,

> *Freedom of the spirit is the real purpose of education, but this is not hindered if students are guided in their work and obliged to pursue studies which enrich and make true freedom possible. We ask for such a sense of educational values as will insist upon courses which afford the student the historical perspective, a scientific method, wide data of the past and present as bases for judgment, a relationship which great truths in many spheres of knowledge to enhance the satisfactions of life and also the hard mental exercise which makes practicable the consideration of hard problems.*[3]

Doney also believed firmly in Willamette's mission of inculcating Christian values and beliefs based on its historical roots in Methodism. As Doney stated his position,

> *Neither do I think a man is able to be good unless God be in his goodness. The motive and strength of a good life are not rooted in the earth. Every age has had its systems of morals which left God out and their record is written in the tragic failure of their followers. The compelling passion by which man is enabled to transcend himself flows from the transcendent, and one is girded with might to do and be good only when he has related himself to the infinite.*

Doney made these beliefs the hallmark of his tenure at Willamette.[4]

Under Doney, the curriculum, organized into three major groups—letters, social science, and natural science—showed no major changes until 1931. Initially, Doney did add a few new graduation requirements concerning religious character and ethics, but the traditional emphasis on liberal arts scholarship remained the academic focus of Willamette. His deep-seated distrust of an overly-broad elective system, moreover, guaranteed that the freedom of choice regarding courses would be kept within strict boundaries. As he once put it, "I see no reason why the four years in college should be given to undirected experimentation or effervescent anarchy." When curriculum change came in 1931, the reorganization centered on both structure and substance. At that time, the courses in a major field were divided into upper and lower levels. The faculty felt that this change achieved a more logical flow of study and better reflected the students' degree of maturity. The adopted changes further required that in order to graduate, a student had to maintain grades at average or above and to pass senior written and oral exams in his or her major field of study. It greatly pleased Doney that Willamette's high academic standards were recognized in 1927 when the Association of American Universities placed the university on the list of approved institutions.[5]

During the Doney years, student enrollment in the

College of Liberal Arts increased from 184 to over 600. The official policy for the early part of the Doney administration stated that enrollment was limited to 450. The board, however, intended to allow enrollment to grow as an enhanced endowment allowed faculty, housing, and equipment to expand. Doney later remarked that his goal had been to make Willamette "the best college in America for five hundred selected students." In 1915, Willamette had 22 professors; by 1934, the number stood at 31.[6]

The Doney administration held a very conservative view about what was permissible in the social life of the students. Shortly after his arrival, Doney imposed a tight rein on the social scene by implementing new conduct rules and strict closing hours for women. Students protested but soon gave in to the new regime. A reporter for the *Collegian* plaintively recorded, "Why, on the morning of Thursday November 6, [1919] somber bands of black crepe ... adorned the left sleeves of all men in school. Ask if you dare why the melancholy expressions of W.U. students—nay W.U. inmates." Doney, reflecting an old-fashioned Methodist opposition to smoking, dancing, and drinking alcohol, tried to forbid such activities on campus as long as he served as president. He wrote a donor in 1930 that:

> *Willamette University is in some respects a bit old-fashioned in its policies. We are trying to produce Christian men and women who will at the same time be great scholars and good citizens. We discourage the dance and have no college dances; we likewise forbid the use of cigarettes and frown upon the use of tobacco at all times. We think that this policy is justified by the results as is evidenced by the fine type of students which are graduated. We, therefore, believe your contribution is an investment of real value to the kingdom and to society.*

As might be expected, students found ways to circumvent the restrictions.[7]

The largest battles between the administration and the students surrounded the ban on dancing. The long struggle between students wanting to hold dances openly on the campus and an administration unalterably opposed came to a climax in the fall of 1933. In response to a request by social organizations to hold the fall sorority formals on campus, the *Collegian* reported that the deans informed the students "that there exists upon this campus a trustee regulation prohibiting dancing in any form, and that that regulation is still emphatically and unswervably in force. This pronouncement, coming shortly before the scheduled dates for two sorority formals, put sorority and fraternity circles in a furor, as last minute changes were made in plans for entertainment." The students would not let the matter rest. To show campus sentiment, they conducted a poll showing 361 students danced and 82 did not. The poll further indicated that 359 thought that dancing should become a recognized part of the social program, while 67 opposed the change. Continued student agitation led the board to formally study the issue and to decide at its June 1934 meeting to lift its ban on student dancing. Even though Doney retired the same year that the board dropped the ban, he never gave in. He admonished the board in his final report that same June:

Named for the popular athletics coach of the period, Sweetland Field occupied the area that is now known as the Quad.

> *I wish to express the judgement that to sanction the dance will introduce a problem more unsoluable [sic] and perplexing than the present one and more fraught with harm to the University. It will change the spirit and the pattern of the school; it will obscure the primary objective and make the secondary more controlling. Willamette heretofore has not been "just another college"; it has had distinctive qualities which have made it appreciated where ever known. You can never get back a bartered birthright."*[8]

Students' interests and activities continued to evolve during the Doney years. Debate and oratory, while still pursued by some students, continued to lose the keen attention they once drew. Drama, choir, and Freshman Glee, on the other hand, attracted much student interest, and a myriad of special activities led to the formation of small group organizations on campus. Publications such as the *Collegian* and the yearbook, the *Wallulah*, gained the steady support of budding journalists who had offices in Waller Hall. Student athletics, both intercollegiate and intramural, commanded strong student interest and support. Sweetland Field, the university athletic field, covered the area where the campus quad is now located, and its grandstand extended over the millstream. Perhaps the biggest change in student social life came with the passing of the old literary societies and the simultaneous rise of sororities and fraternities during the 1920s. Starting in 1919 as boarding clubs because the students feared that the trustees would object to such organizations, sororities and fraternities soon took on expanded social dimensions and broad acceptance. By 1942, Willamette had six such organizations holding an important place in student life.

Doney, again in his autobiography, gave a fascinating sketch of the Willamette campus as he found it in 1915:

> *Across the street from where we lived was the nineteen-acre campus. It was not attractive, save for its lordly trees. The seven buildings had no architectural harmony, being as unlike as animals in a zoological garden. Waller Hall was beautiful, simple and firm; yet poorly adapted for college purposes. Eaton Hall was serviceable throughout, but reminded one of a half-pretty girl beribboned for a party. Science Hall was square and squat, designed*

Map of Willamette University and the civic plaza that encompassed the capitol grounds in 1912. Note the post office facing the capitol building that would later be moved to the Willamette campus to become Gatke Hall.

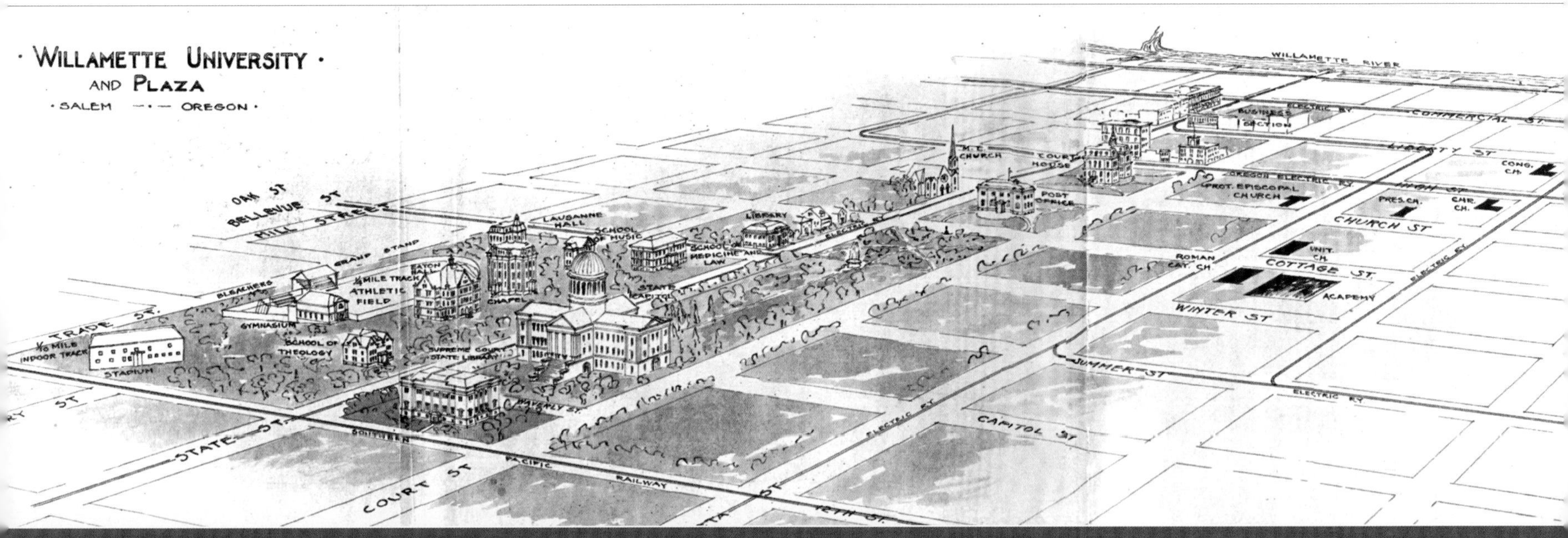

> *to make each dollar go the extra mile. Music Hall had been an aristocratic residence, which a generous friend had placed upon the campus; but the winding stair of rosewood did not make partitions soundproof. The gymnasium was a wooden shell that let in rain and furnished splinters to athletes on the floor. The dormitory for girls heated by a stove in every room, was of wood, saved many times from burning by convenient pails of water which the girls dashed over the incipient flames. Kimball School of Theology had an easement on the campus, was once a part of Willamette, but at this time was wholly independent. … A corner acre was covered by a huge red shed that once had served [as] a nursery and was now abandoned. The library had eight thousand books, one half of which were useful. The laboratories had a fair equipment for the times and for the courses offered.*[9]

Doney also revealed that even with an endowment of $500,000, Willamette still suffered from financial woes stemming from the lack of funds sufficient to meet current expenses:

> *There was a debt, some seven thousand dollars of current unpaid bills and a bank loan of twenty-five thousand and five hundred dollars. But there was the endowment approaching half a million, no mean sum for a college at that time. The obligation at the bank did not bother so long as the interest was paid promptly, but the floating debt to merchants was a jagged pebble in the shoe. Tradesmen called with bills, they waited for me on the street, telephoned at night. … At the beginning of each term when the students paid their small tuition fees there was some money to be divided among the most insistent claimants. Income from endowment was manna from heaven, but never enough; and it could not be gathered every day.*[10]

In fact, Willamette needed many things: a better library, more sophisticated science laboratories, an expanded curriculum and faculty, and better landscaping. While Doney faced many challenges in 1915, the most urgent were the need to increase faculty salaries and the addition of a new women's dormitory. Established professors earned only $1,500 a year and the existing Lausanne Hall, dating from the 1880s, was worn out. Clearly, to meet all of the university's requirements would cost more than the existing endowment and causal gifts could provide. A new fundraising drive would have to be undertaken.

Before firm plans for a major funding effort could be put into place, fire gave a new impetus and direction to the university's program for the future. While the board finally decided in the fall of 1919 that the old Lausanne had to be replaced even though not all of the necessary funding was in hand, fire struck Waller Hall. On the night of December 17, 1919, the roof and much of the interior of the venerable building were destroyed, although the stout brick walls still stood.

The exterior of Waller Fire immediately following the devastating fire of 1919.

An inside view of fire damage to Waller Hall, 1919.

Determined to either replace or rebuild Waller Hall, the board added the cost (approximately $35,000) to its fundraising for the new Lausanne. Architect Fred Legg, who had drawn up the plans for Lausanne, now had the additional task of planning for the devastated Waller Hall. While Legg was finishing up Lausanne and beginning work on Waller, fire once again visited the campus, burning down the old tinder box wooden gymnasium on May 9, 1921. While President Doney "was glad to see it go," replacing the "shabby" gym would require yet another addition to the money raising effort.[11]

After some initial hesitation, the board decided to rebuild Waller rather than replace it. As designed by Legg, the old walls would contain a remodeled and enlarged chapel and the upper floors would house a physics department, library, and space for student literary societies and publications. The remodeled basement received the law library, a bookstore, and student offices. In addition, the restored Waller now boasted steam heat from a central plant and modern lavatories. Best of all, architect Legg proposed that the exterior of the building be returned to its original classical design. This meant replacing the ugly mansard roof imposed on the old structure after the rebuilding following the fire in 1891. The roof lines of the original hall were restored and surmounted once again with a classical-styled lantern tower. The exterior of Waller Hall now returned to the look it had when the building was dedicated in 1867.[12]

While Salem architect Fred Legg designed Lausanne and the rebuilt Waller Hall, the board turned to renowned Portland architect A. E. Doyle for the gymnasium plans. Doyle was responsible for much of the look of early twentieth century downtown

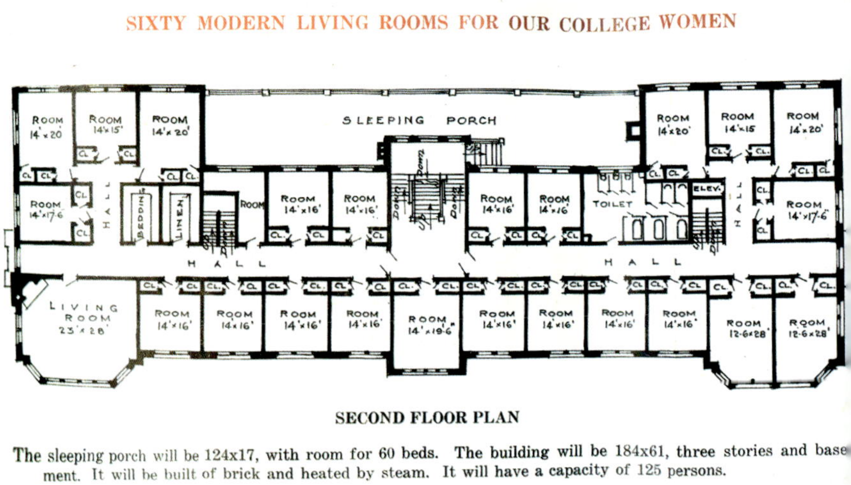

Fundraising flyer showing the architects rendering of the proposed building. In addition to the exterior view, the flyer included floorplans for each of the floors.

The restored Waller Hall.

Fred A. Legg

Fred A. Legg, the architect for Lausanne Hall and the reconstruction of Waller Hall, was a Willamette graduate. Some of Legg's buildings still standing in Salem include the Garfield School, the building now called the Pioneer Bank Building, and Salem High School (now North Salem HS). Many others are now gone, including several that were, until recently, part of Fairview Training Center. His commitment to his work on the chapel in Waller is shown through his donation of nine pieces of Povey Brothers art glass for use in the new chapel door. He prepared the plans and specifications for the Waller reconstruction at no cost to the university.

Lausanne Hall

For the design of Lausanne Hall, Legg produced a Collegiate Gothic-styled, red brick with white stone trim, three-story structure. The front facade was 184 feet wide, divided into six sections, each capped with a pointed gable. The two end-gable sections were slightly larger and contained projecting, two-story bays with stone trim. The slightly projecting center entry bay had an elaborate, two-story stone surround with a Tudor arch over the front doors. Four cast-stone decorative shields sat above the window on the projecting bays. Paired 12-over-1 double-hung wooden windows with stone trim were grouped two sets per bay on each story of the front facade. The side elevations were 60 feet in length, divided into three sections, each capped with a pointed gable. One section on each end held a door with Tudor-styled stone surrounds and a fireplace chimney. The rear elevation featured covered, open sleeping porches on two levels. The building had a concrete foundation with a daylight basement. On the interior, the first floor held common areas, dining and kitchen facilities, and offices for the dean of women. The second and third floors held dorm rooms and bathrooms, while the basement contained laundry facilities and furnace and storage rooms. Doney pronounced Lausanne "beautiful and lacking nothing." The dormitory housed 125 women and cost about $100,000.[13]

The new Lausanne Hall soon after completion.

Portland, designing numerous classical-styled cream-colored, glazed terra cotta office buildings, department stores, hotels, and banks. After an extensive tour of eastern college gymnasiums to get ideas for Willamette's athletic facility, Doyle designed a simple red brick building, according to a newspaper article, "in the English style to conform with the new Lausanne hall." The gymnasium's unadorned, symmetrical proportions also seemed to draw on Waller Hall for inspiration. Finished in 1923, the two-story structure with a full, daylight basement was to have cost around $70,000, but came in just over $80,000.

Willamette's seemingly endless need for money took on a new dimension in the midst of the effort to complete Lausanne, rebuild Waller, and replace the gym. In June 1920, the Rockefeller Foundation's General Education Board gave Willamette a matching grant of $17,500 for two years to increase faculty salaries. In addition, the General Education Board offered the university $350,000 for endowment, provided the board raised $750,000 and paid off all current debt ($250,000). Thinking about the short- and long-term needs, President Doney urged the board to launch a campaign for $1.2 million. He argued

> *Our needs are all pressing, no one can wait long. It is the story of other colleges that campaigns for large sums do not fail as often as campaigns for relatively small amounts. And there is a reason. In a large campaign we recognize the greatness of the task and get ready for it. In a small campaign we make small preparation and let someone else attend to it. Furthermore, people very largely respond in proportion to the amount sought. And still further, a really great program attracts the attention and the giving of persons who cannot be interested in a small movement.*[15]

The Gymnasium

The new gymnasium as completed by A.E. Doyle. A slightly projecting entry bay divided the front facade into two equal sections, each containing four multi-paned, double-hung wooden windows on each floor. On the side elevations, 17 large multi-paned windows furnished abundant light during the day for the playing floor. The entire building was 120 by 116 feet. On the interior, the gymnasium playing floor of polished maple measured 76 by 116 feet, and bleachers accommodated 1,500 spectators. The ground floor also had offices and examination and exercise rooms. The daylight basement level was divided into men's and women's sections, containing showers, lockers, a handball court, and exercise rooms. The top floor contained a trophy display area and several classrooms. Originally, the plans called for an indoor swimming pool, but the board dropped this item as an economy measure. Inflation in building costs eventually drove the price of the building and equipment to slightly over $80,000. Doney later recalled that "in many features it has been a model for some other colleges to follow. Its costs approached a hundred thousand dollars, and while we know it was a noble building that knowledge did not pay for it."[14]

The new gymnasium soon after completion.

The board agreed and, after some preliminary efforts, hired a team of professional fundraisers to direct the work, beginning in the fall of 1922. Generous gifts of $100,000 each from trustees R. A. Booth and E. S. Collins together with the $350,000 from the General Education Board made up over one-half the sum pledged by the close of the Forward Movement Campaign on December 20, 1922. It took another eight years to collect or raise new money to cover the sums due on the almost 6,000 pledges to the campaign. But the end result, a $1.75 million endowment, put the university in a position to increase its faculty and administrative staff and increase salaries.[16]

Amidst all the building and reconstruction on the campus during the early 1920s, President Doney attempted to apply some order to the planning process. He was undoubtedly aware of the campus planning going on at other colleges in the Pacific Northwest. For whatever reason, he hired Portland architect W. C. Knighton to draw up a plan to relate the present and future buildings at the university. In Knighton's 1920 bird's-eye view of the remodeled campus, Eaton Hall served as the axis around which all of the other present and proposed buildings were grouped on the 19 acres of grounds. Science Hall (the old medical school) was to be replaced with a Pioneer Memorial Building which would house a large auditorium, museum, and library. A new science building was to be located east of Eaton Hall, while a boy's dormitory was to be placed on the eastern edge of the campus to complement the women's dorm then under construction on the west side. The new gymnasium stood in the same location as the old gym. The changes and additions were to enable the university to accommodate between 600 and 800 students.[17] Success in the Forward Movement Campaign and Willamette's debt-free condition by 1930 enabled it to survive the worst of the financial ravages of the Depression of the 1930s in relatively reasonable shape, but any implementation of a new

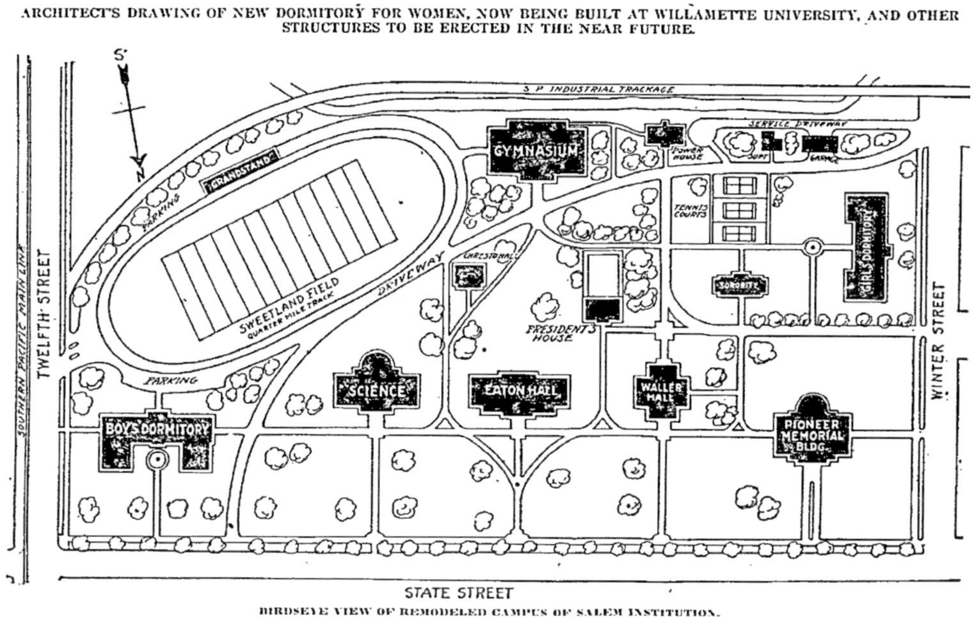

plan that included more buildings would have to wait.

While the building programs of the Homan and Doney administrations added impressive new structures to the campus, the grounds still had a rather scruffy look to them. Little had been done to improve the landscaping and general appearance of the campus. Students complained in the *Collegian* that even three years after completing Lausanne Hall, there still was no lawn around it. Evidently embarrassed by this situation, the board ordered the necessary work to be completed on the grounds adjoining the building. In the World War I era, much of the campus still was laced with old, worn wooden sidewalks. The students, in the late 'teens and early twenties, took it upon themselves to raise money and provide the labor to replace the wooden walks with concrete ones. Still, much work was needed to beautify the campus, and some efforts were made in the late 1920s to improve the grounds. During the financially stringent Depression years, however, little else could be done to further alleviate the situation.[18]

The campus plan including proposals for future development prepared by W.C. Knighton, a very prolific Oregon architect of the time. Among his projects are Deepwood Estate in Salem, from early in his career, and a number of Art Nouveau-style building projects in Portland.

View from the top of the old Capitol building looking south over the Willamette University campus, circa 1923. (The flag in the foreground is on a pole standing at the capitol building.) The small wooden structure just to the south of Kimball Hall was named Cristo Cottage—kind of a student clubhouse that stood for many years. Note the newness of the gymnasium building and the muddy surroundings remaining from recent construction.

In December 1931, still in the depths of the Depression, Doney sadly wrote to a group of Willamette alumni that "there are no new buildings in sight. We need a library building and a science building. We cannot be happy nor efficient fully until we have these. There is not much of a cloud on the horizon, suggesting that these buildings may drop down upon us, … When this terrific depression is over some things will be possible which are now not to be more than dreamed of." At the same time, Doney privately wrote to a trustee that "I had in mind to invite your attention to another very bold and, at this time, seemingly ridiculous idea. Our need for a library building and for a science building is most extreme. … I have long hoped that you might find yourself able to provide one of these buildings." The trustee, E. S. Collins, did not respond favorably at that time, but did a few years later.

Still, hope for addressing some of these pressing needs for new buildings came in the form of a $100,000 bequest at the death of Eric V. Hauser, a Portland businessman. When news of the bequest was published in 1929, the architectural firm of A. E. Doyle and Associates wrote to Doney that the gift to Willamette University would surely mean a new building on the campus, "in which case we would like to be the architects" to design it. Doney responded hopefully that the while the board had made no decision on the disposition of the legacy, "I am, however, confident that within the next five years there will be three or four new buildings on this campus." The long-sought library and science buildings would have to wait for Doney's successor, for he chose to retire in 1934.[19]

Bruce R. Baxter, Willamette's new president, came from the University of Southern California where he served as the Dean of the School of Religion. He had a reputation as a popular public speaker and an energetic leader with great people skills. He quickly won over the students with his personal warmth, accessibility, and devotion to collegiate athletics. Within two years, the editors of the *Wallulah* praised him as "the man who with sincerity, unselfishness, and understanding, has made this school not only an institution of reputable scholastic standing, but also, a school where students are enjoying and will continually appreciate the association of good times and constant friendship." One goal of the new president was to make Willamette better known both regionally and nationally, and throughout his tenure he maintained a heavy schedule of public addresses promoting the university.[20]

President Baxter quickly assessed Willamette's needs. In a mid-year report to the board in February 1935, he expressed appreciation to his predecessor and the trustees for their frugal stewardship that had kept the university debt free during the worst of the Depression. Baxter noted that one survey of a cross-section of American colleges had found a total indebtedness of $40 million, and he went on to remark, "Happily, Willamette makes no contribution to this amount." Baxter also observed that Willamette's enrollment of about 550 was 200 students less than desirable for maximum efficiency. To reach that goal of 750 students, however, it would be necessary to improve the physical plant, especially the library situation. Baxter bluntly told the trustees, "A new library building is our greatest need and I lay upon the Trustees the responsibility of seeing to it that together we find the way to secure such a building." Taking the new president's charge seriously, board president Amadee Smith asked the Portland architectural firm of A. E. Doyle and Associates to prepare gratis a campus layout, with the understanding that the first building to be built would be a library and that the Doyle firm would get the library job.[21]

Before the Doyle firm, under the leadership of architect Pietro Belluschi since the death of Doyle in 1928, could begin its work on a campus plan, fate intervened. In April 1935, the state capitol across the street from the Willamette campus burned to the ground. The governor of Oregon then began a movement to acquire the historic Willamette grounds for the future location of a new capitol building. Willamette University, in turn, would be moved to a new location to the south in Bush's Pasture Park. The Willamette family, embracing students, faculty, alumni, and trustees, after thorough consideration of the matter strongly opposed the proposed move. The trustees, however, realized that the state possessed the right of eminent domain, so they asked the Doyle firm to prepare a plan and cost estimates for a new campus, consisting of at least six buildings, landscaping, and a central heating plant. These would be the facilities and the amount Willamette would expect the state to pay for as a replacement for the existing campus and buildings.[22]

The Doyle firm made a quick study of Willamette's requirements and estimated that a new campus would cost at least $960,000. The trustees decided to seek $850,000, but this amount was at least $250,000 over what the governor and legislature were willing to pay, so the matter was allowed to die. Willamette kept its historic campus, while the legislature ordered a new statehouse built on the site of the old capitol.

Willamette's administration and trustees could now focus on the construction of a new library. In March 1937, the board authorized a new library at a cost not to exceed $100,000. The money came not from a loan but instead from the unrestricted Hauser legacy portion of the endowment. The board specified that the $100,000 be repaid from current income in annual

Bruce Baxter, 1892-1947. A very popular president who did a lot in the short time he was at Willamette. He was elected as bishop of the Methodist Church in 1940, but remained involved at Willamette and cared about its students after Carl Knopf succeeded him in 1941.

Pietro Belluschi, 1899-1994, was one of the founders of the Northwest Regional style of architecture and of the modernist International Style, which made him world famous. Willamette University boasts four buildings designed by him and two remodels .

installments. They chose Pietro Belluschi of the Doyle architectural firm to design the building. At the direction of President Baxter, a faculty committee prepared a report on the present and future library needs of the university. This material, along with his own research and experience in designing college libraries, enabled Belluschi to develop a library that not only served its purpose admirably but also set the architectural style for the next thirty years of building on the Willamette campus.[23]

At the time Belluschi undertook the Willamette library project, he was at the beginning of a long and productive career in which he established himself as one of the leading modernist architects of the twentieth century. Prior to his Willamette work, Belluschi was renowned for his modernist design of the Portland Art Museum in 1930 and had recently designed small libraries for Reed and Linfield colleges. Belluschi's previous work on the plan for Willamette's potential move to a new location communicated the general approach that he would also apply to the library project. In preparing the earlier plan, he told the trustees that "it seems wise in designing a new campus for Willamette University to avoid any useless display of fashionable architecture, but at the same time meet in a creative spirit all conditions arising from various modern requirements." Belluschi would not be a slave to any dead traditions.[24]

Based on the recommendations of the faculty library committee, the architect needed to plan a library that would accommodate 1,000 students and 50,000 books in the short term (5 years) and 1,500 students and 100,000 volumes in the long term (20 years). The seating capacity in the main reading room needed to hold 250 readers. In addition to the book stacks, the library had to include periodical, charging [circulation desk], seminar, and cloak rooms; offices; and a special collections room for rare and archival materials related to the university and the history of the Pacific Northwest. Because all of the existing buildings on the campus represented differing architectural styles, there was no obvious example to follow; the one unifying element stemmed from the red brick used in their construction. Trustees and faculty preferred the Georgian style of architecture as the "best blend with what we already have and... less expensive than certain more ornate styles.... It is a style that wears well. Moreover, it serves to memorialize the temper and the homeland of Willamette's founders."[25]

During the spring of 1937, Belluschi labored through 12 different designs before he was satisfied that he had a room placement and circulation pattern that fit within a compact and properly proportioned Georgian-styled building. Throughout a very collaborative give and take between the client and the architect, Belluschi worked hard to produce a cost-effective solution to the library requirements. As President Baxter described the design process, "We have gone slowly in formulating the plans and we believe that the beauty and the usefulness of the structure will justify this careful procedure." As the final plan took shape, Belluschi reminded the trustees overseeing the project that the effort to accommodate all of their desires had led to a larger building and increased costs. But, as he put it, "We believe that every change has brought about a definite improvement in the workability of the plan, and we do not believe that we should go back to the plan as originally submitted, but we feel that you should be acquainted with our belief as to the final cost of the structure." By early June 1937, Belluschi had arrived at a plan acceptable to all. His final design—referred to in the press as one of "quiet dignity and simple beauty"—represented a stripped or modern version of the traditional Georgian style.[26]

Belluschi took great pains to use quality materials both inside and out and to provide close supervision throughout the library's construction. A good example of his approach was the care taken in the selection, manufacture, and installation of the brick veneer. The library building committee specified that the bricks be the same in texture and color as Belluschi had used in the Portland Art Museum. Because some of the sample bricks for the library did not match the specifications, Belluschi required the Willamina Clay Products Company to refine their process so as to produce bricks that did meet requirements, specifying the exact percentage of color variations that should be produced. He then took equal care to match the appropriate color of the mortar to the bricks. Generally, if the bricks were dark, Belluschi used a lighter shade of mortar, but if a light-colored brick was specified, then he chose darker mortar. The end result of such care in design and construction was a building of timeless quality.[28]

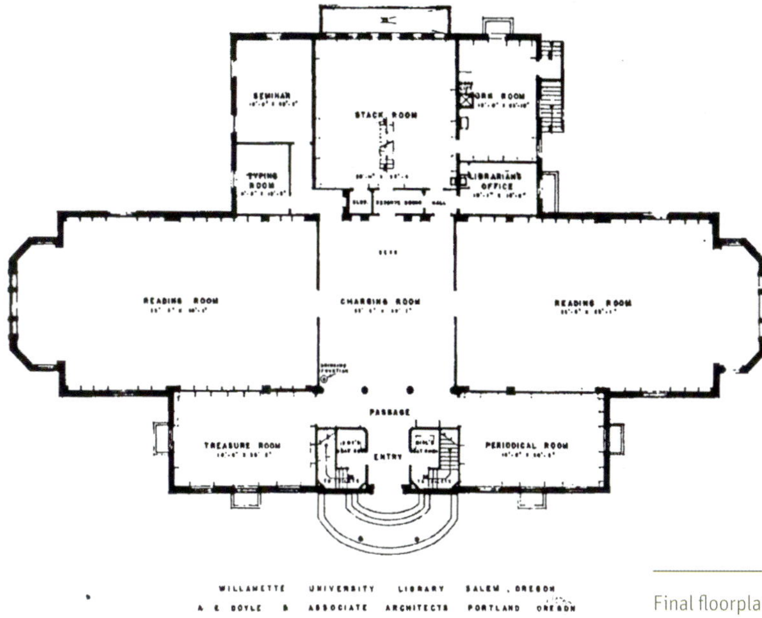

Final floorplan for the library building as designed by Belluschi. Notice how the floorplan speaks to the proportional symmetry of his design for a modern iteration of the Georgian style.

As Willamette's first new building since 1923, the new university library fostered new pride and excitement on campus. President Baxter reported to the trustees, "The firm of A. E. Doyle and Associates, particularly

Belluschi's library building facing State Street.

The Library

Belluschi's Willamette University library provided a functional layout within a symmetrically balanced, rectangular volume. The two-story structure was built of reinforced concrete with a red brick veneer and white wood exterior trim. The building was devoid of the usual decorative elements usually associated with the Georgian style: pilasters, quoining, pediments, columns, and elaborate cornice details at the roofline. Instead, the architect expressed the essence of the Georgian idiom through balanced proportions, tall multi-paned, arched windows with over-scaled keystones, and a hipped roof that fit tightly to the walls. Belluschi cleverly reduced the massive appearance of the steeply-sloped roof by setting it back at both ends of the building. Small, one-story bays at either end of the building held distinctive Palladian windows. The entrance portico was simple and balanced in presentation. It had a slightly outward curving flat canopy supported by slender posts. Modern, multi-paned entry doors were flanked by two, multi-paned porthole windows. As a finishing Georgian touch, a lantern-type cupola surmounted the slate roof. Overall building dimensions were 165 feet by 85 feet with a basement area 90 feet by 20 feet. At completion in September 1938, the library encompassed 12,678 square feet and construction cost $84,592—well under the $100,000 budget. At the time, typical building cost for this type of structure ran about 45 cents per cubic foot; Belluschi's library came in at 33 cents per cubic foot. The project had benefitted from a very competitive contracting market.[27]

Gatke Hall

The moving of the Salem Post Office building (later named Gatke Hall) to Willamette's campus. Hall. In November 1937, Willamette's Board of Trustees authorized the purchase of the building for $750.00 for the purpose of using it to house the University's Law School. Originally constructed in 1902-03 and weighing an estimated 2,000 tons, the "elegant mansion," as it was described, was moved inch by inch by Lebeck and Son down State Street. Bets were placed to see how long it would take to relocate the building from Church St. to the northwest corner of campus. The building, which now houses faculty and administrative offices, was renamed Gatke Hall in the fall of 1967 to honor WU alum, long-time faculty member, horticulturalist, and author of the *Chronicles of Willamette*, Robert Moulton Gatke.

Above: Gatke Hall during the move down State Street. **Below:** The reading room in the new library. The Palladian windows at each end of the room lent natural light and airiness while the wood paneling added warmth.

Mr. Pietro Belluschi have done us a notable service and have set the architectural standard for future buildings." Hundreds of students and many faculty showed their enthusiasm and appreciation for the new facility by carrying the entire collection of books from the old library on the second floor of Waller Hall to the new location. The administration did its part by increasing the library's acquisition budget. At last, Willamette could offer its students reasonably adequate library resources.[29]

When Willamette began planning the new library, it had the opportunity in the fall of 1937 to buy and move on campus the old Salem post office, a two-story, stone classical revival structure built in 1902. The board briefly considered renovating the building to serve as the library, but Belluschi convinced them that such a plan was not practical or cost effective. Instead, the board decided to remodel the old post office to serve as the home of the law school. Even though Willamette purchased the building for its salvage value ($750), moving and renovating the 2,000-ton stone structure cost almost $30,000. The actual move was a painstaking operation. Movers first lifted the massive stone building off its foundation and then placed it on 300 jacks atop a network of pilings and rollers. The next stage required pulling it inch-by-inch down State Street to its new location at the east end of the Willamette campus, opposite the Oregon Supreme Court building. The arduous move took seven weeks and did considerable damage to the walls, floors, and connections between the various structural parts of the building. The board hired Belluschi to prepare the plans for the extensive repairs and renovations and to oversee the necessary work. Given all of the unforeseen difficulties and cost entailed in turning the old federal building into a suitable law school, some trustees expressed regrets that they ever attempted the undertaking. President Baxter, however, put the best face on the process, stating that the renovated home for the law school gave "us a structure that could not have been erected for three times the amount expended."[30]

In addition to completing the library and turning the old Salem post office into a home for the law school, the board also purchased, for $1,600, and moved to campus in 1938 a house that was to be removed for expansion of the state capitol complex. After moving the two-story Craftsman-style house to a site just north of Lausanne Hall, facing Winter Street, the board had it reconditioned for use as the university president's home. President Baxter, after a year's use, reported, "University House offers a most pleasant and comfortable home and a place admirably adapted to entertaining on a large scale."[31]

Having achieved several key building goals in the late 1930s, President Baxter pushed ahead to accomplish the dream of a new science building. As he noted in the President's Annual Report for 1938, "Our laboratories do not measure up to those provided by many small town Oregon High Schools, to say nothing of the laboratories of the better high schools in the state. The need for this new science building is fully as great as was the need for a new library." With a gift of $100,000 from trustee Everrel S. Collins, President Baxter finally realized his dream. While the board did not formally commit to build the science hall until February 1940, preliminary planning began in early 1938. At that time, Baxter had asked architect Belluschi to see if the present science building (the old medical school) could be remodeled into an acceptable science teaching facility and also to study the requirements for a completely new science building. After a thorough examination of the old science building, Belluschi advised, "We have found that its physical condition is very poor and its suitability as a laboratory building very bad ... We also feel that to make such a structure in any way suitable as a Science building, it will require an expense out of proportion with the results." Belluschi then listed in detail the old structures' shortcomings. Belluschi also submitted preliminary plans for a new building that would meet the needs of teaching chemistry, physics, biology, mathematics, and home economics.[32]

Below left: Gatke Hall in place facing State Street.
Below right: University House in position on campus facing Winter Street, just north of Lausanne Hall. It was a graceful example of the Craftsman Style and would be the home of three university presidents.

When the board finally had the funds in early 1940 to move forward with the science hall project, Belluschi prepared the detailed plans and working drawings. As he had done in working up the plans for the library, he consulted extensively with the faculty and conducted his own research into requirements for university science facilities. The trustee building committee and the architect agreed that the exterior of the building should be done in the modern Georgian idiom, following the example of the library. The science building, like the library, would be constructed of reinforced concrete with a brick veneer. The special needs of modern science laboratories determined much of the interior layout. The science faculty and the architect conducted a robust exchange about the dimensions and physical arrangements of the labs and finish details. Trying to finalize the plans and contain costs as the science professors pushed for as much as they could get, a mildly exasperated Belluschi wrote to Professor Cecil Monk of the biology department, "I hope that this correspondence of ours is not going to be too lengthy in the future. Personally, I have been trying to get you as pleased as possible, but I am powerless to disburse the money for the building. You simply must go to see Dr. Baxter … and put up as good an argument as you have with me."[33]

Belluschi's plan called for a large two-story structure with a slightly smaller, setback section with a third floor. The science faculty wanted a full-sized third story for the extra space it would provide. Belluschi, however, felt his plan provided adequate room based on the requirements established by the trustee building committee, with input from the science faculty. On aesthetic grounds, Belluschi argued for a two-story rather than a three-story structure if it met the primary requirements: "We believe that a 2-story is much more desirable and attractive then a 3-story one. The way we will treat the second floor parapet wall will actually make it appear in our scheme to be more a 2-story than a 3-story building. It is not a question at all of harmonizing with the Library Building, but it is a question of relating the openings and walls within the building itself. A 3-story building of such a size and plan would belong already to the Office Building family." Belluschi later wrote that "the third story being set back will take its proper place in the relationship of architectural masses. We feel quite sure that architecturally it will be more interesting than the library building." Belluschi found it challenging to meet all of the technical requirements of the

The Science Hall

As built, the science hall had a T-shaped plan, 142 feet wide on the front and 108 feet deep overall. The main body of the building measured 142 feet wide and 60 feet deep, with the rear wing 50 feet wide and 48 feet deep. The first of three stories held labs and rooms for physics, physical science, geology, and home economics. The second floor housed biology and mathematics, while the chemistry department occupied the entire third level. In describing his design for the science building, Belluschi stated, "The architectural style is Georgian, somewhat modern in execution and made to match as far as requirements allowed with the library building which was designed four years ago." As in the library, the hipped, slate roof, surmounted by a cupola, was tied tightly to the walls and recessed at both ends to reduce its massive appearance. Besides the massing and symmetry that marked the science building as Georgian in style, the double-hung multi-paned windows were the only Georgian decorative elements present. The arched ground-floor windows had keystones, while the second-floor windows were squared off and without keystones. A row of round multi-paned windows (echoing the two porthole windows on the entrance to the library) stretched across the recessed third floor. The slightly recessed front entry consists of modern glass double doors surrounded by large fixed panes. A large Palladian window sits above the entry. Clearly, as Belluschi noted, "The design relies mainly on good proportion and on straight-forward use of materials for its effect rather than expensive ornamentation."[35]

The Science Hall soon after completion.

building and still keep within the $100,000 budget. By mid-May 1940, Belluschi had the plans ready to bid and preliminary cost estimates established. He told the trustee building committee that the total costs, including architectural fees, came to $110,000 and that equipment and fixtures would cost another $30,000. The committee approved the plans and cost estimates and put the building out to bid, receiving favorable responses from contractors.[34]

As completed, the science building cost $151,000 inclusive of architectural fees. The expense of the science equipment and furnishings accounted for $35,000 of the total spent. Belluschi proudly stated, "This surprising economy for a building as large and as well built as this was due not only to the simplicity of the design but also to the plainness of the interior finish. The partitions are solid metal lath and plaster. No furring was used anywhere either in the walls or ceilings. This means, of course, that pipes are exposed and accessible which is a desirable thing in a science building." He expressed equal pride in the collaborative process that went into creating the building: "The plan of this building was arrived at after a thorough study of similar buildings in the country and after lengthy consultations with members of the building committee and the staff. Each of their requirements and desires were considered and incorporated whenever possible." President Baxter agreed that the planning process had been "genuinely a cooperative effort." As the science hall neared completion in the winter of 1940-41, it was revealed that the recently deceased trustee E. S. Collins had been the primary donor and that the building would be named in his honor.[36]

Collins Hall marked the fitting culmination of Baxter's term as president of Willamette. In the summer of 1940, Baxter resigned to become a Methodist bishop but continued to serve as acting president for another year until the board named his successor. Baxter had overseen a period of dramatic growth both in student enrollment and in facilities. Between 1934 and 1940, the student body climbed from 557 to almost 900, an increase of 67 percent. Under Baxter, Willamette built a badly needed library and science hall, while moving to campus structures to house the law school and the president's residence. In addition, the old science building was renovated to serve as the music school. The administration also made a systematic attempt to improve the campus landscaping. With the help of Professor Gatke and a professional arborist, new lawn, trees, and plants were added and, for the first time, the campus grounds received regular watering during the dry summer months. President Baxter, moreover, sought to improve faculty conditions. He instituted, with board approval, faculty leaves of absence to finish the Ph.D. degree and established a retirement plan with university and faculty contributing to the fund. In 1936, Baxter reversed Depression-era salary cuts. Even as he departed, Baxter could not resist reminding the trustees of one unfinished item: "Our next need in buildings is a boy's dormitory and I hope that we may set it as the next objective in new buildings." A highly popular and charismatic leader, Baxter, through his seven-year administration, left a lasting legacy at Willamette.[37]

Throughout Baxter's tenure, Willamette had been preparing for its centennial year in 1942. Unfortunately, the celebration was clouded by a fall in student enrollment brought on by the beginning of World War II and the unhappy events surrounding the brief presidency of Baxter's successor. Dr. Carl Sumner Knopf came to Willamette from the University of Southern California where he served as the Professor of Biblical Literature and Archeology. He was an accomplished scholar with a friendly bearing; the Willamette community had high hopes for Knopf's presidency. Soon after his arrival in December 1941, Knopf, however, privately displayed another side of his personality. The trustees discovered that Knopf could be rather stiff-necked and unbending when he felt he was in the right in a dispute. Belluschi had been tapped by the board to remodel the old science building into a home for the College of Music. The project was just being completed when Knopf reached the campus, and he quickly expressed unhappiness with the cost and quality of the work and the architectural fees. Belluschi, in turn, defended his renovation and appealed for the support of key Willamette trustees. The trustees took Belluschi's side in the controversy and wrote to him that they regretted Knopf's conduct toward the architect and assured him that we "feel you have done a very exceptional piece of work" in converting the old science building. They further assured him that "you are the one person to be consulted when ever we undertake any building on our campus." The renovation dispute quieted down, but Knopf's unbending character flared again a few months later, resulting in his removal as president.[38]

In May 1942, President Knopf went before the Salem Selective Service Board to register for the draft. This was a pro forma appearance because he was 52 years old, an ordained minister, and professing Quaker. Standing before the selective service board, he publicly stated his opposition to war. Subsequently, the local American Legion publicized Knopf's declaration, charging that he had created a disturbance and was unpatriotic. Since the American Legion had made a public issue of the matter and it received wide press coverage, the board had no choice but to investigate. After a thorough examination of the evidence, the board committee concluded the Knopf's pacifist views were historic Quaker convictions and that his statement to the selective service board was not inflammatory. The board committee, however, did feel that Knopf had exercised poor judgment in raising the issue. The committee stated,

Carl Knopf, 1889-1942, esteemed scholar,, controversial president of Willamette, and planter of the Star Trees.

> *We recognize the fact that Dr. Knopf in this, as in other matters, had a clear duty to follow the dictates of his own conscience. We think it clear, however, that the expression of his personal convictions under the circumstances where no such expression was required or called for inevitably created in the public mind the impression that he expressed the views and position of Willamette University. We believe that he owed a duty to the University to refrain from any expression of views or any other action which could be construed by the public as committing the University to any position on such a vital question without consultation with and express authority of the University's governing board.*[39]

On May 29, 1942, the trustees, after a difficult debate—and despite many loyal Knopf supporters on campus—voted to ask for President Knopf's resignation, believing that the affair, and ongoing public outcry against him, had compromised his effectiveness as a spokesperson and leader of the university "by the unfavorable public attention given the registration incident." Although Knopf's tenure as president was brief, it did produce one lasting

The Star Trees, circa late 1940s. It took a couple of decades for them to grow into the campus icons they are today.

positive mark on the university. He conceived and carried out the planting of the sequoia Star Trees in front of Collins Hall as an expression of Willamette's enduring presence on the occasion of its centennial. Named the "Temple of the Centuries," its center held a buried crypt containing terra cotta plaques with quotations from the Bible, Shakespeare, and a history of Willamette. Knopf died of a ruptured aneurism on June 23, 1942, at University House, where he was still residing, less than one month after his resignation.[40]

By almost every measure, the first 40 years of the twentieth century represented a time of tremendous growth for Willamette University. The endowment rose from about $45,000 to slightly less than $2,000,000, with all debt retired. Enrollment in all components of the university increased from 587 to almost 900. The focus on the College of Liberal Arts strengthened with the closure of the schools of medicine and theology and the Academy. In addition, the College of Music was folded into the College of Liberal Arts as a department. After much study and debate, the board made a commitment in 1932 to upgrade the law school from part-time night school to full-time day status and increase the law library to meet standardization requirements. After great efforts by the friends of the law school and the university administration to meet the required standards, the American Bar Association finally accredited the law school in 1938. All of these academic changes were in keeping with the trends in modern higher education.[41]

Willamette's physical plant expanded from a motley collection consisting of one brick and three aging wooden structures (valued at $100,000) to eight substantial brick and stone buildings (valued at $770,000). The total university faculty had grown from 49 to 56 professors and the average salary had advanced from $1,000 to $2,500. By 1940, Willamette had outpaced Oregon's other small colleges in every category. Pacific, Linfield, and Albany (Lewis and Clark) all struggled with enrollments half Willamette's numbers, nagging indebtedness, and small endowments. Key to Willamette's success in building its endowment and expanding its facilities were the efforts of the long-serving members of its Board of Trustees. Two in particular stand out: Robert A. Booth served from 1904 until 1934, and Everell S. Collins from 1912 to 1940. Both were committed Methodist laymen who had made their fortunes in Oregon's booming timber industry during the early years of the twentieth century and became Willamette's two greatest benefactors during its first century. They helped lay the foundations of the modern Willamette University. The board's willingness to embrace the forward-looking application of modern Georgian architecture to the new buildings boldly symbolized Willamette's determination to be the leading small liberal arts university of the Pacific Northwest. In the ever-changing world of higher education, the modern designs of the new library and science hall revealed a confident embrace of the future as Willamette entered a second century.[42]

Endnotes

1 Carl G. Doney, *Cheerful Yesterdays and Confident Tomorrows* (Portland, OR: Binfords and Mort, 1942), 52-112.

2 Quoted in Gatke, *Chronicles*, 562; see also Doney, *Cheerful Yesterdays*, 162-63.

3 Ibid.

4 Ibid.

5 Doney, *Cheerful Yesterdays*, 154-58; Doney instituted in 1926 comprehensive oral exams for seniors to graduate. Report of the President, Jun. 1926 and Jun. 1927, Office of the President Papers, Box 1, Willamette University Archives.

6 Doney, *Cheerful Yesterdays*, 161.

7 *Collegian*, Nov. 12, 1919; Doney to J. C. Luckel, Sep. 25, 1930, Willamette Archives, 2006/14, Box 100, 101, Willamette University Archives; Doney, *Cheerful Yesterdays*, 160-61. Doney also strongly supported national Prohibition; Carl Doney to Fred Squires, Feb. 18, 1931, Willamette Archives, 2006/14, Box 57, Willamette University Archives, Carl Doney to William Atterbury, Mar. 10, 1931, ibid.

8 *Collegian*, Nov. 23, Dec. 7, 1933; quote in Gatke, *Chronicles*, 634.

9 Doney , *Cheerful Yesterdays*, 119.

10 Ibid., 120.

11 *Oregonian*, Nov. 2, Dec. 18 and 24, 1919, Feb. 8, Apr. 25, 1920; *Collegian*, Jan. 7 and Feb. 4, 1920, Mar. 22 and Apr. 12 and 21, 1922; Doney, *Cheerful Yesterdays*, 140.

12 *Oregonian*, Feb. 8, Apr. 25, 1920; *Collegian*, Feb. 4, 1920. University Hall had been renamed Waller Hall in 1912, *Oregonian*, Mar. 3, 1912. Architect Legg prepared the plans and specifications at no cost to the university and also gave as a gift (valued at $150) nine pieces of Povey Brothers art glass (3 transom windows and 6 side lights) for use in the new chapel door; Willamette Archives, 2006/14, Box 57, Willamette University Archives; Doney, *Cheerful Yesterdays*, 138-40.

13 The university actually used students under the supervision of architect Legg to help demolish the old wooden Lausanne Hall; *Collegian*, Oct. 15 and 22, 1919; *Oregonian*, Nov. 2, 1919, Apr. 25, 1920; Doney, *Cheerful Yesterdays*, 138; Fred Legg, Lausanne Hall plans, specifications, and statement of Account, Mar. 30, 1921, Willamette Archives, 2006/14, Box 57, Willamette University Archives.

14 Quote in *Oregonian*, May 20, 1923; *Willamette Alumni Magazine*, vol. I (May 1923), 1; *Collegian*, Apr. 12, 1922, Feb. 7 and 14, Mar. 14, May 23, Oct. 3, Nov. 7, Dec. 19, 1923; Carl Doney to A. E. Doyle, Oct. 21, 1922, Feb. 15, 1923, Pietro Belluschi Papers, Box 44, File II, Job No. 387, Syracuse University Library; A. E. Doyle to Carl Doney, Oct. 28, and Nov. 27, 1922, Jan. 24, 1924, ibid; see also *Oregonian*, Feb. 14, 1923, Feb. 24, 1924. Doney, *Cheerful Yesterdays*, 140; Receipts and specifications for gymnasium, 1923, Willamette Archives, 2006/14, Box 57, Willamette University Archives.

15 Quote in Gatke, *Chronicles*, 569; *Oregonian*, Jun. 16, 1920; *Collegian*, Apr. 12, Sep. 27, Dec. 3 and 21, 1922.

16 *Oregonian*, Dec. 19 and 24, 1922, Jun. 11, 1928; Doney, *Cheerful Yesterdays*, 140-43; on the struggle to raise the endowment funds, see for example, Carl Doney to Laura Goltra Starr, Aug. 2, 1930, Office of the President, Doney Papers, Willamette University Archives, Carl Doney to Amedee Smith, Sep. 27, Oct. 2 and 11, 1930, ibid.; Carl Doney to Guy Atkinson, Feb. 20, 1930, ibid.

17 *Oregonian*, May 30, 1920.

18 *Oregonian*, Oct. 26, 1919; *Collegian*, Oct. 24, 1917, Apr. 24, 1918, Nov. 5 and 26, 1919, Oct. 19, 1921, Mar. 21, Apr. 4, 1923; Report of the President, Feb. and June 1927, Office of the President Papers, Box 1, Willamette University Archives.

19 Doney to Robert Story, et al., Dec. 8, 1931, Willamette Archives, 2006/14, Box 100, 101, Willamette University Archives; Doney to E. S. Collins, Nov. 24, 1931, ibid; A. E. Doyle and Associates to Doney, Feb. 7, 1929, Pietro Belluschi Papers, Box 114, File II, Job 595, Syracuse University Library; Doney to A. E. Doyle and Associates, Feb. 9, 1929, ibid.; for the Hauser bequest, see *Oregonian*, Feb. 1, 2, 4, 1929.

20 *Wallalluh*, 1937; President Baxter, President's Mid-Year Report and Annual Report, 1935, Smith Papers, Box 76A, Willamette University Archives.

21 President Baxter, President's Mid-Year Report and Annual Report, 1935, Smith Papers, Box 76A, Willamette University Archives; David Jack, Memo for the File, Jun. 30, 1935, Pietro Belluschi Papers, Box 114, File II, Job 595, Syracuse University Library.

22 David Jack, Memo for the File, Jun. 30, 1935, Pietro Belluschi Papers, Box 114, File II, Job 595, Syracuse University Library; A. E. Doyle and Associates to Amedee Smith, Aug. 19, 20, 1935, Ibid.; *Oregonian*, Jul. 28, 1935, 1. Initially, the students were somewhat receptive to the possibilities of a new campus with up-to-date facilities, but they soon cooled on the idea; see editorials in *Collegian*, Sep. 19 and Oct. 3, Nov. 21, 1935.

23 A. E. Doyle Associates to Amedee Smith, Aug. 19, 1935, Pietro Belluschi Papers, Box 114, File II, Job 595, Syracuse University Library; the controversy over the potential move of the campus can be followed in *Oregonian*, Sep. 6, 7, 10, 24, 27, 28, Oct.

23-27, and Nov. 6, 10, 16, 1935; see also *Salem Statesman*, Sep. 6, Oct. 26, Nov. 3, 9, 1935; Robert Gatke Notes on Trustees Minutes, Mar. 6 and Jun. 1937, vol. 13, Gatke Papers, Box 1, Folder 10, Willamette University Library Archives; Report of Faculty Library Committee, Smith Papers, Box 108B, Willamette University Archives; *Collegian*, Mar. 19, 1937.

24 Meredith L. Clausen, *Pietro Belluschi: Modern American Architect* (Cambridge, MA: The MIT Press, 1994), 1-79; A. E. Doyle Associates to Amedee Smith, Aug. 20, 1935, Pietro Belluschi Papers, Box 114, File, Job 595, Syracuse University Library.

25 Report of Faculty Library Committee, Smith Papers, Box 108B, Willamette University Archives.

26 Pietro Belluschi to Charles Sprague, Mar. 27, Apr. 7, Apr. 24, Jul. 28, 1937, Feb. 28, 1937, Smith Papers, 108B, Willamette University Archives; Report on the Special Committee on the Library Building, Mar. 31, 1937, ibid.; Amedee Smith to Charles Sprague, Apr. 26, 1937, ibid.; Pietro Belluschi to Charles Sprague, Apr. 24, 1937 (see additional notes on letter) and Jun. 11, 1937, Belluschi Papers, Box 114, File II, Job 595, Syracuse University Library; Pietro Belluschi, Memo for the File, Jun. 1, 1937, ibid.; Pietro Belluschi, Library plan and square footage, Sep. 9, 1937, File I, ibid.; President Baxter, President's Annual Report, 1937, Jun. 12, 1937, Smith Papers, Box 76A, Willamette University Archives; *Oregonian*, Sep. 17, 1937, p. 7, Sep. 19, 1937, p. 9, Feb. 22, 1939, p. 79; *Collegian*, Oct. 1, 8, 1937, May 6, Oct. 8, 28, 1938; "Willamette University Library in Typical Georgian Style," *Pacific Builder and Engineer*, vol. 45 (May 20, 1939).

27 The total cost including furnishings and architectural fees came to $93,000; Pietro Belluschi to Charles Schofield, Dec. 4, 1942, Pietro Belluschi Papers, Box 114, File III, Job 595, Syracuse University Library. "Willamette University Library in Typical Georgian Style," *Pacific Builder and Engineer*, vol. 45 (May 20, 1939); Pietro Belluschi, Library plan and square footage, Sep. 9, 1937, Pietro Belluschi Papers, Box 114, File VII, Job 595, Syracuse University Library; Pietro Belluschi to Forrest Mills, Aug. 12, 1938, Pietro Belluschi Papers, Box 114, File I, Job 595, Syracuse University Library.

28 L. H. Hoffman to A. E. Doyle and Associates, Oct. 7, 1937, Pietro Belluschi Papers, Box 114, IV, Job 595, Syracuse University Library; Pietro Belluschi to L. H. Hoffman, Nov. 12, 1937, ibid; personal communication between William Willingham and Anthony Belluschi, Jul. 17, 2012.

29 President Baxter, President's Annual Report, June 11, 1938, Smith Papers, Box 76A, Willamette University Archives; *Collegian*, May 19, 1938.

30 Pietro Belluschi to Amedee Smith, Oct. 24, 1936, Pietro Belluschi Papers, Box 114, File II, Job 595, Syracuse University Library; Robert Gatke, Notes on Trustees Minutes, Mar. 6, Nov. 5, 16, 1937, Feb. 28, 1938, vol. 13, Gatke Papers, Box 1, Folder 10, Willamette University Archives; L. H. Hoffman to Charles Sprague, Sep. 30, Dec. 6, Dec. 10, 1937, Smith Papers, Box 108B, Willamette University Archives; Sprague to Library Building Committee, Oct 2, 1937, ibid.; Pietro Belluschi to Charles Sprague, Nov. 1, 1937, ibid.; Bruce Baxter to Charles Sprague, Nov 19, 1937, ibid.; Charles Sprague to A. D. Moodie, Dec. 11, 1937, ibid.; Leo Hanley to Charles Sprague, Dec. 17, 1937, ibid.; W. E. Kennery to Charles Sprague, Dec. 15, 1937, ibid.; Sprague to C. E. McCulloch, Dec. 18, 1937, ibid.; Charles Sprague to Pietro Belluschi, Dec. 18, 1937, ibid.; Charles Sprague to L. H. Hoffman, Jan. 22, 1938, ibid.; Charles Sprague to Lebeck and Sons, Jan. 22, 1938, Nov. 16, 1938, ibid.; David M. Jack to Charles Sprague, May 27, Jun. 3, Jun. 16, 1938, ibid.; Philip Chipman to Charles Sprague and attachment, Jun. 29, 1938, ibid.; William Crowell to Charles Sprague, Aug. 22, Oct. 6, Oct. 27, 1938, ibid.; William Crowell to Lebeck and Sons, Aug. 22, Oct. 1, 1938, ibid.; Arbitrators to Lebeck and Son, Sep. 19, 1938, ibid.; Lebeck and Son to Willamette Building Committee, Nov. 14, 1938, ibid; *Collegian*, Nov. 24, Dec. 3, 1937, Jan. 21, Feb. 4, Apr. 22, 1938; President Baxter, President's Annual Report, Jun 11, 1938, Smith Papers, Box 76A, Willamette University Archives; *Collegian*, Jan. 21, Feb. 4, 1938.

31 Building Committee to Board of Trustees, Report on Purchase of House, Feb. 25, 1938, Smith Papers, Box 108B, Willamette University Archives; Charles Sprague to A. E. Doyle and Associates, Mar. 7, 1938, ibid.; President Baxter, President's Annual Report, Jun. 11, 1938, Smith Papers, Box 76A, Willamette University Archives; President Baxter, President's Annual Report, Jun. 10, 1939, ibid.; Robert Gatke's Notes on Trustees Minutes, Feb. 28, 1938, Jun 11, 1938, vol. 13, Gatke Papers, Box 1, Willamette University Archives.

32 President Baxter, President's Annual Report, Jun. 11, 1938, Smith Papers, Box 76A, Willamette University Archives; Pietro Belluschi to Bruce Baxter, Apr. 5, 1938, Pietro Belluschi Papers, Box 116, File 3, Job 624, Syracuse University Library; *Collegian*, Feb. 23, 1940.

33 Pietro Belluschi, Memo for the Files, Feb. 15, 1940, Pietro Belluschi Papers, Box 116, File 1, Job 624, Syracuse University Library; Professors Peck and Monk to President Baxter, Feb. 28, 1940, File 3, ibid.; Pietro Belluschi to Professor Monk, Oct. 25, 1940, ibid.

34 Professors Peck and Monk to President Baxter, Feb. 28, 1940, Pietro Belluschi Papers, Box 116, File 3, Job 624, Syracuse University Library, Pietro Belluschi to Pres. Baxter, Feb. 28, Mar. 7, 1940, File 3, ibid.; Pietro Belluschi, Memo for the File, Mar.13, Apr. 18, Jun 24, 1940, File 1, ibid.; Chester Luther to President Baxter, Mar. 13, 1940, Smith Papers, Box 67A, Willamette University Archives.

35 Pietro Belluschi to President Baxter, Mar. 31, 1941, Pietro Belluschi Papers, Box 116, File 3, Job 624, Syracuse University Library; Pietro Belluschi to Prof Pullias, Aug. 1, 1941, ibid.

36 Pietro Belluschi, Statement of Cost, Willamette University Science Building, May 19, 1941, Pietro Belluschi Papers, Box 116, File 3, Job 624, Syracuse University Library; Pietro Belluschi to President Baxter, Mar. 31, 1941, ibid.; President Baxter, President's Annual Report, Jun. 20, 1940.

37 President Baxter, President's Annual Report, Jun. 7, 1941, Smith papers, Box 76A, Willamette University Archives.

38 Robert Gatke's Notes on Trustees Minutes, Jun. 7, Jun 8, (letter from Charles Sprague to Paul Wallace, Jun. 25, 1941, entered into Board minutes), Jul. 10, 1941, vol. 14, Gatke Papers, Box 1, Folder 11, Willamette University Archives; Carl Knopf to Pietro Belluschi, Dec. 4, 1941, Feb. 4, 1942, Petro Belluschi Papers, Box 132, Job 695, Syracuse University Library; Pietro Belluschi to Carl Knopf, Dec. 18, 1941, ibid.; Pietro Belluschi to Paul Wallace, Dec. 19, 1941, ibid.; Pietro Belluschi to Amedee Smith, Dec. 22, 1941, ibid.; Paul Wallace to Pietro Belluschi, Dec. 20, 1941, ibid.; President Baxter, President's Annual Report, Jun. 7, 1941, Smith Papers, Box 76A, Willamette University Archives; *Collegian*, Dec. 5, 1941.

39 Quote in Gatke, *Chronicles*, 682.

40 Ibid., 683; Robert Gatke, Notes on the Minutes of the Trustees, Mar. 29, 1942, Gatke Papers, Box 1, Folder 12, Willamette University Archives. Professor Robert Gatke sadly noted in private his opinion that "Dr. Knopf received very unfair treatment at the hands of his Board who rendered a great disservice to Willamette by not standing with him. He went thru the trial of fire with a brave spirit—and while I don't believe in broken hearts causing death in the sense that expression is used I don't think there can be the slightest doubt that the fearful nervous strain he was under is what brought on his death. ... There had been rough spots in Dr. Knopf's administration but the faculty with very little exception felt that no man could be judged as an administrator in seven months and we felt that with a decent chance and support he would prove an effective president." Robert Gatke to Dr. Roy Smith, Jul. 3, 1942, Willamette Archives, Box 8, Willamette University Archives; *Oregonian*, May 12, 14, 30, Jun. 25, Jul. 2, 1942. See also, *Willamette Scene* (Spring, 1991), 13-17.

41 For the law school changes, see *Collegian*, Oct.28, 1938.

42 For the condition of Oregon's other small colleges by 1940, see Hitchman, *Liberal Arts Colleges*, 43-45, 62-66, 82-88.

5

World War II and the Postwar Period

When G. Herbert Smith stepped into the presidency of Willamette University in the summer of 1942, he had two major tasks before him: restore the morale of the Willamette community and cope with the effects of World War II on university operations. The Knopf affair had shaken confidence in the university's leadership, and the war had devastated male enrollments. Amidst this gloom and tension, Smith quickly had to assert leadership and convey his vision for the future. Smith came to Willamette with a background in college administration at the University of Illinois and DePauw University in Indiana. At the age of 37, he was the youngest president since Willis Hawley in 1893, who also had become president during a critical moment in the university's history. Like Hawley before him, Smith, while not a Methodist minister, had served as a lay leader in the church. Over time, Smith demonstrated a strong commitment to Willamette's religious heritage by reaching out to the Oregon Conference of the Methodist Church and reminding the ministers that of the 162 surviving colleges founded by Methodists before the Civil War, Willamette was one of 14 that still maintained a connection to the church.[1]

Upon his arrival in Salem, President Smith immediately took control of the university administration, worked to improve student morale, and reinvigorated dormant alumni relations. Assessing the immediate need to convey a sense of stability and continuity, Smith declared to the Willamette Board of Trustees in February 1943 his full devotion to the ideal of the small independent liberal arts college, which "has characterized the University for a century, and which has been the foundation of American college

G. Herbert Smith, 1904-1980, was the president of Willamette University from 1942-1969. A chronicle of his presidency is captured in Gregg's book, *Chronicles of Willamette, Volume 2; Those Eventful Years of the President Smith Era.*
Facing page: Architect's rendering of Smith/Fine Arts

Below left: This photo of a Willamette professor with Admiral Tom Gatch, with the then recently-planted Star Trees in the background, illustrates the partnership of the campus and the military training program. Admiral Gatch was the grandson of former Willamette president, Thomas Gatch.
Below right: Cadets lined up in an academic procession at Willamette University during the WWII V12 program.

education." President Smith would prove to be an astute administrator, fundraiser, and builder for the university.[2]

President Smith wasted little time in addressing the effects of the war on Willamette. He noted to the trustees that the draft law "in its operation will have far reaching effects on the colleges and universities of America. Unless some counter program is developed, the present draft will strip the colleges of the male students who are now on the campus and who might be expected to come to the campus in the future." In fact, Willamette's enrollment between the fall semesters of 1941 and 1942 declined from 697 to 582, with the resultant loss in tuition. Across the United States, severe enrollment declines hit small colleges the hardest, and many had to close their doors. To meet the crisis, Smith raised a wartime emergency fund to supplement the regular budget and went to Washington, D. C. to seek government approval for Willamette to join the military college training program then being established. After determined lobbying, and careful scrutiny by the Navy, Smith succeeded in securing a Navy V-12 unit for the university in April 1943.[3]

To carry out the V-12 naval program, the university increased its math and science offerings and operated on an accelerated schedule of three terms a year. The program began on July 1, 1943 with 258 men, 90 in pre-medical courses and 168 studying the basic curriculum for deck officers. To house the V-12 students, the administration moved the women out of Lausanne Hall and placed the program offices in the Law School building. Military discipline and a heavy schedule of physical conditioning prevailed on campus throughout the life of the program. In spite of the heavy demands of the training, the naval personnel participated fully in campus athletics and other extra-curricular activities. In late 1945, the V-12 program ended and the university returned to normal peacetime conditions, especially with women

again taking up residence in Lausanne. During the life of the V-12 program, 577 naval men attended Willamette University.

With careful planning and fiscal prudence, Willamette made it through the war years better than most small private colleges and universities, either regionally or nationally. In the Pacific Northwest, Linfield and Lewis and Clark colleges and Pacific University all saw enrollments decline below 200 students and suffered from small endowments and operating deficits. Whitman College, like Willamette, however, managed to obtain a V-12 program and kept its enrollment at around 500. The picture was much the same on the national level: Those schools that won a coveted campus military training program or provided some specialized science research or language instruction program survived the war in better shape than their peers.[4]

While President Smith contended with the immediate challenges of keeping the university afloat during the war years, he actively planned for the future. In a report to the board in February 1944, Smith gave his view of what Willamette should strive for in the future. As it had in the past, he believed that the university should focus on a well-defined program of liberal arts with a selective student enrollment. He thought that faculty salaries needed to be raised from the average of $2,500 to $3,000. At a minimum, necessary facilities included additional on-campus housing for men and provision for health services and an infirmary. He also proposed moving the athletic field off campus to free up badly needed space for a new classroom building, an auditorium, student union, and central heating plant. Of course, he called for an expanded endowment as well. In response to Smith's report, the trustees adopted most of his recommendations at their spring 1944 meeting. All agreed that the first priority should be on-campus housing for men, and then an infirmary. The minimum amount thought necessary for the two buildings came to $321,000. In the context of postwar inflation and material shortages, this proved to be wildly optimistic. The board also pledged that once the first two items were accomplished, they would increase the endowment by $500,000 and create an off-campus athletic field. The board envisioned accomplishing these goals over a ten-year period.[5]

President Smith wasted no time, despite the war, in beginning plans for the new dormitory. He asked architect Pietro Belluschi to prepare some preliminary sketches. Belluschi started work immediately, offering some cautionary advice about the building process timeline:

> *One thing we would like to bring out is that it takes a long time to arrive at a decision. It takes even longer to determine the nature of all details, and after those are settled the preparation of the working drawings and specifications is a longer process than the average client realizes. If this work is to be done, as we assume your board intends to in the immediate post-war, the building committee should begin to act in earnest now, as we estimate that it will take not less than five or six months from the time the preliminary drawings are accepted, until the time the working drawings and specifications are ready to go out for bids.*[6]

Even with this foresight, as will be seen, the realization of the new housing would be rushed to accommodate the influx of students immediately following the war.

The immediate impetus for the surge of students into higher education stemmed from the return of military veterans. To ease their transition into civilian life and keep from flooding the labor market, the federal government provided funding for higher education through the GI Bill. By 1950, two million veterans had taken advantage of the offer, which cost the government $5.5 billion. This represented 16 percent of the 14 million eligible veterans.

Under the GI Bill, military personnel could receive up to 48 months of education at an accredited institution, covering tuition, fees, books, and supplies up to $500 a year. At the time, private universities typically charged about $300 for tuition and state universities less.

Postwar Growth in Higher Education

The postwar years would present a new set of challenges for higher education in the United States. For a quarter of a century, colleges and universities would experience heady expansion and great turbulence during a period marked, as one historian has noted, "by the 'three P's' of prosperity, prestige, and popularity." Colleges and universities had to cope with rapid increases in enrollments as returning war veterans took advantage of the GI Bill for education. After this wave subsided, a new expansion began in the 1960s as the "baby boom" generation came of age and a greater proportion of the population went to college. Given the apparent national commitment to expanding educational opportunity, the extent of the federal government's role in the process also had to be clarified over time.[9]

The sheer increase in the numbers flocking to colleges and universities after World War II revealed the impact that higher education would have on American society in the future. In 1870, the country had 311 institutions of higher education, while in 1960 the number stood at 2,026. Of those persons between the ages of 18 and 21 in 1870, 1.7 percent were in college; by 1960, the percentage had risen to 50. In the decades after the Second World War, enrollments in higher education dramatically increased:

1940	1.5 million
1950	2.7 million
1960	3.6 million
1970	7.9 million

Single veterans also received a monthly subsistence allowance of $50 and eligible married veterans, $75. As an entitlement, the GI Bill guaranteed all eligible servicemen the benefit, which they could use at any accredited institution as determined by existing accrediting associations' standards.

In an interview with the *Oregonian* in April of 1945, President Smith stressed that Willamette's immediate postwar expansion would be tightly focused. As Smith put it, "We do not propose to expand and expand and expand. We want to be the very best medium-sized college that can be found and do our part in preservation of the independent college as the balance wheel in American higher education." The board had determined that enrollment for three years after the war would be held at about 800, allowing the university to accommodate about 300 ex-servicemen and women. Smith emphasized that traditional academic standards would be maintained: "We do not intend a lot of specialized short courses for veterans. We will retain our regular curriculum, giving, of course, credit for educational experience in the service proven by examinations in the subject and credit for studies under the Armed Forces institute." Events soon showed that the Willamette administration was overly optimistic that it could hold down enrollment. In the fall of 1946, the university admitted 1,100 full-time students, including 558 returned veterans. The academic year 1948-49 marked Willamette's peak enrollment of 1253 students. The numbers would drop to 1096 in 1950 – still well over the initial ceiling of around 800 – and they would stay there through the mid-50s. In this situation the university desperately needed a men's dormitory.[7]

The presence of large numbers of older veterans brought a new dynamic to campus, at least for a few years. More mature mentally and emotionally, they

Baxter Hall, as proposed.

Baxter Hall

Belluschi's dormitory design, while adhering closely in look and feel to the stripped or modern Georgian aesthetic displayed in his other two campus buildings, had its own distinct characteristics in detail. The central portion of the dormitory has a hipped roof tightly tied to the front of the building and set back on both ends where the roof is flat. This design element reduces the bulky appearance of the large structure. A Georgian-styled cupola surmounts the roof. Belluschi's arrangement of the large amount of glazing necessary in the dormitory serves to lighten the building's appearance and heighten its modern feel. To accomplish this design objective, he stretched the three floors of flat-profile windows in bands across each major elevation. The rectangular wood-framed windows consist of a fixed central portion with casement openings on either side. Painted brick surrounds each window frame, providing an understated definition to the whole arrangement. As in his other Willamette campus buildings, Belluschi's dormitory achieved much of its modern Georgian sensibility through a skillful use of materials and a fine sense of proportion and symmetry in overall design.

wanted, as Dean Gregg of the College of Liberal Arts, noted, "an education and a career as quickly as possible." He also observed, with some relish, that in class, the veterans were "real leaders and brought about some lively discussions."[8]

Belluschi eventually produced five different schemes by the summer of 1946. His preferred option presented a three-story, H-shaped structure in modern Georgian style, compatible with the library and science buildings previously designed by him. A complicating factor in the design of the building was that it had to accommodate four fraternities with 31 students each, while the main portion of the dormitory housed 100 independent students. The final design, with overall dimensions extending 246 feet in width and 204 feet in depth, would be built of reinforced concrete clad in red brick, with the center portion housing independent students while the wings contained the four fraternity units. The three-story center section stood 172 feet wide and 72 feet deep; the wings measured 204 feet by 37 feet each and reached only two stories in height.[13]

The plan for Baxter Hall provided a somewhat unusual arrangement for housing and governance of the national fraternities that it contained. The

Baxter Hall

The interior of Baxter Hall provided an efficient layout with a large central area that included a main kitchen that provided food for the central dining room as well as for each of the four fraternity dining rooms. The housing for the independent students would be in the central area, which contained four triple rooms, four single rooms, and 42 double rooms on the upper floors. The central area also included a large lounge, recreation room, office, and a house mother's suite on the first floor. Each of the four fraternity wings had a lounge, library, dining room, serving kitchen, chapter room, and house mother's suite. The fraternity units each had 15 double rooms and one single. The board named the new dormitory in honor of ex-president Bruce R. Baxter, who had recently died.[14]

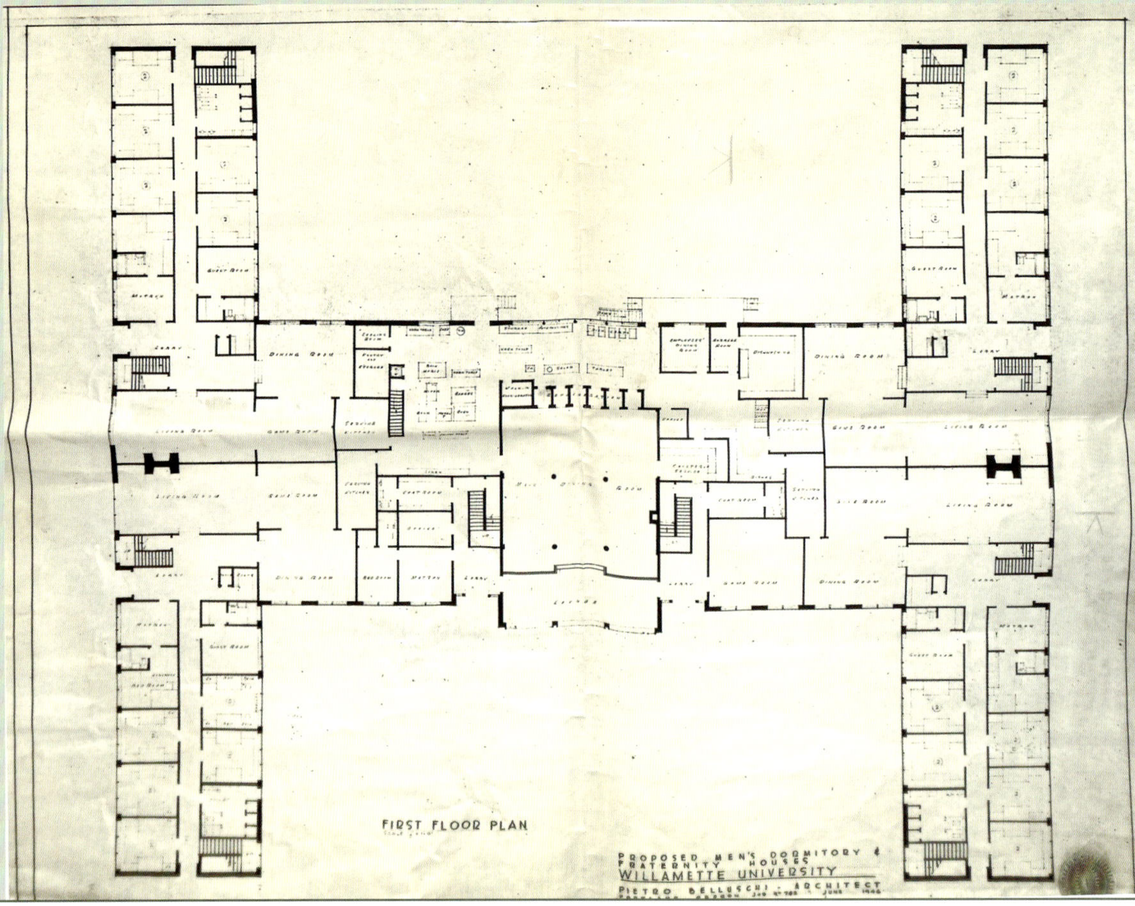

Floorplan for the first floor of Baxter Hall.

promotional literature for the new dormitory indicated that while each fraternity would handle its own internal management, dues, and finances, the new on-campus housing plan was "designed to make the fraternity an integral part of the educational and social program of the University rather than student organizations simply tolerated and loosely 'attached' to the parent educational institution." The Willamette administration wanted to take the fraternities out of the rooming house business and the attendant burdens of mortgages, property taxes, and inadequate financing. Moreover, since living conditions for all men on the campus would be the same, the administration hoped that "there is little chance for artificial differences to develop between groups which often have led to misunderstandings and ill will." The administration wanted to "promote a democratic, friendly spirit on the campus ... with fraternities having the best possible opportunities to encourage high ideals, develop real brotherhood and forward the educational program of the college."[15]

The actual construction of Baxter Hall proved to be difficult. As the university vice president for finance reported with a certain understatement, "Many difficulties were encountered in order to complete this project on time." First, it was a busy time for Belluschi and he was not able to devote as much personal time to the Willamette project as he would have liked. His office had a tremendous body of work in design and/or under construction during the late 1940s. These projects included major Portland commercial buildings such as the Equitable, Oregonian, Pacific Telephone and Telegraph buildings, and the Portland branch of the San Francisco Federal Reserve Bank. In addition, he designed significant residences for the Burkes and Menefee families, and pace-setting churches in Portland, such as St. Philip Neri, Zion Lutheran, and Central Lutheran. His firm also worked on numerous other large and small commissions during this period. Through it all, Belluschi tried to remain in tight control of design, client negotiations, and most aspects of the business operations of his architectural practice. He was also increasingly involved in professional affairs on the national level. As his biographer Meredith Clausen has noted, "By the late 1940s, he was one of the most highly respected architects in the country."[16]

Second, if Belluschi's other commitments were not enough to complicate the construction of Baxter Hall, building conditions in the country at large contributed to the difficulties involved. The early postwar years were a confounding time to attempt a major building project. Inflation, material shortages, and labor unrest all bedeviled Willamette's dormitory undertaking. In addition, the construction timeline was short, as the need for on-campus men's housing was great. Two hundred and twenty men had been admitted in the fall of 1947 with the promise that they would be housed on campus at the beginning of the second semester. Bids would come in on March 7, 1947.[17]

The Guy F. Atkinson Company of San Francisco submitted the low bid as general contractor, and there was a good reason that such a distant corporation would take an interest in bidding on the dormitory project. George Atkinson, chairman of the company, also served as a Willamette trustee and wanted to assure that the university could get the project completed at a reasonable price on a

Postwar Changes in Higher Education

While some higher education administrators were skeptical that many ex-soldiers would take advantage of the GI Bill, many others began vigorously recruiting servicemen. As a result of the aggressive outreach, many schools saw enrollments double between 1943 and 1946. Colleges and universities needed expanded facilities to meet the crush of students and had to adjust to a cohort older than the traditional college age. The GI Bill also temporarily shifted the gender mix on campuses. In 1940, women accounted for 40 percent of undergraduate enrollment; by 1950, their proportion had declined to 32 percent of the total. It took until 1970 for women to regain the 40 percent proportion of higher education enrollments.

Policy makers envisioned the GI Bill as a temporary program to smooth the transition from a wartime to a peacetime economy. For more permanent approaches to the future relationship between the federal government and higher education, President Harry Truman established in 1946 a Commission on Higher Education. The Commission sought to find the best way to expand higher educational opportunities nationwide. Implicit in this charge was the assumption that improved access to higher education promoted the national interest. Among the Commission's many recommendations was a call for an expanded, long-term federal policy to increase investment in higher education. While initially the idea of massive programs for a heightened federal role in post-secondary education met political resistance, over time, the federal government gave increased support for scientific research at universities and then gradually directed funds to other areas of academia.

The impetus for an expanded federal role in scientific research came from science advisor Vannevar Bush's 1945 report entitled "Science, The Endless Frontier" and from the anxieties stemming from the advent of the Cold War. In supporting scientific research, the federal government established permanent laboratories and agencies, such as the National Science Foundation and the National Institutes of Health, and funded large-scale scientific research by universities through competitive grants. In time, leading research universities became dependent on federal science funding and lost a measure of independence, but the external money proved too tempting to turn down. By 1960, institutions of higher education had received about $1.5 billion from the federal government, with twenty universities accounting for 79 percent of

continued on next page

Postwar Changes in Higher Education *continued*

the grants. A few fields, particularly the physical and biological sciences, health sciences, and engineering benefitted the most from federal funds. Just as the initial wave of federally supported research started to plateau in the mid-1950s, the Soviet launch of Sputnik sparked a new round of federal scientific funding that lasted through the 1960s. The new age of expansion in higher education after World War II led to an explosion of Ph. D. programs to provide qualified faculty. For example, in 1940, enrollment in graduate programs stood at about 106,000 students; by 1950, the numbers in graduate schools reached 237,200. Many universities expanded existing programs or entered the graduate arena for the first time. The number of doctorates awarded rose from 6,420 in 1950 to about 30,000 in 1970.

To address the imbalances within universities and colleges created by the heavy federal investments in the sciences, private foundations attempted to direct their funding to the social and behavioral sciences. The Ford Foundation, for example, was especially active, committing $560 million in 1955. The grants went to raising faculty salaries, strengthening instruction at private medical schools, improving business administration programs, and aiding historically black colleges and universities. All of the postwar growth and innovation assisted by the federal government and private foundations led to a need for new and expanded physical plants at colleges and universities.

The nation's public and private colleges and universities had to engage in major building programs on existing campuses, and many states embarked on establishing new campuses, vastly expanding their systems of higher education. States such as New York and California invested heavily in developing new campuses. In New York, for example, the State University of New York (SUNY) grew to encompass 64 diverse campuses, enrolling 300,000 by 2000. California, on the other hand, chose to create both a University of California system of nine campuses and a California State University arrangement of 19 institutions. Both states had thriving private colleges and universities as well. Prior to 1970, both California and New York provided generous public tax support for their higher education programs. Many private institutions felt that public universities enjoyed an unfair advantage because of per student subsidies from the state. Private schools responded by building strong fundraising efforts and trying new approaches to student financial aid, such as need-blind and need-based admissions policies. Small private liberal arts colleges also attempted to stand out with unique curriculums that offered prospective students honors programs, independent study abroad options, and small class sizes.

The changes in American higher education after World War II brought new directions in campus planning. The increased enrollments and more complex pattern of education encouraged new designs to accommodate both growth and change. Nearly all of the approximately 2,000 institutions underwent physical expansion, and by 1962, 200 entirely new campuses were either planned or under construction. The increasing diversity of academic offerings at both undergraduate and graduate levels combined with the expanding role of grant-supported research required a host of new special facilities. The ubiquity of the automobile also had to be addressed in campus planning. The scale and complexity of the higher education campus challenged the ingenuity of architects to successfully sort out high density, conflicting land-use patterns, traffic congestion, and diverse academic goals to produce a coherent college or university campus. As one architectural historian put it, "The complex, fluid, and unpredictable nature of many schools required a type of planning that was itself fluid and flexible, unhampered by formal preconceptions of what a campus should look like."[10]

compressed schedule when building conditions were so problematic. Financing the project put President Smith and the Board of Trustees under great pressure. While the basic construction bid came in at $526,500, by the time the dormitory opened the entire project cost had inflated to almost $750,000. Initial fundraising produced only $450,000, so the trustees had to borrow $300,000 to cover the finished cost of the building. President Smith considered repaying the bank loan a major goal of his administration, reminding the board in November 1948 that "we should push additional gifts as rapidly as possible to pay off this mortgaged indebtedness at the earliest date." Smith also pointed out that "it was fortunate that we completed this building when we did. Present estimates indicate that the building would cost a quarter of a million dollars more if we had to erect it today."[18]

Although students moved into Baxter Hall in February 1948, much finish work remained incomplete. Indeed, when representatives from Belluschi's office inspected the building in late January 1948, they reported much unfinished or substandard work. They stated in an office memo that "the general reaction to the job from a distance is good at first appearance. Closer inspection brings out the poor quality of glass and brick work." They also complained about the inadequate quality of the millwork for doors and window frames and the poorly executed sheet metal work. Repairs and adjustments continued until late in 1948, when final acceptance of the contract occurred.[19]

While pushing completion of Baxter Hall, President Smith also scrambled to acquire war surplus buildings from the Army's Camp Adair, which closed following World War II. As a result of President Smith's persistence, the university received a badly needed infirmary facility, which Belluschi remodeled to meet Willamette's needs. In the summer of 1947, President Smith was able to get two other structures from Camp Adair and place them at the southwestern corner of the campus near the millrace. Each was a one-story building constructed of wood and measured 25 by 90 feet. One became an annex of the Music Building to house the band department, while the other was used by the art department. While the federal government made the buildings available under a program providing facilities to schools affected by large numbers of returning veterans, the re-erection and remodeling of the buildings still cost the university $55,000. The structures alleviated overcrowding in the Music Building and Eaton Hall and remained a part of the campus until the university completed the Fine Arts building and the Bishop Infirmary in 1955.[20]

Rear view of Baxter Hall under construction. The photo was taken from where Matthews Hall now stands.

In the late 1940s, the Bishop family of Salem—long-time benefactors of Willamette—contributed a home for the university president. Located on Court Street, the house was never actually used by the president. Student housing needs were so great that the university used the old Victorian home as a dormitory for 18 women. Finally, in 1955, the trustees sold the home and used the funds to purchase a residence at 325 Lincoln Street South, for the president.[21]

Another major building project in the late 1940s encompassed the development of a new athletic field and stadium. When President Smith arrived to take up his post, he quickly surveyed the shortcomings of

Crown Hall at the Illinois Institute of Technology, opened in 1956, represents one of the earliest, and most influential, examples of modernist International Style on college campuses.

Modernism in Architecture and Postwar Campus Planning

With its emphasis on functionalism and flexible planning, architects of modernism should have been well-suited to meet the new challenges facing higher education during the rapid growth following World War II. Initially, however, most colleges and universities resisted modern design, preferring the traditional architecture of their existing buildings. While a few International Style buildings appeared here and there on campuses in the 1930s and 1940s, its major success came in Ludwig Mies Van der Rohe's design for the Illinois Institute of Technology in Chicago (1938-49), which proposed an exposed steel-frame structural system for buildings. The plan of the campus, however, with its symmetrical and axial layout of buildings, reflected traditional Beaux-Arts collegiate design principles. Frank Lloyd Wright's design for the new campus of Florida Southern College, begun in 1938 and executed in the 1940s and 1950s, represented another application of modernist design to campus planning.

In the 1950's, college administrators contemplating new buildings showed increasing enthusiasm for the Modern style as an antidote to dull traditional Georgian or dismal Gothic Revival style buildings. In part, college officials liked the fact that Modern designs (form follows function) came without complex, expensive surface ornament, emphasizing instead clean, simple, hard-edged lines and flat roofs. Economies in materials and construction made Modern style buildings attractive to cost-conscious higher education officials.

Modernism in collegiate architecture went through three phases in the last half of the twentieth century. Writing in 1998, architectural critic Richard Dober phrased it thusly: "Early Modern purged the system [of traditional styles]. Middle Modern, with its move away from sanitary surfaces and interest in textured and sculptured effects, demonstrated the range of possibilities. Late Modern, with more elaboration and segmentation of building forms, laid the foundation for today's contemporary campus design and architecture." Willamette University would experiment with the Modern idiom in its own way with varying degrees of success.[11]

Architectural historian Paul Turner has noted that "traditional college planning in the twentieth century whether a conception for an entirely new campus or a development plan for an existing campus, usually produced a unified design, specific in its overall form and architectural character." After World War II, college planning began to drop comprehensive master plans in favor of flexible general guidelines allowing future growth. Formal master plans no longer adequately dealt with complexity and unpredictability that higher education administrators experienced in the mid-twentieth century. The emphasis shifted from grand, static campus designs to focusing on the character of individual buildings and their ability to meet the needs of change and growth. The problem in such an open planning process was to avoid aesthetic chaos in erecting and placing new buildings in the open spaces on an existing campus.[12]

The new emphasis on flexibility in campus planning with each building an independent architectural statement was in a sense a return to pre-Beaux-Arts master planning which simply placed separate buildings in large open spaces. Now, as before the Beaux-Arts period, college buildings differed from one another because they represented the popular architectural styles of the times in which they were constructed. The preference in the nineteenth and early twentieth centuries was for unity rather than disparity of style, but in the 1950s and 1960s architectural variety became a fully acceptable design principle on the college and university campus. Unified master plans and stylistic conformity seemed to make little sense for institutions in flux and made up of diverse and often conflicting academic interests. Within this context of dynamic growth and change in higher education, and the resulting experimentation in campus planning, Willamette University had to find its way as it grew and built during the post-World War II period.

the existing old athletic field on Willamette's campus. As Dean Robert Gregg noted in his book about the President Smith era, Sweetland Field was "less than desirable. It was a sea of mud for six or eight months, including the football season, and a 'dust bowl' during the dry season. The old wooden stands leaked and were drafty. Valuable land in the path of campus expansion was at stake." To improve the athletic field and provide badly-needed expansion room on campus, President Smith entered into a complicated three-way negotiation involving the City of Salem, the prominent Bush family, and the university. As a result of the talks, in June 1946, the city paid $50,000 for 90 acres and the Bush House, while the Willamette gained 10 acres directly south of campus for $25,000. Over the next four years, the university graded and cleaned the land and added a quarter-mile cinder track and baseball diamond. Finally, in 1950, the trustees voted to build a modern concrete and steel, covered stadium to seat 3,500 at a cost of about $132,000. Lighting and fencing for the stadium field came to another $10,000. The

McCulloch Stadium in 1950.

trustees named the new athletic complex and stadium McCulloch Field in honor of long-time board member and chairman, Charles McCulloch.[22]

In the early 1950s, President Smith declared that the board development plan of 1944 had been successfully completed. Baxter Hall dormitory provided badly needed on-campus housing for both independent and fraternity men. Acquisition of federal war surplus buildings aided the university in providing a student infirmary and alleviating over-crowded facilities in the art and music programs. The creation of McCulloch Stadium and field gave the athletic program modern facilities for the first time in the university's history. Other, less visible, additions to existing buildings also improved the learning and social life of the campus. For example, the library gained new, badly needed, lighting and two more levels of book stacks, while an anonymous donor paid for expanding folding bleachers in the gymnasium. This latter improvement enabled the entire student body to attend convocations on campus instead of at the First Methodist Church, several blocks away. Finally, after two years of effort, the unsightly hole left by the removal of Kimball Hall in 1942 was finally filled and landscaped in 1947.[23]

As happened so often in Willamette's history, barely would one massive effort be completed before the need for new buildings, more endowment, and a look at curriculum standards became critical. President Smith would have his hands full in the years to come, but as he had ably proven in the difficult 40s, he was the man to get the job done.

Endnotes

1 Quote in Robert D. Gregg, *Chronicles of Willamette, Vol. II: Those Eventful Years of the President Smith Era* (Portland, OR: Durham and Downey, Inc., 1970), 10; for this chapter, much of the background information on the Smith era at Willamette is drawn from the Gregg volume.

2 Ibid., 11.

3 Ibid.

4 Hitchman, *Liberal Arts Colleges*, 46, 66, 89, and 130; Thelin, *A History of Higher Education*, 257-59.

5 *Willamette Alumnus*, vol. II, Dec. 1944.

6 Pietro Belluschi to G. Herbert Smith, Mar. 25, 1944, Belluschi Papers, Box 141, File 1, Job 782, Syracuse University Library.

7 Quotes in *Oregonian*, Apr. 1, 1945.

8 Mid-term Report of the President, Feb. 1949, Smith Papers, Box 35A; Gregg, *Chronicles, II*, 57.

9 Much of the background information on higher education in the postwar years is based on Rudolph, *The American College*, 294-ff; Thelin, *A History of Higher Education*, 260-316.

10 Quote in Turner, *Campus*, 250. The following discussion of campus architecture and planning is based on ibid., 249-305. See also, Dober, *Campus Architecture*, 1-51 and Carole Rifkind, *A Field Guide to Contemporary American Architecture* (New York: Penguin Putnam, 1998), 230-250.

11 Dober, *Campus Architecture*, 11.

12 Quote in Turner, *Campus*, 260.

13 Pietro Belluschi to G. Herbert Smith, Mar. 25, 1944, Jul. 13, 1946, Belluschi Papers, Box 141, File 1, Job 782, Syracuse University Library; G. Herbert Smith to Robert Gatke, Aug. 3, 1945, Gatke Papers, Box 2, Willamette University Archives; G. Herbert Smith, Application for Authority to Construct Housing under Veterans' Housing Program Order 1 and attachments, Sep. 30, 1946, Gatke Papers, Box 1, Willamette University Archives.

14 Dedication Brochure for Baxter Hall and Fraternity Residences, Mar 19-21, 1948, Smith Papers, Box 108B, Willamette University Archives.

15 Ibid.

16 Annual Report of the Financial Vice President, 1947-48, Smith Papers, Box 36B, Willamette University Archives; Meredith L. Clausen, *Pietro Belluschi: Modern American Architect* (Cambridge, MA: The MIT Press, 1994), 187.

17 *Collegian*, Oct. 3, Dec. 5, 1947, Jan. 16, 30, 1948; *Oregonian*, Jan. 26, 1948; Mid-term Report of the President, Feb. 1948, Smith Papers, Box 76A, Willamette University Archives.

18 G. Herbert Smith to The Guy F. Atkinson Co., Mar. 22, 1947, Smith Papers, Box 108A, Willamette University Archives; Pietro Belluschi to Robert Fenix, May 18, 1948, Belluschi Papers, Box 141, File 4, Job 782, Syracuse University Library; G. Herbert Smith to Board of Trustees, Oct. 1946, quote in Nov. 8, 1948, Smith Papers, Box 37, Willamette University Archives. Belluschi received a fee of $40,198.15 for the dormitory project (6 percent) but also gave a donation of $7,000 to the project: Smith to Belluschi, Mar. 13, Jun. 16, 1947, Belluschi Papers, Box 141, File 1, Job 782, Syracuse University Library; Mid-term Report of the President, Feb. 1948, Smith Papers, Box 76A, Willamette University Archives.

19 Memorandum Re: Willamette University Dormitory, Jan. 23, 1948, Belluschi Papers, Box 141, File 4, Syracuse University Library; Belluschi to Guy F. Atkinson, Co., Jan. 26, Nov. 8, 1948, ibid.

20 G. Herbert Smith to L. R. Durkee, Oct. 23, Nov. 4, Dec.14, 1946, Feb. 21, 1947, May 13, 1948, Smith Papers, Box 108B, Willamette University Archives; L. R. Durkee to G. Herbert Smith, Dec. 2, 1946, Feb. 17, 1947, ibid.; G. Herbert Smith to L. R. Durkee, Jul. 7, 11, 1947, Smith Papers, Box 108A, Willamette University Archives, L. R. Durkee to G. Herbert Smith, Jul. 8, 1947, ibid; Pietro Belluschi to G. Herbert Smith, Dec. 5, 1946, Belluschi Papers, Box 141, File 1, Job 1037, Syracuse University Library; Robert Fennix to Pietro Belluschi, Dec. 18, 1946, ibid.; G. Herbert Smith to Pietro Belluschi, Dec. 27, 1946, ibid.; Annual Report of the Financial Vice President, 1946-47, 1947-48, Smith Papers, Box 35A and 36B, Willamette University Archives; Mid-term Report of the President, Feb. 1948, Smith Papers, Box 76A, Willamette University Archives.

21 Annual Report of the Financial Vice President, 1949-50, Smith Papers, Box 35A, Willamette University Archives.

22 Gregg, *Chronicles, II*, 45; Your Gifts to Willamette, [no date, late 1940s], Smith Papers, Box 108A, Willamette University Archives; Robert M. Bonney to Pittsburgh-Des Moines Steel Co., May 7, 1950, Smith Papers, 110B, Willamette University Archives; David Thompson to G. Herbert Smith, Mar. 6, 1947, ibid., David Thompson to Robert Fennix, Nov. 15, 1948, ibid.; G. Herbert Smith to David Thompson, Jul. 25, 1946, May 1, 1947, Smith Papers, Box 108B, Willamette University Archives, David Thompson to G. Herbert Smith, Jul. 6, 1946, May 9, 1947, ibid., G. Herbert Smith to Common Council, May 7, 1946, ibid.; Annual Reports of the Financial Vice President, 1947-51, Smith Papers, Box 35A and 36B, Willamette University Archives; *Collegian*, Mar. 3, May 19, Jun., 2, Sep. 15, Oct. 20, 1950.

23 Annual Reports of the Financial Vice President, 1947-50, Smith Papers, Box 35A, Willamette University Archives; *Willamette Alumnus*, Mar. 1952, 4-5.

EATON HALL

Leadership and Growth 6

The late 1940s were a tumultuous time at Willamette, not only as a result of the physical expansion, but also because of the changing student demographics and curricular revisions. As President Smith put it in his mid-year report to the board in February 1949, "Just as the subject Plant Development ranked first consideration in the president's report last year, so the leading section this year should be The Educational Program—since primary attention has been given to internal functioning of the University." Challenged by the debate over the future direction of higher education contained in President Harry S. Truman's Commission on Higher Education, Willamette's administration reevaluated the university's proper educational role. Once again, the debate centered on the relative emphasis between a liberal arts versus a vocational or pre-professional education. The commission report urged a broadened higher education for all capable high school graduates so as to strengthen the democratic foundations of society and contribute to international order and peace. The commission, moreover, proposed a financial role for the federal government in achieving these educational goals. President Smith, however, had grave reservations about an expanded federal involvement in higher education, stating that "any wide program of federal assistance will result in changing our educational pattern in the United States so completely that the result should give us real reason for concern." He feared that with federal funds would come federal control.[1]

Most importantly, President Smith firmly believed that there was still a place for the small liberal arts college within American higher education—one that provided depth as well as breadth in educational experience. To make sure that Willamette continued

Facing page: Eaton Hall

to achieve its educational goals, Smith instituted a reexamination of its curriculum and graduation requirements. Out of this self-study came a phasing out of the Home Economics major and a merging of economics and business administration programs with an emphasis on theory over applied courses. The university strengthened foreign language, science, and math requirements and tightened the comprehensive written and oral examinations for graduation. In addition, department course offerings were pruned, and better student counseling and guidance practices became the norm. Above all, Smith wanted to avoid an undergraduate education that simply collected unrelated fragments of knowledge or created a sequence of courses in overly narrow fields of study. President Smith summed up his thinking for the board by stating that "the more I see of mass education, the more convinced I am that there is a continuing place for outstanding educational institutions which select students upon the basis of ability to profit by the educational experience, and which stress excellence of teaching rather than any other phase of educational activity. To this type of education Willamette should continue to dedicate itself."[2]

As before, increased enrollment and an evolving academic structure required expansion of the physical plant. As Dean Gregg so aptly stated it:

> *Most educators realize that the heart of a university is the student-teacher relationship .... Buildings, however, are the necessary setting in which this meeting of minds can take place to best advantage. With the growing complexity of life in a technological age, education for living naturally becomes more complex. Thus, more adequate and better equipped classrooms, laboratories, libraries, living, and recreational areas must be provided.*

In his 1953 mid-year report to the board, President Smith succinctly listed the "needs of the University, both immediate and for the long future":

> *At the present we have a portion of the Music School and all of the art Department housed in temporary buildings, which must be replaced. We are woefully in need of a satisfactory auditorium and area for the work of our Speech and Drama Department. As we look ahead we must anticipate greater capacity for our women's dormitory. As soon as we erect another building, we must think in terms of the needs in the heat and maintenance plant to adequately take care of the needs of the campus. Other buildings, which we must anticipate in the future, are a Student Union Building, a permanent Health Service and Infirmary, a Worship Chapel and another general classroom building.*[3]

Based on a presentation by President Smith and the trustee committee on development, the board voted in February 1953 to launch a $1 million Challenge Fund campaign to construct a new fine arts/auditorium building and a women's dormitory. This action represented the first step in a $5 million long-range program which ultimately sought $2.5 million for buildings and $2.5 million for the endowment. The board also agreed with President Smith that the proposed new buildings would allow enrollment to increase 25 percent to a total of 1250 full-time students. To kick off the initial fund drive to raise the initial $1 million, President Smith announced that two trustees, Truman Collins and George Atkinson, had each pledged $250,000. With half the needed amount in hand, Smith pressed to get the buildings moving forward. By the spring of 1954, the project was bid at $1.15 million and construction began soon thereafter.[4]

When planning for the new buildings, President Smith had to find a different architect. Pietro Belluschi, who had designed all of the campus buildings built between 1937 and 1950, had left Oregon to become dean of the School of Architecture at the Massachusetts

The auditorium and fine arts building under construction in 1954.

Institute of Technology. After interviewing a half dozen firms, President Smith and the trustees settled on a local Salem architect, James Payne. Payne, after earning a degree in architecture from the University of Arkansas and doing military service during World War II, had moved to Salem and established a thriving architectural practice. In addition to his Willamette buildings, Payne's firm designed many prominent commercial and public buildings in Salem, including the Salem Civic Center (1972), Meier and Frank Department Store (1956), the Pacific Northwest Bell Telephone Company building (1972), and the State Department of Agriculture Building (1965). In choosing Payne, President Smith especially appreciated his "willingness to work with us, and his excellent abilities as an architect." What most pleased Smith was Payne's ability to design the auditorium/fine arts building, the health center, and a women's residence hall in such a way as "to achieve harmony in relationship to the older buildings at Willamette." Additionally, Payne's work evidenced the same attention to detail his predecessor had displayed.[5]

As early as September 1952, President Smith and the board executive committee had instructed Payne to prepare plans for the three buildings that would form a new quadrangle on the southern portion of the campus where Sweetland Field once stood. In order of importance they listed first a fine arts building that would combine an auditorium and space that would house classrooms for the music, art, speech, and drama departments. The second building was a women's dormitory for 75 students. This structure would sit at the west end of the quad near Lausanne Hall. The third building sought by the Willamette leaders initially appeared uncertain. Smith instructed Payne to think in terms of either a student center or infirmary. Longer range plans included moving the music building south to the location of the University House and putting a chapel in its place.[6]

By the spring of 1953, Willamette University had firmed up its development plans. The immediate goal of the first phase of development would focus on completing the auditorium/fine arts building and the women's residence hall. Payne's architectural drawings of the proposed buildings detailed his version of Belluschi's stripped Georgian style. As trustee Robert Notson noted approvingly in a talk before a Salem crowd gathered to launch the Challenge Fund drive, Payne's plans "reflected the very best features of Collins Hall, the Library and Baxter Hall." As designed, the two new buildings had symmetrically balanced facades with plain, metal sash windows set flush on the surface. The designs employed little surface decoration, and, in order to save money, the specifications called for painted brick detailing instead of ornamental stone trim. Both structures were clad in Belluschi's favorite warm-colored red bricks with contrasting mortar. The bricks were to come from the same Willamina Clay Products Company that previously had supplied Belluschi.[7]

Fine Arts/Smith

Payne designed the auditorium/fine arts building in a U shape with the central, 85-foot- high auditorium portion of the structure flanked by two-story wings containing the class and practice rooms. Each wing has an entry porch covered by a flat roof supported by plain, slender pipes. The back of the building sits flush with the mill stream that crossed the southern edge of the campus. Seven tall rectangular panels in outline break up the plain brick exterior of the front elevation of the central section that houses the auditorium. At the base of the center section, underneath the stylized panels, Payne's plan provides a covered outdoor passageway to visually connect the two wings. This design element helps to provide additional relief from the massive blank brick face of the building. To further reduce the bulky appearance of the building, Payne set back the massive hipped roof from the ends of the central section; the wings have flat roofs. Of the three buildings Payne placed around the quad, only the auditorium/fine arts building has a Georgian-styled cupola in the manner of Belluschi's library, science building, and men's dormitory.

View of Fine Arts/Smith from across the quad.

This floorplan of the ground floor of the auditorium and fine arts building demonstrates how the space interconnects.

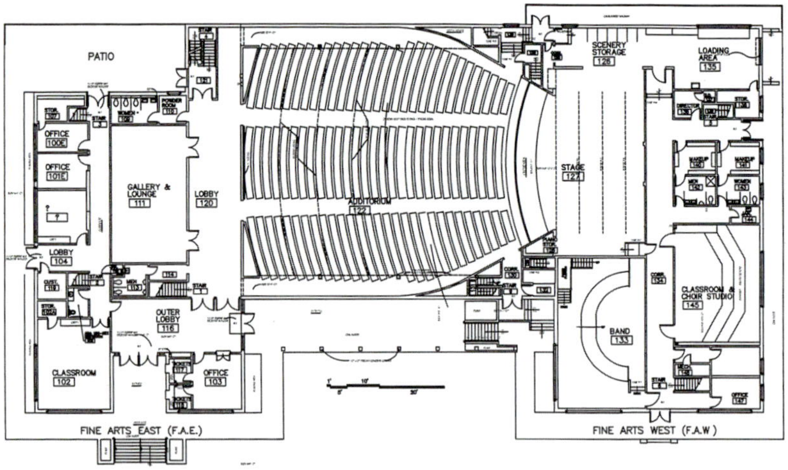

An interior view of Smith Auditorium from the stage.

Smith Auditorium

Smith Auditorium seats 1250 people (950 on the main floor and 300 in the balcony), claiming at the time, according to a university press release, "the most modern construction of its kind in the Northwest." The stage contains 1,672 square feet of floor space and an organ loft sat in a chamber at the upper left of the stage. An orchestra pit is recessed at the front of the stage, and the backstage area housed what was then the latest in modern theater equipment. For convenience, a passageway leads directly to the orchestra pit from the band practice room in the west wing. Payne paneled the interior walls of the auditorium with Philippine mahogany. The acoustical treatment directed "sound through the shaping of ceiling and walls. Excess sound is absorbed through baffles." Payne relied on a nationally recognized acoustical consultant, Dr. Vern Knudson of the University of California at Los Angeles, to achieve the desired sound properties for the auditorium.[8]

Doney Hall, named after the twelfth president of Willamette. Parallel to Lausanne Hall, it formed the west end of the new quad.

The most difficult design challenge faced by Payne was how best to accomplish the task of combining in one structure the requirements for a modern theater and concert stage of a fine arts center with the space needs of class and practice rooms for teaching art, music, drama, and speech. In the end, Payne skillfully created a multipurpose building that accomplished the diverse programmatic needs in a dignified and balanced manner. Set on raised ground at the south end of the new quad, and ultimately flanked on either side by Doney Hall and Bishop Health Center, the large auditorium/fine arts building became the focal point for the campus.

In January 1954, while the Challenge Fund effort proceeded, the board announced that the Bishop family, long-time supporters of the university, had decided to fund the erection of a new student health center. This was the second major gift to Willamette by the Bishop family. They had previously given a residence in 1948 for the use of the president of the university.[9]

Willamette's long-range expansion plans received a boost early in the Challenge Fund drive when the California Packing Company donated a 1.5 acre triangular tract of land along with a recently

Doney Hall

Architect James Payne's take on Belluschi's stripped Georgian style, the three-story women's dormitory contains 25 double, 18 single, and 3 triple rooms. The rectangular, symmetrically balanced structure is clad in the same warm red brick and cream-colored painted trim to conform with the other recent stripped Georgian-styled campus buildings. The third floor is set off by a cream-colored cement band. At the residence hall's corners, the architect designed full height, shallow projections from the main volume to break up the blocky appearance of the dormitory. The building's entry has a two-story flat roofed portico with slender supports, while a low, hipped roof that sits back from each end covers the structure. The front facade holds banks of windows that differ in height on each floor; all are rectangular in shape and symmetrically grouped but vary from four- to single-pane in layout. On the interior, the first floor contained a lounge, a dining room, and the head resident's suite, while the upper floors hold the dorm rooms. A large recreation room filled the basement.

An interior shot of the lounge in Doney Hall at completion.

The Original Bishop Student Health Center

Located on the east end of the new quad and near the old gymnasium, the health center had facilities for 18 bed patients, four baths, treatment and physical therapy rooms, a kitchen, and office space. The T-shaped building sat on high ground and had a projecting center section with an entry porch and symmetrical wings on either side, each having its own separate end entrances. The brick and cream-colored trim cladding conformed to the other stripped Georgian styled buildings on campus.

The original Bishop Student Health Center when it was completed in 1955.

abandoned canning plant located on the southeastern edge of the campus along 12th Street. The university had owned the property until 1891 when it was sold for the development of a fruit and vegetable cannery; at the time of sale, Willamette desperately needed money to keep its doors open in the face of competition from the rival Methodist university newly opened in Portland. After receiving the property in late 1953, the university cleared it, hoping ultimately to build another men's residence facility on it, and decades later Mathews Hall would stand on the site. In the short term, it served as an intramural sports field.[10]

When construction on the three buildings got underway in the summer of 1954, the trustees had raised $743,000 and felt the remainder would be in hand by the time the buildings were finished. In September 1955, however, when the three additions to the campus neared completion, the Challenge Fund drive remained $142,000 short of its goal. To close the gaps, the trustees took out a bank loan to complete the then most ambitious expansion yet undertaken by the university. Several more years of fundraising enabled the university to pay off the bank loan and to raise $30,000 for a dormer addition under the backside of the roof on Baxter Hall's center section to accommodate an additional 18 men.[11]

A growing enrollment and physical plant were not the only large challenges facing Willamette in this period, however. Educational costs also continued to rise. President Smith worried about the ability of the existing endowment to meet constantly rising educational costs. In the early 1950s, Willamette's tuition stood slightly below average compared to six other private liberal arts colleges in the Pacific Northwest. A strong endowment would enable Willamette to hold the line on tuition increases, but high inflation in the late 1940s and early 1950s had made it difficult for endowment returns to adequately support the university's growing financial needs. President Smith pointed out in his February 1953 report to the board that "most endowed colleges would consider themselves fortunate if their endowment would take care of twenty-five to thirty-five per cent of those costs." He went on to say, "Currently, our present increased income from endowment now provides but seventeen per cent." He further stated that in a study of 12 Methodist-related colleges having more than $2 million in endowment, Willamette ranked in the bottom one-half of the schools in the percentage of income derived from endowment. All of this information reinforced President Smith's call to increase Willamette's endowment to $5 million. By 1957, Smith and the board had pushed the endowment to $2.9 million, an increase of 40 percent in seven years. They did not limit their efforts just to boosting the endowment. During that same time period, they increased faculty salaries by 54 percent, which put Willamette at the average for similar private colleges nationwide. Willamette's faculty salaries, however, still remained behind those of the Oregon system of higher education.[12]

Even with these accomplishments, two factors still challenged the board as it looked to the future: a long-range inflationary trend and predictions of a wave of students that was expected to double enrollments at Oregon's colleges and university by the mid-1960s. The board recognized that it might have to commit to a student body larger than the authorized 1250 and, accordingly, would need to grow the endowment further to support such an expansion. In 1958, Robert Notson, Chairman of the Willamette Trustee Development Committee summed up the situation by asking:

> *What kind of an institution do we want to have by 1965? It is well enough to say that we shall not be pressured into a student body expanded beyond the limits that we have set for a small but strong, liberal arts institution. ... But the day will surely come when the sons and daughters of our Willamette alumni, of our Methodist constituency, of our cultural community will seek admission in greater numbers than we had desired. What then? When the day comes that we reject young people in large numbers, young people otherwise qualified for admission, because we do not desire to expand, will we continue to enjoy the full support of our present friends or of the business community in general? Will we then be told that we are not doing our share to meet the need of youth for college training?*[13]

While the board pondered Notson's questions related to the future, he went on to remind his fellow trustees that they must provide, in the short run, for a faculty, staff, and finances of a university of 1250 to which they had already committed. The first priority had to be men's housing, since the university was already short rooms for 175 men. In fact, architect Payne had already prepared preliminary plans for a men's residence hall to be located on the newly acquired California Packing Company property. A second priority was a residence hall for 75 women, sited near Lausanne and Doney Halls. Unfortunately, the university lacked the funds to cover the estimated $1.1 million for the two dormitories. Additional needs identified by the Development Committee included replacing the outmoded existing gymnasium and the outgrown law school building. Finally, in preparation for future expansion on the southern edge of campus, the board purchased 17 parcels (3.83 acres) of land and had its eye on nine other tracts in the area.[14]

As the board looked at present and future financial and physical needs to accommodate growth, President Smith had a plan for responding to the university's immediate and pressing housing needs. He felt that the university was at a crossroads in how best to meet the university's student housing requirements. Smith told the board in February 1959 that "we are rapidly coming to the place where we need expanded facilities for housing our sorority houses for women as well as additional [men's] dormitory space." He reminded the board that when Baxter Hall was built, he had been neutral on whether or not Willamette should have fraternities and sororities. As he put it, "If at that time, we had decided to eliminate all fraternities and sororities I would have been just as happy as I am under our present situation." After careful consideration, the board had decided that such organizations should be a part of Willamette's housing and social structure and had made fraternities an integral part of the new plan for housing men in Baxter. Smith now averred that fraternal organizations were making a positive contribution to campus life and should continue as a part of the university's overall housing program. In fact, he boasted that "I know of no program where fraternities and sororities are involved which is more constructive than that at Willamette." He also urged that future plans insure that comparable housing be provided for independent students as well.[15]

The question then became how to best carry out the housing program for men and women, both fraternal and independent, given the university's tight finances. Smith estimated that housing for women students would require at least $1.5 million. The issue required immediate resolution because the sororities were rapidly outgrowing their current facilities off campus and new women's dormitory space was needed on campus as well. While Smith did not think that the university could afford to provide housing for women as it had for men, he proposed that the university acquire land next to the southern edge of campus so that sororities could build on university-owned property. As he suggested,

> *by providing an area in which to build we could encourage our women to develop an overall housing program that would be very much more beneficial to the University than to have houses scattered throughout the community. In addition, we would have the women students located in a desirable area, so far as the campus is concerned, and we would also be assisting in the financial problems which go to acquiring a site, as well as building chapter houses. This, it would seem to me is the minimum which the University should attempt as we face the new program of housing construction on the part of the sororities.*[16]

President Smith pointed out to the board that it might be possible for the university, as a result of recent changes in federal housing policy, to take out low interest federal loans to finance both regular dormitories and fraternal facilities if they were university owned and operated. As Smith stated, "It would be possible for Willamette to enter into a program with its sororities to plan housing which could take advantage of the low cost loans available through the Federal Housing program and pass this savings on to the women students of the university who ultimately have to pay the cost of construction of any sorority houses, as long as these are not provided outright by the University." The board ultimately took Smith's advice and used federal loans to build sorority housing on campus as a part of the university housing program.[17]

Before bringing the sororities on campus, Willamette pushed ahead immediately with a plan to provide independent, junior- and senior-class women's housing. By June 1960, Willamette had construction underway on women's housing units for 96 upper-class, independent women. The trustees named these dormitories Lee and York Houses in honor of Jason Lee's only daughter, Anna Lee, and Willamette's first college graduate, Emily York.The two dormitories cost about $506,000 to build, and Smith had great hopes that the new housing complex would improve the university's physical appearance, stating "the erection of this new building in the area just South of the campus is changing the entire aspect of this area adjacent to the campus, which in the past has been so undesirable." Trustee George Atkinson and his wife were the major donors for the Lee and York Houses.[18]

While work proceeded on the new women's dormitory, the board decided to move ahead with construction of a badly needed $1.2 million residence hall for men. After borrowing $950,000 from the Federal Housing and Home Finance Agency, the board set about raising the approximately $300,000 necessary to complete the project. In the search for funds, the board made a special appeal to the Oregon Conference

Above: The front entrance to Emily J. York House, which embodies mid-century residential design.
Below: Residents of York House in their state-of-the-art dorm room for women, circa 1960.

Emily J. York House

In designing the buildings, the university architect James Payne departed from the traditional, institutional dormitory style of housing. To achieve an informal, home-like living atmosphere for the young women, Payne designed the structurally linked (by a common kitchen) one- and two-story buildings to appear as a large, mid-century modern home. The use of low pitched, gable roofs helped to convey the sense of a home-like living space in the dormitories. Each building encompassed about 11,000 square feet of space with separate recreation and dining facilities and had separate entrances on Winter Street. A common courtyard area separated the dining areas of the buildings. Payne clad the dormitories with a brick veneer and stucco surface, once again using the mellow-hued Willamina bricks to tie the exteriors to the other brick buildings constructed on the campus since the late 1930s. Strikingly, the architectural style of the dorms marked Payne's first break from the prevailing stripped or modern Georgian style laid down by Belluschi. Perhaps Payne felt emboldened to introduce the new look because the new structures sat on the recently acquired land at the southern edge of the campus, well away from the existing modern Georgian buildings at the heart of the university layout.

Architect's rendering of the Matthews/Belknap complex showing a perspective difficult to capture with photography.

Matthews-Belknap Hall

Matthews-Belknap Hall sits directly south of Baxter Hall and exhibits the same general shape and materials as its older neighbor—that of an H with the exterior faced in brick. Payne, however, differentiated the stylistic expression of the new dormitory from that of its predecessor, giving it a more explicitly modernist look. He chose to downplay the Georgian features of the older dormitory and, instead, emphasize the more contemporary modern elements of design. Payne broke up the plain horizontal brick surface and bands of windows with exposed flat concrete piers that express the inner structure of the building. A completely flat roof replaced the Georgian hipped roof and cupola found on Belluschi's Baxter Hall. The center section of the reinforced concrete building stands three stories tall, while the two wings on either side are two stories high. The building's east-west axis measures 230 feet and the north-south sections, 206 feet. Payne did specify that Belluschi's favorite Willamina brick again be used on the new dormitory, thus giving both the Baxter and Matthews-Belknap residential complexes the same warm finish.[20]

of the Methodist Church and the Salem business community. One part of the new men's residence hall, named in honor of James T. Matthews—a beloved and much respected, long-time professor—housed freshmen, while another portion set aside for independent upperclassmen was named for Dr. Lewis Franklin Belknap, a prominent Methodist minister and benefactor of Willamette. Altogether, Matthews Hall housed 98 freshmen in the center section of the structure, while the eastern arm of the building held two new fraternity units of 32 men each. Belknap Hall served 78 upperclassmen in the western portion of the structure.[19]

While the ambitious building program during the 1950s positioned the university for a new round of growth, other aspects of Willamette's collegiate life during that decade seemed more traditionally bound. The academic and social affairs of the students during the 1950s continued along well-worn paths. The reaccreditation of the university in 1959—the first reevaluation in over 30 years by the North West Association of Secondary and Higher Education Schools—indicated that Willamette continued to provide a quality education. The effort to maintain educational standards was reflected in the requirement that, starting in 1951, all students seeking admission as freshmen take College Board aptitude tests. In 1957, to enhance the undergraduate offerings for the most academically successful students, the university started an honors program, initially limited to selected juniors and seniors. In his annual report for 1959, President Smith considered the inauguration of the honors program "the most exciting innovation in Willamette's education during the past decade." Another indication that Willamette provided a solid educational foundation could be seen in the fact that the university sent 52 percent of its graduates on to graduate or professional school. Also, Willamette graduates compiled one of the two best records in the Northwest for earning doctoral degrees in the sciences, arts, and humanities. Between 1935 and 1956, Willamette alumni earned a total of 96 doctorates.[21]

Social activities also followed well-worn paths that focused on fraternities and sororities. Freshman Glee, Homecoming, and May Court represented the highlights of student activities. Athletics continued to provide opportunities for males and in the late 1950s Willamette won two consecutive Northwest Conference basketball championships. The president also sought to rejuvenate religious life on the campus. With board approval and a grant from the Atkinson Fund, President Smith appointed a university chaplain in 1957. The chaplain carried a program of student counseling, community outreach, and teaching courses in religion and philosophy in those departments' regular schedules. The establishment of a campus chaplaincy also accomplished one of President Smith's larger goals, which was to bring about a

1962 interior of the public lounge area in the recently completed Matthews Hall. The raw brick and concrete materials left uncovered show a modern aesthetic as well as being a cost-cutting measure.

Aerial photo of the campus circa 1969. The dotted black line indicates the extent of the campus in 1941. The solid line indicates Willamette's portion of the the urban-renewal area.

1 College of Music
2 E. S. Collins (science)
3 Collins addition
4 Waller (chapel, liberal arts)
5 Eaton (liberal arts)
6 Walton (foreign languages)
7 Library
8 Gatke (economics, political science)
9 Baxter (men's residence)
10 Matthews (men's residence)
11 Belknap (upper class men)
12 Gymnasium
13 Bishop Health Center

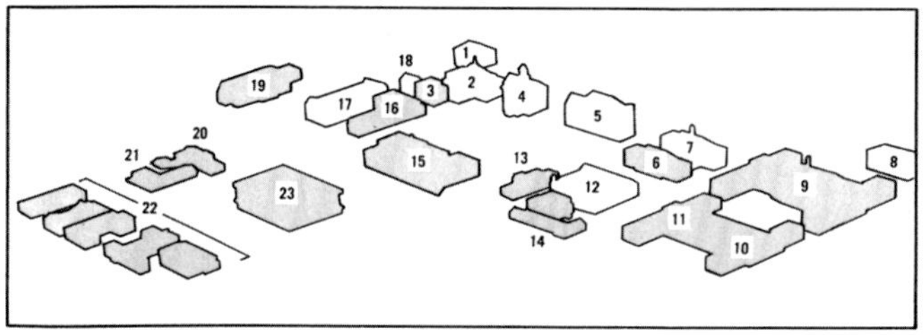

14 Heating and maintenance
15 Auditorium, Fine Arts
16 Doney (women's residence)
17 Lausanne (women's residence)
18 University House
19 Truman W. Collins Legal Center and administrative offices
20 York House (upper class women)
21 Lee House (upper class women)
22 Housing for upper class women
23 George Putnam University Center

McCulloch Stadium was built in 1950 on a ten-acre athletic field four blocks south of the campus.

closer relationship between the Methodist Church and the university. In financial terms, he apparently succeeded in this effort; in 1942, when he arrived at Willamette, the Methodist Church was contributing little or nothing to the university. By 1960, it was giving $25,000 annually.[22]

Once President Smith completed the new men's and women's residence complexes, he immediately initiated the next round of needed building projects. To bolster his new recommendations to the board, he used the accreditation report prepared by the North West Association of Secondary and Higher Schools. In granting Willamette reaccreditation in 1960, the North West Association pointed out university facilities that could stand improvement. The most critical needs included an expansion of Collins Hall to increase space for more laboratories, classrooms, and special projects work; additional stack space for the ever-expanding library collections; and a new college of law building. Smith believed that improved science facilities required the board's immediate attention. He noted in February 1961 that "Collins Hall was erected at a time when our enrollment was about half of the present, and the emphasis on science was far less than at present … . The Board is aware that we now have a completely new concept of the importance of science as compared to 1941. If we are to attract and hold outstanding faculty members in this area, it is going to be necessary for us to provide office-laboratory facilities to encourage research." Smith estimated that Collins Hall initially required an additional 8,000 square feet and twice that much over a ten-year period. He wryly noted that "with present building and construction costs, to add even the minimum of 8,000 square feet would require approximately as much as it did in 1941 to erect Collins Hall."[23]

President Smith and architect Payne proposed to add a new wing on the south side of Collins Hall, changing the footprint of the building from a T to an H shape. Only half of the new three-story wing would be built initially. Smith also announced that Tektronix, a large science technology firm in Portland, offered the university a gift of $36,000—about one-third of the then estimated cost—toward constructing and equipping the addition. After the bids came in, however, the new addition's construction cost alone came to $195,000. When finally completed and furnished, the total cost reached $215,000.

A key part of President Smith's plan to increase the educational plant depended upon the expansion of the campus's acreage. When he came to Willamette the university comprised only 18 acres. Gradually through gifts and purchases, Willamette, by 1961 had grown to 42 acres. Smith wanted the university to include all land from one-half block beyond Winter Street on the west to 12th Street on the east and extending south from State Street to the Shelton Ditch. To complete this plan, Smith urged the board to join with the City of Salem in a federally-subsidized urban renewal project. The urban renewal process would allow the university and city to condemn the blighted land on the south of the campus at fair-market prices, with the federal government paying two-thirds of the total cost. Willamette would assume the city's financial requirements of the remaining one-third of the cost and acquire title to the property after the land was cleared. In addition, Willamette was able to get credit for all of its previous purchases of land within the urban renewal boundaries for the five years prior to the signing of the renewal contract, thus further reducing the cost to Willamette.[24]

An aerial photograph of the southwest corner of campus circa 1970. Notice the double railroad tracks running through the campus, and the parking in front of Putnam University Center where Hudson Bay is now. Sorority row shows in the upper right corner. Note Lee and York; their mid-century design is apparent even from above.

While the urban renewal process—dependent on the formal approval of the city—proceeded slowly, the university began development of the properties it already owned in the renewal area. The administration established tennis courts and an intramural field, named for benefactor and trustee Dr. Frank Brown, on the land between Winter and Capitol Streets. While the Salem City Council voted in late 1961 to make itself the city's urban renewal agency, it did not activate the renewal program until 1965. In the meantime, an impatient university administration moved ahead where it could. In early 1962, it made plans to erect two sorority houses for Pi Beta Phi and Alpha Phi on land within the urban renewal area already owned by the university. These living organizations arranged the necessary financing through the federal housing program, and the university hoped to complete the sorority houses by the fall of 1963. By the time all of the urban renewal acquisitions had been completed, the university had grown by almost 30 acres at a total

The façade of Walton Hall mirrors Belluschi's library building which was connected to Walton by the stack space.

cost of $750,000. Willamette was given credit for the $400,000 it had previously spent on land acquisition in the renewal area, and this money was applied to the city's share of the project's expense.[25]

On the additional urban renewal land, the university built three more sorority houses—Chi Omega, Delta Gamma, and Alpha Chi Omega—financed by federal loans. Designed by James Payne, each house on sorority row had its own unique architectural style, ranging from Colonial Revival for the Delta Gamma house to variations on contemporary suburban split-level styles in the case of the Phi Beta Phi and Alpha Chi Omega houses. Each house served between 40 and 48 women students. The complete ensemble of sorority houses cost approximately $1.1 million, with each sorority contributing $15,000.[26]

Just as the urban renewal effort began in earnest, the board and President Smith launched a new $12.5 million development program. Announced in the spring of 1965, the key components of the program, to be achieved by 1973, included an increase of the undergraduate student body from 1250 to 1500, an expansion of the law school from 180 to 300 students, a commitment to raise the funds for a graduate program in public and business administration, an additional 22 new faculty members in the colleges of liberal arts and music, and continued improvement of faculty salaries. President Smith labeled this grand development campaign the Fund for Educational Excellence. His new push for further growth was grounded on the previous 20 years of steadily strengthening all aspects of the university. As President Smith reminded the board in June 1964,

> *it should be recognized that Willamette has been in a continuous development program since the start of our work to secure funds for the erection of Baxter Hall in 1945. We have seen the tempo increased in the challenge fund drive and we have been anticipating another emphasis to meet our current needs. This should be not simply an intensive drive but rather a general improvement of methods, staff and ability to attract continuing support for the University.*

He felt sure that the new plan for development would "influence the history of the University for the next quarter of a century" and, coupled with the adoption of the 4-2 academic plan (discussed below), "will set the pattern for the educational program of Willamette for the immediate future."[27]

To address the badly needed expansion of the university library, President Smith—working with the building committee of the board and architect James Payne—devised a plan to triple the stack space and connect it to a new addition south of the existing library that would house modern language laboratories, classrooms, and faculty offices. The addition—named in honor of Salem philanthropist William Walton, whose estate gave nearly $145,000 toward the cost of the building—closely duplicated Belluschi's stripped Georgian design for the library to which it was connected by the new section holding the increased stack space. The two-story addition's dimensions, brick color, and finish details all sympathetically related to the existing library building. The university sought and received a loan and grant under a new program of federal aid for academic facilities to help pay for the library-language building expansion. At the same time that the university added to its academic facilities, it also increased student living space. In the fall of 1966, an addition to Doney Hall connected that dormitory to Lausanne Hall at a cost of $450,000. The two-story connecting section provided new kitchen and dining facilities and housing for 40 women students.[28]

Along with the new buildings and physical expansion of the campus to accommodate growth and renewed emphasis on undergraduate academic advancement, Willamette also responded to pressing needs of its law school. By the early 1960s, the law school had outgrown its existing home in what had been Salem's old post office. Moved to the campus in 1937 and renovated into classrooms and a law library, the old law school building (now called Gatke Hall) could no longer meet the requirements of a modern law school. In addition to having no mock courtrooms, the old building had insufficient space for the law library, classrooms, and offices as well. Smith also pointed out that other law schools in the West had

Thetford Lodge

In 1963, the university received another notable addition to its facilities. Trustee and former Oregon Governor Charles Sprague gave his summer home on the Little North Fork of the Santiam River, called Thetford Lodge, to Willamette. Designed by Pietro Belluschi during 1944-46 and built in 1947-48, this quintessential Northwest Regional style summer home became a retreat for student and faculty groups. Beautifully sited so as to overlook the forest, stream, and a sheer rock cliff, the 30- by 38-foot split-level floor plan contains a living room, dining room, and kitchen placed around a great raised, brick fireplace. The downstairs also has two bedrooms, while the loft holds other sleeping quarters. A large deck fronts the board and batten wood and expansive glass exterior. The home rests on concrete piers setting on bedrock. To better accommodate student and faculty groups, the university installed a second bathroom and updated the kitchen but otherwise maintains the home as Belluschi designed it.[29]

recently completed new college law buildings, placing Willamette "in an unfavorable position competitively." He told the board that it was his "hope and plan that Willamette may be able to secure the resources necessary to develop a great legal center for the Pacific North West."[30] A new law school thus received priority in the university development program undertaken in 1965. Financed chiefly by a large private gift from the Collins family to honor Truman Collins, long-time trustee and board president, Willamette was able to erect a new building for its law school in 1967. The new law center allowed the school to expand from 180 to 300 students. In preparation for designing the new law school, Payne undertook extensive research of law schools around the country, personally visiting a number of them.[31]

Designed in a more traditional Georgian Revival style by university architect Payne, the handsome building was located on the newly acquired urban renewal land along Winter Street across from Lausanne Hall. President Smith took great interest in the design of the interior and gave Payne detailed suggestions to consider in arriving at the best use of space for classrooms, the library, and student facilities. Smith told Payne, "I hope I shall not appear unreasonable in my requests on this building but I am eager that this be the finest building we have ever built and the one most suited for the needs." The interior is highlighted by fine

Truman Wesley Collins Legal Center

The traditional Georgian Revival style chosen for the law structure represented an interesting contrast with the stripped or modern Georgian style that Belluschi and Payne had employed for the buildings in the core of the campus. The three-story brick building's symmetrical facade has evenly spaced, double-hung, six-over-six-paned windows on the first and third floors and nine-over-nine-paned windows on the second floor, all of which dominate the front exterior. The center point of the front is a dramatic entry under a projecting, pedimented portico supported by four, full-height Doric columns. The three entryway doors and their surrounding side lights sit under two-story round arched portals and are separated by plain brick pilasters. The low-pitched pediment atop the portico has a lunette, or multi-paned semi-circular window, within it. Other typical classical elements found on the building include a cornice with dental course and full balustrade along the hipped roof.

The Truman Wesley Collins Legal Center.

Putnam University Center from the Mill Street side soon after completion. Notice the circular drive and the staircase leading to the main entrance on the second floor.

Putnum University Center

The architectural style of the Payne and Settecase design can be characterized as expressionist modernism or brutalism, emphasized through the use of exposed concrete framing and prominent, poured-in-place concrete columns that support both a flat roof and concrete porch, which wraps entirely around the building at the first floor above the ground level. Both the main volume and wrap-around porch are recessed under a roof marked by a bold, plain concrete cornice. In a nod to Willamette's past use of brick as its chief building material, the architects designed three, widely spaced red brick panels to rise the full height of the building and break up the surface of large sheet-glass windows filling each floor. The brick served to soften and warm an appearance otherwise dominated by the exposed cold, hard concrete and extensive glass on the structure's exterior.

woodwork throughout, with the entry space especially notable for walls of dark walnut. The south half of the first floor has an elevated auditorium that seats up to 300. Sliding panels allow dividing the auditorium into two classrooms. The north half of the building houses a three-floor library, capable of holding 100,000 volumes. The remainder of the second and third floors is taken up with study rooms, lounge area, and faculty and administrative offices. A focal point of the ground floor is a practice court. Student organizational offices, lockers, and another lounge are also located on the ground floor. The building cost about $1.1 million, and its completion marked the 100th anniversary of the Willamette Law School.[32]

The construction of the long-sought student center in the late 1960s marked the last major addition to campus facilities undertaken in the Smith years. Named for Salem newspaper publisher and editor, George Putnam, whose estate gave Willamette $380,000 toward financing the project, the $1.4 million center was sited across the Mill Stream behind the Fine Arts Auditorium on land acquired through the urban renewal process. Architect James Payne and his new partner, Phillip Settecase, planned the 48,300 square-foot building to house a student lounge; recreation area; coffee shop; bookstore; music listening area; conference and meeting rooms; offices for various deans, chaplain, and financial aid director; and student

Regional Growth at Private Institutions 1945-1970

Willamette University's growth between 1945 and 1970 was typical of other small liberal arts colleges and universities in Oregon and Washington. As the following tables indicate, Willamette, Pacific, Linfield, Lewis and Clark, and Whitman all increased their faculties, expanded their physical plants, and grew their endowments and enrollments. In addition, as historian James Hitchman found, all modernized their curriculums, adopted tenure and promotion policies, and reaffirmed their commitment to the liberal arts tradition. At each institution, moreover, while church ties loosened, they continued to seek church financial support. Like Willamette, all the schools had strong presidents who served lengthy terms and left solid legacies on which their successors could build. Finally, all of these colleges and universities were relatively unscathed by strident student protest or dramatic upheaval during the 1960s, reflecting the general homogeneity of the class, race, values, and geographic origins of their respective student bodies. As historian G. Thomas Edwards of Whitman College noted, students at Willamette and Whitman "were more likely to be protesting policies such as *in loco parentis* and dormitory curfews instead of protesting the Vietnam War."[43] The solid growth and development of Willamette and her sister institutions of higher education in the Pacific Northwest during the 1950s and 1960s positioned them to survive the challenging times ahead for small colleges and universities dedicated to the values of the liberal arts education.

1939	Institution	Enrollment	Faculty	Endowment	Physical Plant
	Willamette	883	56	$1.7M	$770K
	Linfield	592	37	$927K	$678K
	Pacific	348	24	$288K	$420K
	Lewis and Clark	*	*	*	*
	Whitman	601	43	$1.1M	$400K

Source: Hitchman, *Liberal Arts Colleges*, 246-48. *No data

1971	Institution	Enrollment	Faculty	Endowment	Physical Plant
	Willamette	1,714	129	$10.3M	$10.1M
	Linfield	1,058	89	$2.5M	$10.M
	Pacific	1,249	127	$650K	$10.4M
	Lewis and Clark	2,188	179	$2.9M	$17.4M
	Whitman	1,105	86	$18.4M	$12.9M

Source: Hitchman, *Liberal Arts Colleges*, 255-56.

body chambers and student publications offices. The student center would bring together under one roof facilities then scattered about the campus and would be the center for nearly all non-academic campus-related student activities.[33]

Clearly, starting in the 1960s, Payne was taking the architecture of Willamette University's new buildings ever further in the direction of then-current contemporary modernism. Even so, as Settecase later argued, the move away from "the established 'Georgian Style' on campus ... [was accomplished] with sensitive conservatism." He and Payne took a novel approach to arriving at the design for Putnam Center: "A design competition was held within our office, three totally different solutions were brought to a campus presentation, and the building now in place was selected by unanimous Board action."[34]

While President Smith pursued his development plans, the faculty took the initiative to revise the curriculum in the mid-1960s. With support from the administration and after much study and discussion, the faculty proposed that the university adopt a 4-2 plan. This plan required that students take four courses each semester during the academic year. To make this adjustment practical, the faculty revised and reduced the number of courses offered. The plan established majors in six concentration areas and limited each faculty member to six courses. The focus on concentration areas did tend to diminish the importance of traditional academic departments. The concept sought to provide a more focused and concentrated plan of study toward graduation, while giving the faculty flexibility to continuously review and evolve their course offerings. As Dean Robert Gregg put it, the hope among the faculty was to produce a "spirit of experimentation and new vigor" in the undergraduate liberal arts program.[35]

While buying land for campus expansion, planning new buildings to carry out Willamette's educational mission, and raising money to finance his growth initiatives, President Smith also had to deal with the stirrings of the students and a number of assertions of the faculty during the 1960s. Motivated by the social and political ferment sweeping the United States, the Willamette students left behind the insular, apathetic outlook of the previous decade. As Smith observed to the board in October 1968,

> *In keeping with the tenor of the times, the present generation of students are impatient, properly or improperly as the case may be, with the universities and colleges as they find them, and they are demanding immediate solutions to the problems as they see them. The ability of a college or university to continue to carry out its educational function in the face of mounting dissatisfactions has depended upon the degree of responsibility with which the students and faculty have acted in advocating and effecting change on campus.*

While the level of unrest at Willamette never reached that experienced at larger, more diverse institutions of higher education, such as the University of California at Berkeley, Kent State, Columbia University, or the University of Oregon, students did recognize and discuss issues surrounding racial equality, free speech, and the Vietnam War. President Smith acknowledged that "there is no doubt that Willamette students, in keeping with their peers all over the country, have sought a stronger voice in forming their educational and social environment. Opportunity has been given for expression of these thoughts as long as this expression has been responsible and has been channeled through legitimate channels of student government."[36]

The relatively homogeneous nature of the Willamette student body probably accounted for the muted response to the political and social ferment of the times. Willamette's students, after all, were overwhelmingly white, middle class, and chiefly from the Pacific Northwest and California. What the students wanted, as President Smith noted, was a greater say in their own educational experience at Willamette—both academic and social. They, for example, took a keen interest in the implementation of the 4-2 program and sought a liberalization of the convocation requirement. They also challenged the prevailing structure of rules and regulations governing drinking alcohol and closing hours for women's living organizations. The Greek fraternity and sorority system came in for its share of criticism, as well. Some felt that fraternities and sororities lacked relevance to modern life and that they had too great a dominance over the campus social life, given their declining proportion of the student body.[37]

While Willamette students of the 1960s increasingly challenged the paternalistic notions embodied in the century-old concept of "the Willamette Family," they found the administration and board open to reasoned arguments for change. Again, as President Smith observed, the board had shown a willingness to take the students' concerns seriously:

> *In years gone by most college boards of trustees have depended upon reports of the faculty and president to keep them abreast of the problems of the campus. Under today's conditions, this is not sufficient. Students are demanding direct opportunities to know the members of the Board of Trustees and to be able to express some of their opinions to the Board. Fortunately, our Board of Trustees has responded by having held certain joint meetings of Board committees with students and during the last year, Board members have accepted invitations of students to visit the campus and become personally*

An anti-war demonstration in 1969 that began on the capitol grounds and proceeded to the Willamette campus.

acquainted. The reaction of the Board last spring to join in a conference to be participated in by students, faculty, and Board members was a further step in this direction.

By the end of the 1960s, students had made considerable progress in modernizing the rules governing campus life. The administration and Board of Trustees gave way to reasonable student demands on eliminating compulsory convocation attendance and liberalizing university policy regarding closing hours for women and coeducational visiting hours in dormitories under certain conditions. A student government committee also gained participation in faculty meetings when student matters were under discussion.[38]

Just as the students asserted themselves, so did the faculty. In addition to the usual push for salary increases, the professors wanted a program of regular sabbatical leaves and a tenure policy. By the mid-1960s, a sympathetic President Smith convinced the board to establish the former and by 1970, the latter. Over the course of his time at Willamette, Smith had made it a personal crusade to boost faculty salaries in a frustrating attempt to keep up with inflation and competition from other higher educational institutions, business, and government. Between 1960 and 1968, for example, Willamette doubled its salaries for all ranks. But this upgrading, as Smith lamented, meant that "we have been able to do no more than try to keep within range of the general increase in salaries."[39]

Properly maintaining the campus grounds and buildings grew ever more costly as the university expanded in size and number of facilities. Dormitories needed regular repairs or renovations, while utilities and the heating plant required periodic upgrading. Lawns and plantings had to be groomed and renewed. Roofs needed to be replaced and building trim, classrooms, and offices had to have fresh coats of paint. Unanticipated weather events could add to the maintenance burden. In October 1962, a powerful windstorm swept through the Willamette Valley, causing almost $17,000 in damage to university buildings and landscape. Unfortunately, because of burdensome maintenance costs, the administration removed the cupola and corner tower caps on Eaton Hall in 1967. This considerably diminished the significant character-defining features of the historic structure. At the same time that Eaton Hall lost its cupola, the administration wisely decided to rebuild the cupola on Waller Hall, realizing that this was an essential architectural feature of the historic building. Campus buildings also continued to undergo changes in use over time. When, for example, the college of law moved to its new building across campus, the administration turned its old quarters into a home for the departments of economics and political science. Ultimately, the repurposed building became Gatke Hall in honor of the long-serving professor and author of the history of the university's first one hundred years.[40]

President Smith's retirement in 1969 marked the closing of a remarkable period of growth at Willamette University. Smith began his presidency in the university's centennial year, 1942. After serving 25 years, he took stock of his accomplishments on the eve of Willamette's 125th year. He told the university trustees in January 1967 that he saw his term as president as a "Period of Enlightenment" after the previous eras he labeled as "Founding," "Struggle to Survive," and "Fulfillment" made possible "by the loyalty, devotion, and leadership of a dedicated group of trustees, able faculty, and a growing constituency interested in the welfare of Willamette." With not a little pride in his stewardship, Smith noted in his final report in 1969 that he had increased the endowment

Above: An example of the damage done by the Columbus Day Storm in October of 1962. Taken from about where the bridge between the present-day Hatfield Library and Mary Stuart Rogers Music Center now stands, the photograph shows the end of the original Bishop Health Center building in the background.
Below: Eaton Hall missing the caps on the towers and the cupola. (Compare with view of the original elements shown in Chapter 3.)

from just under $2 million to over $9 million (book value) and expanded the campus from 18 to almost 60 acres. The value of the university's physical plant had increased from $1 million to over $9 million and the annual budget had risen from $179,000 to almost $4 million. Enrollment had doubled and full-time faculty and staff had increased from 38 to 117. The curriculum had been revised and strengthened and the Board of Trustees reorganized. Much of the physical growth, moreover, had been achieved without the university incurring heavy, long-term debt. Except for $1.5 million in self-liquidating federal government loans taken out to build or add on to dormitories, Willamette had paid for its ambitious expansion program through gifts.[41]

But as President Smith was quick to note, Willamette's past success as a small liberal arts university was no guarantee of its future survival. Some educational leaders at the time doubted that small liberal arts colleges would be able to—as Smith paraphrased the argument—"command the resources to meet the rising cost and thus keep pace with the quality which higher education must have in America today." Smith, on the other hand, remained "convinced that there is, and will continue to be a place for the well-equipped and well-staffed institutions designed primarily as a teaching institution on the undergraduate level." Smith was certain that Willamette would have an even greater future if it continued to focus on: increasing its financial support; emphasizing good teaching; continuously supporting faculty improvement; setting clear educational objectives and plans to achieve them; maintaining an academically selective student body; and providing an adequate library, laboratories, and other modern educational equipment. Smith declared that if Willamette accomplished those tasks, "there is no doubt in my mind that Willamette's future will far exceed the past."[42]

When President Smith arrived in 1942, the Willamette campus contained eight permanent buildings; by his retirement in 1969, it had grown to an ensemble of 25 well-built and attractive structures, as well as an athletic stadium south of the main campus. The value of this physical plant had grown from $965,000 to approximately $12 million over the same time period. The architectural style of the buildings constructed in the core of the campus exhibited a remarkable consistency. Pietro Belluschi's three buildings established a modern or stripped Georgian style, while James Payne's four buildings surrounding the quad and in close proximity to Belluschi's retained that architectural idiom. However, Payne's buildings on the southern perimeter of the campus expressed a more pronounced modern, non-historical sensibility, by emphasizing the structural elements of the buildings or, in the case of the women's residential facilities, a mid-century modern or suburban housing aesthetic. The one exception to the variations on modernism was Payne's law school building, designed in the traditional Georgian Revival style. Regardless of style, the use of brick as the main surface treatment served as a unifying feature of all the buildings put up during the 27 years of Smith's tenure. As one alum remarked in 1965, "The half-dozen buildings of a half century ago have tripled in number. Brick is still the favorite building material and there is no 'far out' architecture." In the next decade, however, Payne would go on to design two more large buildings for the university that moved in the direction of ever-more modern architectural style.[44]

Endnotes

1 Mid-term Report of the President, Feb. 1949, Smith Papers, Box 76A, Willamette University Archives.

2 Ibid.; Gregg, *Chronicles, II*, 62-65.

3 Gregg, *Chronicles, II*, 70; Mid-term Annual Report of the President, Feb. 1953, Smith Papers, Box 76A, Willamette University Archives.

4 Willamette University, The Challenge Fund, No. 1 (May 1953); ibid, No. 2 (Aug. 1953). The campaign sought to raise 20 percent of the entire fund ($200,000) from the Salem community. President Smith reminded the Salem Chamber of Commerce that university operations and student expenditures annually added $1.375 million to the local economy.

5 G. Herbert Smith to Al Loucks, March 19, 1957, Smith Papers, Box 15B, Willamette University Archives; Ritz, *Architects of Oregon*, 311-13.

6 G. Herbert Smith to James Payne, Sep. 26, 1952, Smith Papers, Box 15B, Willamette University Archives.

7 Willamette University, The Challenge Fund, No. 1 (May 1953); G. Herbert Smith to Robert Bishop, May 17, 1956, Smith Papers, Box 4A, Willamette University Archives.

8 Willamette University, The Challenge Fund, No. 5 (Sep. 1955); Dedication Brochure for Bishop Memorial Health Center, Doney Residence Hall, and Auditorium/Fine arts Building, Oct. 1, 1955, Willamette University Archives.

9 This building was removed in the late 1990s for Rogers Hall. Willamette University, The Challenge Fund, No. 3 (Jan. 1954); Mid-term Annual Report of the President, Feb. 1954, Smith Papers, Box 76A, Willamette University Archives; Willamette University, The Challenge Fund, No. 4 (Jun. 1954).

10 Willamette University, The Challenge Fund, No.2 (Aug. 1953); ibid, No. 4 (Jun. 1954).

11 Annual Report of the President, June 1956, Smith Papers, Box 76A, Willamette University Archives.

12 Mid-term Annual Report of the President, Feb. 1953, Smith Papers, Box 76A Willamette University Archives; Annual Report of the President, Jun 1957, ibid. Faculty salaries also benefitted from a gift of $216,600 from the Ford Foundation. This sum was earmarked for the endowment fund with interest to be used to increase faculty salaries; G. Herbert Smith, "President's Message," *Willamette Alumnus* (Winter, 155-56), 2.

13 Report of the Willamette Trustee Development Committee, Jun. 7, 1958, Smith Papers, Box 29A, Willamette University Archives; see also G. Herbert Smith, "High Tide in Admissions Ahead," *Willamette Alumnus* (Spring, 1957), 4-5.

14 Report of the Willamette Trustee Development Committee, Jun 7, 1958, Smith Papers, Box 29A, Willamette University Archives; Mid-term Annual Report of the President, Feb. 1958, Smith Papers, Box 76A, ibid.; Annual Report of the President, Jun. 1958, Smith Papers, Box 8, ibid. By June 1959, President Smith could report additional land purchases, bringing a total of 5.42 acres south of the main campus available for future development; Annual Report of the President, Jun. 6, 1959, Smith papers, Box 8, Willamette University Archives.

15 Mid-term Annual Report of the President, Feb. 1959, Smith Papers, Box 76A, Willamette University Archives.

16 Ibid.

17 Ibid.

18 *Collegian*, Oct. 23, 1959; Annual Report of the President, June 1960, Smith Papers, Box 76A, Willamette University Archives; Summary of Construction Costs, Lee-York House, Willamette University Records, Box 4, ibid.

19 Annual Report of the President, June 1960, Smith Papers, Box 76A Willamette University Archives; Summary of Construction Costs, Matthews-Belknap Hall, Willamette University Records, Box 4, ibid.; *Collegian*, Sep. 22, 1961.

20 *Collegian*, Feb. 19, Mar. 4, 1960.

21 Mid-term Report of the President, Feb. 1959, Smith Papers, Box 76A, Willamette University Archives.

22 Annual Report of the President, June 1956 and 1957, Smith Papers, Box 76A, Willamette University Archives.

23 Mid-term Report of the President, Feb. 1961, Smith Papers, Box 76A, Willamette University Archives.

24 Ibid.; Annual Report of the President, June 1961, Smith Papers, Box 76A, Willamette University Archives; *Collegian*, Sep. 22, 1961; Lawrence E. Davies, "Willamette Now," *Willamette Alumnus* (reprint, 1965), 16.

25 Annual Report of the President, June 1962, June 1963, June 1965, June 1967, Smith Papers, Box 76A, Willamette University Archives; *Collegian*, Sep. 29, 1961, May 11, 1962, May 10, 1963, Dec. 4, 11, 17, 1964, Oct. 22, 1965, Dec. 4, 1966.

26 Annual Report of the President, June 1967, Smith Papers, Box 76A, Willamette University Archives; *Collegian*, Sep. 24, 1965, Sep. 8, 1967; Petrie to Pres. Smith, Jan. 26, 1962, Smith Papers, Box 16B, Willamette University Archives.

27 As early as 1961, President Smith outlined for the board this next phase of expansion for the university; Development Committee Minutes, Nov. 27, 1961, Smith Papers, Box 29A, Willamette University Archives. Annual Report of the President, June 1964 and 1965, Smith Papers, Box 76A, Willamette University Archives.; see also Annual Report of the President, June 1962, ibid; *Collegian*, Feb. 26, 1965, Sep. 9, 1966; Davies, "Willamette Now," 18-19; Willamette Development Program and Willamette Enrichment and Development Plans, n. d., Smith Papers, Box 29A, Willamette University Archives.

28 Walton Hall ultimately cost $575,000. Annual Report of the President, June 1964 and Jan. 1967, Smith Papers, Box 76A, Willamette University Archives; *Collegian*, May 25, Sep. 17, Oct. 8, Dec. 22, 1965, Feb. 4, 18, Apr. 1, 1966, Dec. 16, 1966; Annual Report of the Business Office, Smith Papers, Box 35A, Willamette University Archives; G. Herbert Smith to Glenn Lathrop, Mar. 10, 1966, Facilities Records, Willamette University.

29 Annual Report of the President, June 1964, Smith Papers, Box 76A, Willamette University Archives; Pietro Belluschi to Charles Sprague, Sep. 1, Oct. 13, 1944, Feb. 7, Mar. 2, Jun. 3, 5, 14, 27, Nov. 13, 1945, Mar. 13, 1946, Aug. 14, 28, Oct. 10, Nov. 4, 20, 1947, Belluschi Papers, Box 147, Job 859, Syracuse University Library; *Collegian*, Feb. 24, 1967.

30 Ibid.

31 *Collegian*, Oct. 16, 1964, Feb. 5, 19, 1965, Apr. 1, 1966; Davies, "Willamette Now," 12-13; Seward Reese, to James Payne, Apr. 18, 1963, Smith Papers, Box, 16B, Willamette University Archives; James Payne to G. Herbert Smith, Sep. 4, 1963, Smith Papers, Box16B, Ibid.

32 *The Willamette Lawyer*, vol. 4, no.1 (Sep. 1967); G. Herbert Smith to James Payne, Mar. 14, 1963, Smith Papers, Box 16B, Willamette University Archives; quote in President Smith to James Payne, Feb. 1, 1965, ibid.

33 Annual Report of the President, Mar. 1969, Smith Papers, Box 76A, Willamette University Archives; *Collegian*, Mar. 10, Sep. 15, 1967, Mar. 29, Nov. 8, 1968, Sep. 19, Nov. 14, 21, 1969.

34 Phillip Settecase to Brian Hardin, Jun. 14, 1990, Goudy Box, Facilities Records, Willamette University.

35 The concentration areas were American Studies, Fine Arts, Humanities, Letters, Natural Science-Mathematics, and Social Science. Communication Arts and Religion made up the two special areas, while Teacher Preparation and Physical Education and Aerospace Studies comprised the professional areas. Course offerings dropped from 610 under the old system to 120 under the new; quote in Gregg, *Chronicles, II*, 183. *Collegian*, Apr. 8, 1966; Davies, "Willamette Now," 8-10.

36 Quotes in Annual Report of the President, Oct. 1968, Smith Papers, Box 76A, Willamette University Archives; see also, *Collegian*, Oct. 15, 17, 1969.

37 The discussion of student attitudes and conduct is based on a close reading of the *Collegian* during the 1960s; Davies, "Willamette Now," 5-6.

38 Quote in Annual Report of the President, Oct. 1968, Smith Papers, Box 76A, Willamette University Archives. The struggle over student control of their living circumstances can be followed in the *Collegian*; see, for example, Oct. 11, 18, 25, 1968, Feb. 6, 20, 1970; "Willamette University New Ideas Stirring The West's Oldest University," *Northwest Magazine* (Feb. 16, 1969), 8-15.

39 Quote in Annual Report of the President, Mar. 1969, Smith papers, Box 76A, Willamette University Archives; Davies, "Willamette Now," 18.

40 Annual Report of the President, Jun. 1963, Oct. 1967, Smith Papers, Box 76A, Willamette University Archives; *Collegian*, Oct. 19, 1962, Oct. 6, 1967.

41 Annual Report of the President, Jan. 1967, Smith Papers, Box 76A, Willamette University Archives; G. Herbert Smith, "Another Hundred Years ... the first twenty-seven" (Willamette University, 1969), ibid.

42 Annual Report of the President, Jan. 1967, Smith Papers, Box 76A Willamette University Archives.

43 Hitchman, *Liberal Arts Colleges*, 211-36; G. Thomas Edwards, "Student Activism at Whitman College and Willamette University, 1965-1971," *Pacific Northwest Quarterly* (Fall, 2008), 173-80.

44 Davies, "Willamette Now," 4.

7

Storm and Transition

Between 1970 and 2010, a number of developing trends affected how colleges and universities operated in the United States. Many of them had their start in the late 60s and early 70s, but have become ever-increasing factors in the structures of higher education. Chief among the long-term changes was the steady bifurcation of the work of large public and private research universities and their big-time athletic programs from that of small, traditional liberal arts colleges and universities focused on providing accessible and affordable undergraduate education. Other long-term developments that affected all institutions regardless of their size or mission stemmed from diversity, gender, and equity concerns. Other common matters causing anxiety included availability of federal grants and loans for student financial aid, effective curriculum, financial solvency, competition from for-profit schools, and, more recently, long distance learning via the internet.[1]

Of more immediate focus, after a quarter of a century of growth following World War II, were concerns about student unrest over campus governance issues, demographic projections that questioned future enrollment growth, and inflation that drove up costs while income was flat or declining. The proliferation of problems caused one commentator to refer to higher education as a "Troubled Giant."[2]

The common denominator for nearly all of these challenges was finances. The question of money was acute, especially for those large public and private universities seeking to achieve or maintain their status as high-powered research institutions. Competition for federal research grants, especially in the sciences and medicine, was fierce and costly. Such externally-

Facing page: Interior of Seeley G. Mudd building

funded research programs had high overhead costs, which resulted from having to recruit and maintain star researchers, their support staffs, and necessary facilities and equipment. Changing priorities of federal granting agencies added to the cost and insecurity inherent in pursuing "soft money" research, which might disappear at any time in the future.

Often these same institutions had the added financial burden of supporting expensive, big-time intercollegiate athletic programs. Winning sports programs required high-priced coaches, support staffs, and elaborate facilities. Added financial pressure for public universities arose from steadily declining state support beginning in the 1990s and continuing into the first decade of the twenty-first century. For their part, both large and small private colleges and universities fretted over endowments that suffered from periodic declines in the value of stocks and annual budgets that had to account for ever-increasing costs and demands for greater student financial aid.

In addition to these more predictable financial stresses, all institutions of higher education had to respond to a new student profile and expectations. More women and minorities entered colleges and universities, with women accounting for 40 percent or more of the undergraduates. Student unrest of the early 1970s waned in time, but a lasting legacy of collective action was a student realization of their rights as part of the campus community. Their role became institutionalized through representation on governing boards and faculty and administration committees. A brief enrollment decline in the mid-1970s forced administrators throughout the nation to pay closer attention to students and their parents in the provision of services and academic course offerings. Competition for students required better campus living and learning conditions through improved dormitories and food options, state-of-the-art health and fitness centers, up-to-date media facilities, overseas study programs, and the option for coeducational living arrangements.

The change in student profile and interests also affected the curriculum. The increased interest in so-called vocational subjects such as business and computer science led to new majors. Within traditional fields, new perspectives and multidisciplinary approaches came to the fore. Ideological debates within the liberal arts led to questioning existing definitions of a field. What constituted the canon for study in the field of literature or the relevance of multiculturalism in history became hot topics for faculty and student debate. Amidst all of the changes buffeting colleges and universities in the late twentieth century and beyond, all of them—large or small—had to maintain a clarity of educational mission and remain financially solvent. They had to attract and retain students, while adjusting to changing government regulation and student needs. Willamette University would not be immune to these demands.

Campus design in the late twentieth century was directly affected by all of these diverse, often conflicting forces. Accommodating new growth while holding down costs and making the best use of existing facilities challenged academic administrators, architects, and planners and caused them to question some of the modernist concepts of campus form adopted immediately following World War II. The campus plans and buildings that had rejected traditional styles and embraced the contrast and hyper-individuality of eclectic expression found in various forms of modernism or contemporary style began to fall out of fashion by the late 1960s.

A constantly growing interest in energy conservation, sustainability, and historic preservation offered new possibilities for the design of college buildings and campus layouts, whether traditional or modern in sentiment and style. The diversity of academic fields and emphasis on student-faculty research in the sciences often required special facilities. Conflicts in land-use patterns and commuter-pedestrian traffic circulation also had to be addressed. These and other matters greatly complicated campus planning. Flexibility and a willingness to experiment became necessary in shaping the built and landscape environments of colleges and universities after 1970.

In particular, as ambitious and often freewheeling expansions of higher education in the 1950s and 1960s gave way to levelling enrollment and financial stringency, campus planners demonstrated a new attitude toward their role. They sought to identify and preserve the spatial and formal character of the historical campus setting for which they would be designing new additions. Wherever possible, architects and planners sought to remodel or repurpose existing or underutilized buildings, especially if they held historical significance to the institution. Additions were usually modest and compatible with existing architecture and placed within the existing campus layout. Despite growth and change, one factor generally remained constant at most campuses and that was the desire to remain open and outward-looking toward the surrounding community, with buildings set in a landscape rather than clustered around inward-turning quadrangles.[3]

At Willamette, the decade of the 1970s served as a time of transition and adjustment as the university passed through two presidents in the immediate aftermath of the 27-year presidency of G. Herbert Smith. This unsettled period in Willamette's history occurred against a national backdrop of financial and social disruption. Energy shortages, surging economic inflation, and a declining student population as the wave of "baby boomers" passed through created challenging times for Willamette. In addition, unrest among faculty over pay and institutional governance, issues surrounding affirmative action and minority rights, and questions about the adequacy of the college's curriculum also buffeted the university—as such matters did at other colleges across the nation. In the early part of the decade, students continued to press concerns related to rules governing social conduct and dormitory living arrangements. Remarkably, through all of the tumult of the 1970s, the trustees, administrators, and faculty continued to plan, finance, and construct new buildings for the university's athletic and academic programs, while beginning the renovation of older structures to extend their useful lives.

The initial time of transition after the long tenure of a strong leader is often a period of uncertainty and instability, as the constituent parts of an organization test the new institutional boundaries and jockey for power. Willamette was no exception to this truism. The trustees, unfortunately, made the transition even more fraught in their choice of a successor to President Smith. The board selected as the new president Roger Fritz, a corporate executive with a background in management development and educational administration. He promised to bring the efficiencies and decision-making processes of the business world to an academic setting that prized its long-standing traditions and decisions reached through collaboration and consensus.[4]

Making administrative reorganization his first order of business, Fritz unfortunately pushed his reforms in a high-handed and preemptory manner. Over time, his blunt approach and forceful directives applying the principles of business operations to running the university ignored long-standing governance practices and called into question the abilities of respected administrators and faculty members. During his first year as president, Fritz seemed to get off to a promising start, appointing student and faculty committees to lay the foundation for his program of academic change and a widened the role for students role in determining their governance and living arrangements. In his second year, however, Fritz—apparently impatient with the speed of change—unilaterally began to implement his view of what should constitute the new administrative structures, academic programs, and student governance.

As a student leader later astutely observed:

> *Fritz named numerous committees—both student and faculty—to help work on problems and shape goals. But he viewed these committees as strictly advisory. He figured his role was to either accept or reject the advice. But the people on these committees felt they were working and submitting recommendations which would, in large part, be implemented by the president. The committee members viewed themselves as policymakers. The president, whether he was aware of it or not, viewed them as advisory and not a policy voice.*

A respected faculty member succinctly stated the situation by noting that "the necessary trust, cooperation and mutual confidence never developed" between President Fritz and the Willamette community.[5]

In the spring of 1972, matters came to a head when both students and faculty felt that President Fritz had unfairly forced the resignations of Jerry Whipple, the popular Vice President for Student Affairs, and Chaplin Phil Harder. The student senate condemned Fritz's actions and the faculty decisively voted 79 to 2 for Fritz's resignation. The faculty informed the Board of Trustees that the main issue was a lack of confidence in the administration and leadership of the president and urged them "to restore the health of the institution" by replacing Fritz. After careful deliberation, the board bowed to this campus-wide expression of a loss of confidence in Fritz's leadership and called for his resignation in April 1972.[6]

In spite of the campus turmoil caused by Fritz's methods, much of his program continued. Improvements in academic offerings and faculty salaries, coupled with board-approved policies recognizing academic freedom and tenure provisions, moved forward. In addition, the final buildings in the expansion program launched by President Smith in the mid-1960s were pushed along by Fritz and then carried on by his successors. The groundwork for a badly-needed, modern physical education and recreation facility and an innovative graduate school of administration was well under way when President Fritz took office, but he and his team started the process of raising funds for the projects.

At the time, Willamette's physical education facilities were the least adequate among competing Northwest Conference institutions of higher education. The existing gymnasium had been built in 1923 for a student body of 500. At the time of its construction it was considered to be the finest gymnasium of its type in Oregon. By 1970, however, the facility's shortcomings had become evident. Willamette now enrolled over 1,200 undergraduates, and the gym could serve only 50 percent of the university's physical education classes; others had to be held at the local YMCA and YWCA. At the same time, the administration saw an opportunity for outreach to the Salem community by designing a physical education and recreation facility that could offer public access during weekend and summer months when student use likely would be less. With these requirements in mind, architect James Payne prepared preliminary plans for a new physical education and recreation center (PERC) that carried a price tag of approximately $2.1 million. A pledge of $300,000 from the board and a $400,000 2-for-1 challenge grant from the Truman W. Collins Foundation kicked off the funding drive for the PERC project.[7]

In seeking to meet the physical education and recreation needs of the students and the greater Salem community, the physical education and athletic departments worked closely with the architect to devise a flexible, multipurpose facility. The resulting design by architect Payne produced a 12,757 square-foot building divided into three distinct blocks: the east section held a field house; the west unit contained a multi-purpose gymnasium; while the connecting center section housed the swimming facilities, various offices, class and locker rooms, and the main entryway to the entire structure. The field house contained the 120- by 160-foot basketball court with a synthetic floor surface and bleacher seating for 3,000. The gymnasium provided a 120- by 130-foot maple floor capable of accommodating two basketball or eight badminton or three volleyball courts, gymnastics or dance, and other floor activities. The natatorium and adjacent area held a 45- by 75-foot, six-lane "L" shaped swimming and diving pool; four handball courts; dance, wrestling, exercise/fitness, and locker rooms; offices; and a varsity lounge. The building sprawls across the southeast corner of the campus, bordered by 12th and Mill Streets.[8]

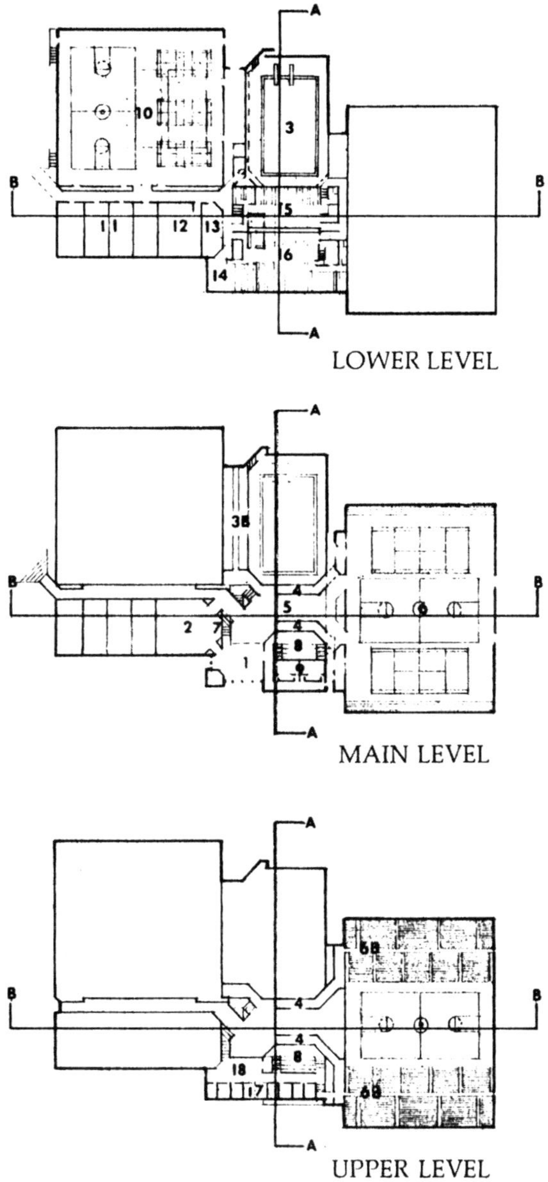

PERC Building

1. Entry
2. Multi-purpose Room
3. Pool
3B. Pool Bleachers
4. Ramps to Field House Bleachers
5. Ramp to Field House Main Floor
6. Field House
6B. Field House Bleachers Corridor
7. Concessions
8. Auditorium (Theater-Classroom)
9. Rest Rooms
10. Gymnasium
11. Handball Courts
12. Exercise Room
13. Equipment
14. Therapy
15. Women's Lockers
16. Men's Lockers
17. Offices
18. Secretarial

A document from the Lestle J. Sparks Physical Education and Recreation Center dedication showing the original configuration of each of the floors.

The university administration encountered many challenges in raising the full funding for the PERC. Throughout the planning phase, inflation kept pushing up the cost estimate, even though the architect struggled to keep within the budget by eliminating items or proposing cost-saving design alternatives. All involved in the project expressed considerable shock when the bids came in $600,000 over the architect's estimate in April 1972. The board required that the architect find $250,000 in savings without sacrificing program objectives. Payne, after a thorough reexamination of the plans, came up with a revised, less costly approach. The main savings came from changing the roof system from a truss-spanned building to a joist system. This change also allowed lowering the masonry walls by about six feet in all areas except the office wing and handball courts,

The architect's rendering of the PERC (Sparks).

Lestle J. Sparks Center

The requirements of the various athletic and recreational activities included in the Physical Education and Recreation Center (PERC) largely determined the interior layout and external shape of the building. As originally constructed, the blocky, brick-clad building encompassed three distinct volumes. Plain red brick topped by a concrete fascia, similar to that of Putnum University Center, covered the exterior surface of the building. Other key features included a flat roof supported by wooden trusses and narrow bands of windows on the front facade of the center section, which provided light to the swimming area and visually broke up the massive expanse of plain masonry walls. Overall, the architectural style of the PERC continued Payne's application of expressionist modernism, first employed in his design for the student center a few years earlier. Note the outline of Matthews Hall in the background on the left, and the Thomas Kay Woolen Mills in the background on the right.

thereby reducing masonry costs. Other cost savings came from using a concrete fascia on the building instead of stucco, electrical and mechanical revisions, redesigning the parking lot, and postponing the purchase of certain items of equipment. In sum, the architect proposed changes that would reduce costs by slightly over $200,000. This satisfied Willamette officials and the project was rebid, with the new cost coming in at $2.6 million in June 1972.

All of this occurred in the midst of the furor over President Fritz. As an interim replacement, the board appointed James H. Corson—a well-respected California educational administrator and friend of George Atkinson, chairman of the Board of Trustees. President Corson's collegial and steady manner brought a welcome calming to the campus atmosphere, and the project continued.

While the university had raised approximately $2 million in cash and pledges, the board and administration found themselves under considerable pressure to complete the PERC project funding well before finishing construction because they planned to launch another major campaign in the fall of 1973 for establishing a graduate school of administration and a building to house it. To keep the PERC construction on track while raising the remaining funds, the university had to take out two short-term bank loans of $400,000 each.[9] The PERC, formally named the Lestle J. Sparks Physical Education and Recreation Center—for Lestle Sparks, the grand old man of Willamette sports—opened in March 1974, after almost two years of construction.

After an eleven-month search, the university found a new president. The board chose Dr. Robert P. Lisensky, an educator from Ohio Wesleyan University, to become Willamette's 19th president. Lisensky was known for his open style and collaborative approach to decision-making. The new president wasted no time leading Willamette in the search to find solutions to questions of relevance and value that confronted institutions of higher learning nationwide. In an era of inflation surpassing ten percent, the costs of running a university were spiraling out of control. The population of traditional "college aged" students was on the downswing as the tail end of the baby boom passed through the system and, to further heighten the competition for students, many people were wondering if a college degree held real value in the job market.

In his first address to the faculty, Lisensky confronted the two main problems of enrollment and finances then generally facing higher education and especially private liberal arts colleges. Noting the interrelationship of the two issues, he optimistically called for internal changes to address them, stating "we must be a vigorous and exciting institution of learning, to preserve our own sense of integrity, to attract those kind of students that we want to be co-workers in our community of scholars, and as well, to seek donors to support the new and interesting [learning environment] that we create."[10]

It was a pivotal moment in Willamette's history, and President Lisensky immediately sought answers to the problems confronting the university. To improve Willamette's governance structure and increase the number of people involved in the decision-making process, Lisensky established a faculty council to weigh in on policies affecting the faculty, set up a separate academic council to give the faculty involvement in setting the direction of the entire academic undergraduate program, and constituted a budget advisory council to give all constituencies opportunities to influence university policy. In addition, he convinced the board to reorganize its deliberations to include student and faculty representatives. It took time for these new structures to work effectively and to achieve wide acceptance of the need for hierarchical governance for the institution.[11]

The board, in particular, became more engaged with campus issues as a result of the leadership upheaval around Roger Fritz during the early 1970s and the threatening external environment in which Willamette had to operate. In the spring of 1974, the board—in response to recommendations from the ad hoc Committee for Institutional Change that Lisensky had created—established three special task forces. One explored modes of campus inquiry, emphasizing analytical and synthetic reasoning ability; another looked into the relationships and interaction among the university's four colleges; while the third group explored potential changes to the undergraduate program. The faculty engaged in its own self-examination by looking at its process for development and renewal. The faculty also revisited the undergraduate curriculum, which would eventually lead to recommendations for tightening the requirements for graduation and reducing electives. The result of the institutional change process was a reinvigorated governance system that rebuilt trust among the various constituent elements of the campus community. As the administration, faculty, students, and trustees worked through the various issues, the project to establish a graduate school of administration came to fruition.[12]

The initial idea for a graduate school of administration had been put forth in the mid-1960s by undergraduate professors Ted Shay, political science, and Richard Gillis, economics. The board and Smith administration, after careful consideration, agreed to establish such a program. The need, as stated to the board by its Special Committee to Consider a Graduate Center in Administration, came from an:

> *increasing complexity of business-government relationships at all levels [which] has been marked by*

Named for the foundation that gifted the project, the Seeley G. Mudd building sits just south of the Collins Legal Center on Winter Street.

Seeley G. Mudd Building

The 19,485 square-foot Seeley G. Mudd building is a three-story, modified cube clad in a brick veneer on metal stud walls. The bottom floor of the building, set below grade, could be considered a daylight basement. The corners of the stark structure are clipped, partially exposing round, reinforced concrete columns. The four sides of the building present a complex expression of the Modernist style of architecture as practiced in the 1970s. A portion of the north elevation projects from the main volume and contains on the upper floors a two-story band of plate-glass windows set in thin aluminum muntins and framed by two exposed concrete columns, which extend all the way from the ground to the top of the third floor. Wide, board-formed concrete spandrels divide the two floors of north facing windows. The three-story, east-facing facade is most notable for its two, large brick veneer panels surrounded by narrow windows. The brick panels project slightly, giving the appearance of floating in front of the windows. Three partially exposed, round concrete columns symmetrically divide the space occupied by the attractive brick panel-and-window composition. The south elevation is mostly brick with a narrow band of inset windows on three floors. The west side continues the plain brick veneer walls and also contains a narrow band of recessed windows on each of three floors. An aggregate terrace extends from the below-grade first floor lounge toward the Mill Stream. A water feature originally fronted the terrace but was later removed. The second-floor building entry is approached from the street at an L-shaped angle by a raised concrete ramp. The building has a fourth level consisting of a penthouse for mechanical equipment and is capped by a flat roof.

an aura of suspicion and at times open hostility. The well-being of our capitalistic system in the modern world demands cooperation and understanding between government and business. This can only come about through trained executive personnel of both groups who have an understanding of the needs and operations of both government and business. In addition, there has been a decline in moral responsibility in both government and business which may in part be eliminated by attracting men of integrity to both government and business.

The Special Committee further argued that Willamette's graduate program would meet this need by:

A. *Training administrators ... with a specialized competence in either business or government, within the Christian and Liberal Arts tradition of Willamette.*

B. *Integrating the professional training so as to provide the future business leader with an understanding and appreciation of the objectives, problems and procedures of the public administrator, and the future public official with a similar understanding and appreciation of business.*

C. *Providing a trained reservoir of professional manpower to fill responsible positions in both business and all ranges of government; local, state and national.*[13]

The graduate program proposed to accomplish its goals by "developing a first rate curriculum leading to a two year graduate degree, Master of Arts in Administration." The proposal also noted that the close proximity of state government would enable the development of internships as an integral part of the graduate experience and assist in eventual job placement of graduates from the school. The curriculum would focus in the first year on a study of administration, while the second year the students would concentrate in either business or government administration. The proposal also called for locating the program in a new building near Willamette's law school. The board approved the proposal, estimated to cost $1.4 million for a building and equipment. President Lisensky selected Stephen Archer, an academic with a background in both business finance and public administration, as the Dean to organize the program, hire the initial four faculty, and select the first class, which was expected to number between fifty and one hundred students. To pay for the building and establish an endowment for the graduate school of administration, Willamette had to undertake a $5.2 million campaign—its single most expensive fundraising effort up to that time.[14]

Trustees of the Seeley G. Mudd Fund of Los Angeles agreed to support the Graduate School of Administration (GSA) with a $1 million challenge grant, while trustee and Chairman of the Board George Atkinson and his foundation gave another $800,000 toward the capital campaign. With the fundraising moving ahead, the architectural firm of Payne, Settecase and Smith worked up the building plans. As explained by Philip Settecase, the lead architect on the project, the structure was to be "of modern Georgian style," complementing other campus buildings. When finalized, Settecase's design placed the emphasis more on the modern than the Georgian aspect of style. It has more in common with the firm's move into expressionist modernism as represented by their Putnam University Center and the recently completed PERC then the stripped Georgian-style buildings in the core of the campus. Settecase assured the trustees that his modern, boxy design would provide about 15 to 20 percent more usable space than one more similar to the traditional Georgian design used in the adjacent Collins legal center. He also indicated that a less elaborate external design, along the lines of the university center, would save money.[15]

The Mudd building houses the George H. Atkinson Graduate School of Management, which the board named in honor of the long-time chairman and donor. On the upper two floors are class and seminar rooms, an auditorium, faculty offices, and a library (later discontinued), while the first floor contains a computer center, administrative offices, and staff and student lounges. The original plans called for a building that would house an enrollment of 150, but the program grew to accommodate more than 200 students and 45 faculty. At the Mudd building dedication, Dean Archer pronounced himself pleased: "It adapts well to our aim of providing the common core curriculum in administration as well as serving the diversity of the second year offerings. We also have projected several continuing education programs for the facilities which should serve the greater Salem community."[16]

An interior view of the Seeley G Mudd building soon after the building opened showing a cast aggregate staircase and study area.

The dedication of the Seeley G. Mudd building in September 1975 represented the successful conclusion of the Fund for Educational Excellence campaign initiated by President Smith in 1965. A decade of building had produced the Truman W. Collins Legal Center (1967), William Walton Hall (1967), the intertie between Doney and Lausanne halls (1967), George Putnam University Center (1970), Lestle J. Sparks Physical Education and Recreation Center (1974), Willamette Playhouse (1974), and the Seeley G. Mudd Building (1975). The playhouse involved the initial conversion of the old gymnasium into a theater department facility. Virtually all of the planning and design of these buildings or renovations had been the work of the architectural firm of Payne, Settecase and Smith. President Lisensky declared their design work "both aesthetically sound and functional" and noted that they "strive for the best possible in all situations." James Payne retired after the completion of the Mudd building, ending a 20-year collaboration with the university. While Lisensky spoke highly of the firm's work for Willamette since 1953, other architectural firms soon took over most of the future building on the campus. Philip Settecase, however, would return to do work for the university in the late 1980s and early 1990s.[17]

In the spring of 1978, Lisensky looked back over the previous five years of his administration to assess the success of his various initiatives. In an unfortunate accident of timing, three new deans had been selected just prior to his becoming the president. As he recalled, "The feeling on campus was that 'outsiders' were in charge and they had little respect for the past." At first, he found the faculty resistant to change and to an administrative team that was new to Willamette. While governance improved, by virtue of the inclusive committees he initiated soon after his arrival, the attempt to achieve immediate major changes in the direction of the university failed. Over time, however, the planning process did encourage the faculty to engage in experimentation, which resulted in new interdisciplinary programs and a realization that faculty complacency would not help the university meet future educational challenges. As he looked ahead, he felt that the continued vitality of Willamette would depend upon thorough planning, clarifying and reaffirming the university's mission, and strengthening the decision-making process by basing the assertion of presidential leadership on widespread consultation. Lisensky's planning process also succeeded in getting major foundation grants to fund new curricular programs and identify the new facility needs of the university.[18]

In the late 1970s, a major part of the planning effort focused on making better use of existing facilities for the educational program. The initiative got underway in 1977, as the board approved a six-year, three-phase, $2.3 million renovation of buildings. The plan sought to upgrade facilities for the departments of music, theater, and art, and the library. Phase one involved moving the music department from the old Music Hall to the Fine Arts Building (both wings of the Smith Auditorium Building). The east wing of the Fine Arts Building was remodeled at a cost of $300,000 to accommodate offices and practice rooms; the west wing already held music faculty offices, a recording studio, band and choir rooms, and a music library. After a complete reconstruction, the old 9,700 square foot Music Hall (formerly the Medical School and a science building) housed the art department. The Salem architectural firm of Chrisman/Grimms designed the new art facilities and oversaw the reconstruction process.[19]

Phase two of the renovation program aimed to turn the Willamette Playhouse into a better theater facility. The administration considered the preliminary conversion of the old gymnasium into a playhouse for the theater department in 1974 as only a first step. New plans called for an almost $600,000 remodel to better serve the growing theater program. Led by a $150,000 Kresge Foundation challenge grant, the university ultimately raised the funds necessary to convert the existing space into a 280-seat thrust theater and a black box experimental theater. In place by 1979, the thrust theater contained tiered amphitheater style seating around three sides of the stage. The black box theater has no fixed seating plan, allowing the space to be adapted to experimental productions. The remainder of the renovated space included offices, classrooms, a set construction area, a dance studio, dressing rooms, a make-up laboratory, and a green room.

Again, the Salem architects Chrisman/Grimms carried out the conversion of the old gymnasium into a modern theatrical performance space. Grimms also sought advice from San Francisco theater consultants Landry and Hunt, who had designed successful theaters for Lewis and Clark College and Lane Community College. The goal of the theater project according to Robert Peffers, chair of the theater department, was to create "the most effective use of theatre space in the region," and support the growing theater program at Willamette.[20]

Phase three—the library expansion—did not progress as smoothly as the other two renovation projects. The university had outgrown the existing library facilities and hoped to increase capacity by adding a second floor within the existing space and expanding the west side of the south wing of the building to gain 30 percent more floor space and 100 percent more stack space at an estimated cost of $1.5 million. The more the university studied the problem, the more it became evident that merely renovating and expanding the existing library would never produce an effective facility. A 1978 campus development

While the exterior to the gymnasium remained unchanged in its transformation into theater space, the interior underwent a complete renovation. Note the new sound baffles hanging from the ceiling. The names of the three men pictured were not documented.

study carried out by the Portland architectural firm Martin, Soderstrom, Matteson found the library to be functionally inadequate and little more than a book storage facility. They considered the library as a place to be endured rather than efficiently used by students and faculty because of noise levels, crowded book stack areas, poor ventilation and heating, bad lighting, and an inflexible building design that made remodeling almost impossible. The architects concurred with the earlier findings of Ralph Ellsworth, a nationally recognized authority on university libraries, who had visited Willamette in 1977 to inspect the library. At that time he had recommended "that the University abandon the present building entirely and construct a new building."[21]

In 1979, Lisensky and the board decided to proceed with a new library building. As Lisensky put it in a funding request to the Arthur Vining Davis Foundation, "The single most compelling need at Willamette is for a modern library facility; the present library is not adequate for a university of Willamette's stature and for the caliber of students and faculty members who make up our campus community." After a thorough national search, the board selected the St. Louis architectural firm of Murphy, Downey, Wofford and Richmond, which specialized in academic libraries. Ted Wofford, the lead architect from the Murphy firm, impressed the library committee with his knowledge of and experience in library design and his suggestion that the new library could serve as a bridge between the old and new parts of the campus. His preliminary scheme called for a three-story building to straddle the Mill Stream, approximately where Goudy Commons now sits. The building plans laid out 55,000 square feet of floor space (the existing library had 32,000 square feet) at an estimated cost of $5 million. Fundraising took longer than expected, and by the time construction began in 1986, the building plans had changed considerably.[22]

A key part of Lisenky's long-range planning rested on the campus development study conducted by the architectural firm of Martin, Soderstrom, Matteson. Their work had been done in conjunction with a campus facilities planning committee consisting of faculty and administrators. The study assessed the existing campus building conditions and made recommendations for cost-effective improvements to the physical plant. In general, the architect's final report focused on efficient use and energy cost-savings and revealed their lack of regard for the existing historic character of many campus buildings. The report described Belluschi's Collins Hall as a decaying remnant of an earlier age of science education "with neither architectural grandeur nor historic significance." To the authors of the report, Collins "was outstanding only in its lack of positive or noteworthy characteristics."[23]

The report condemned Eaton Hall for its "ever-present brown linoleum floors and painted wood trim," institutional pastel green paint [on the walls]," [and] "the dark feeling in the hallways." In general, the location of some administrative offices on Eaton's first floor "contributed to the fragmentation of University administrative efforts." While admitting that Eaton Hall played a major role in meeting the needs of the university, the architects concluded that "the overall use of available space, classroom conditions, building amenities and interior appearance leave much to be desired. [However,] the building has the structural potential for remodeling."

The architects were equally unsparing in their criticism of Waller, asserting with alarm that its primitive fire protection system "constituted a public safety hazard." Among other short-comings, they noted that Waller had noisy plumbing, sagging second- and third-story floors, poorly configured classrooms, and energy-leaking large single pane windows. The report did admit that "Waller is the symbol of the University" and as such, "While exact structural potentials and limitation are not yet known, ... [it] appears to have potential to remain an integral part of Willamette." Upon receiving the report, President Lisensky hastened to reassure the campus community that the venerable old building would remain, agreeing with the architects: "We can't touch Waller Hall, it is the symbol of Willamette."

Based on the report, however, the administration decided that Eaton, Collins, and Waller all needed significant renovation. Additionally, they determined that once the new library was completed, the old library would be converted to academic offices. In all, the total package of building renovation and new library carried an estimated price tag of $12-18 million. The board felt some urgency to proceed rapidly with a larger building program due to the fear that if the university waited too long, inflation would drive cost up to unacceptably high levels. Another factor was the recognition that existing science facilities were not meeting the current teaching needs.[24]

Operating costs in the face of continuing inflation were a primary factor for President Lisensky in his planning.

Energy costs were rising at an alarming rate. (The energy bill for the university in 1977-78 was $289,000. By 1980-81, it would be an estimated $519,000.) In his view, Gatke Hall was a liability that should be eliminated. Since the law school had moved out in 1967, Gatke had housed political science and economics classes. He suggested that once the fourth-floor attic in Eaton Hall was renovated, the political science and economics classes could be moved and the building razed. Ultimately, Lisensky did not succeed in removing Gatke Hall, and its fate would still be undecided when a new president arrived after his term ended.[25]

In late 1979, the university achieved a long-sought goal when the Southern Pacific Railroad finally removed its tracks bisecting the southern portion of the campus. A spur line tracing a westerly route off the main north-south rail line paralleling 12th Street originally ran along the southern border of the campus adjacent to the Mill Stream. This spur line served industrial plants west of the campus and along the Willamette River on the southern edge of Salem's downtown commercial district. Until the 1960s, Willamette was not especially bothered by the tracks and periodic freight cars intermittently passing along the edge of the campus. This situation, however, changed when the university acquired almost 40 acres of urban renewal land south of the tracks and began building facilities, especially the student center and living units, on the new portion of the campus.

The university began in earnest to pressure the Southern Pacific to cease using the spur line, remove its tracks, and give the right-of-way back to Willamette. Several developments aided the university's request. In 1870, the Board of Trustees had given the railroad land upon which to build its Salem Depot with the stipulation that said property would revert to the university if the depot at any time was removed or abandoned. This reversionary clause was still valid and gave Willamette a means of pressuring the railroad over the use of the spur line, which began just a few hundred yards north of the depot. The railroad, at the time, was in negotiations with Salem for the sale of the depot and surrounding land, and its bargaining position with the city would be much stronger if Willamette's reversionary interest did not cloud the title. Another factor in Willamette's favor was that many of the industrial and commercial customers served by the spur line had relocated, lessening traffic over the tracks. The Southern Pacific, moreover, could serve its remaining customers by securing trackage rights from a competing railroad company. Finally, the Salem community generally supported the removal of the Southern Pacific spur line so that the Trade Street area could be redeveloped from its then deteriorating, semi-industrial condition. The Southern Pacific, for its part, wanted the university to trade the 60-foot-wide strip of land through the university in exchange for all rights to the depot property held under the reversionary clause, but the board demurred.[26]

A view of the railroad tracks and original mill race as it cut through campus on the south side of Smith Fine Arts Center. The photo was probably taken from the recently-completed Putnam University Center balcony.

By the mid-1970s, the Willamette community had become increasingly agitated about the spur line, asserting that the tracks created:

> *an absolute distraction and deterrent to accomplishment of the educational and community*

service objectives of Willamette University. It limits our educational effectiveness and provides a restriction on growth. Although the restriction is easy to see in a physical sense, the psychological situation is becoming serious as well. ... It is very difficult to hide a set of tracks and noise which disrupts classes, programs being held in the Auditorium and new University Center, and study in student residences continues to be a problem. Also, interruption of foot traffic in what are now heavily-used routes is becoming a serious safety and morale problem. ... Everyone related to Willamette University would be most appreciative if the Southern Pacific would soon take the necessary steps to eliminate the trade Street rails which divide our campus.[27]

Under continued pressure from both the university and Salem, the railroad finally gave in and agreed to remove its tracks during the summer of 1979 and deed the cleared roadbed to the university without any contingencies. Subsequently, the railroad company transferred the depot to the City of Salem without any objection by the university.[28]

Before funds could be raised for a new library or to initiate building renovations, President Lisensky resigned in February 1980. New leadership would need to reevaluate university priorities. In leaving Willamette after eight years, Lisensky believed he had achieved his main goals and that it was time for a change in leadership. He expressed pride in what he had accomplished in long-range planning and fundraising, which he felt laid a strong foundation for the future of liberal arts education at Willamette. Under his leadership, the endowment had increased from $16 million to nearly $35 million and an improved governance structure had been put in place. Above all, he thought he had helped the university clarify and reaffirm its commitment to a values-centered liberal arts education.[29]

Endnotes

1 This overview of national trends in higher education is based on John Thelin, *A History of American Higher Education*, 2nd ed. (Baltimore, MD: The Johns Hopkins University Press, 2011), 317-98.

2 Quote in ibid., 318.

3 Turner, *Campus*, 249-305.; Richard P. Dober, *Campus Architecture: Building in the Groves of Academe* (New York: McGraw-Hill, 1996); Rifkind, *Contemporary Architecture*, 251-62.

4 Hitchman, *Liberal Arts Colleges*, 28-29; "Willamette University: New Ideas Stirring the West's Oldest University," *Oregonian*, Feb. 16, 1969; *Collegian*, Feb. 9, 1971.

5 Quotes in "Willamette U. Firing Analyzed," *Oregonian*, Apr. 18, 1972.

6 Ibid.; "What Next at WU?", *Oregon Statesman*, Apr. 11, 1972; *Willamette Scene*, Oct. 1971; Apr. 1972, 3-4, 37-38.

7 Memo: Location of the New PERC, Nov. 16, 1970, Smith Papers, Box 29B, Willamette University Archives ; PERC Facts Sheet, Aug. 20, 1970, ibid.; A Proposal From Willamette University for the Support of it New Physical Education and Recreation Center, Jun. 23, 1970, ibid.; Report of the PERC Planning Committee, Apr. 21, 1970, PERC Box, Facilities Records, Willamette University; PERC Preliminary Analysis and Design Phase, Jul. 31, 1970, ibid.; PERC Estimate of Costs, Apr. 12, 1972, ibid.; *Collegian*, Oct. 24, 1969, Feb. 15, Oct. 21, Nov. 4, 1971; *Willamette Scene*, Oct. 1970.

8 Program of Dedication for Sparks Center, May 11, 1974, Facilities Records, Willamette University; A Place to Play on the Willamette Campus (n.d.), ibid.

9 When the board took out the short-term loans, the university's only long-term debt consisted of $2.5 million in self-liquidating bonds incurred for the construction of dormitories and the library expansion. Debt service was covered by housing revenues and library fees; Memo: PERC Bid and Financing, May 3, 1972, Facilities Records, Willamette University; James Payne to Board of Trustees, May 5, 1972; ibid.; Milo Harris to Pres. James Corson, Jun. 12, 1972, ibid.; Milo Harris to Pres. James Corson, Jul. 6, 1972, Ibid.; Memo: PERC Architectural and Engineering Fees, Aug. 3, 1972, ibid.; Milo Harris to James Payne, Jan. 10, 1973, ibid.; PERC: Supplementary Financial Data, Jun. 8, 1973, ibid.; PERC Project Budget, May, 17, Oct. 2, 1974; ibid.; *Collegian*, Sep. 7, 1972, Sep. 20, 1973, Jan. 17, Mar. 7, 1974; *Willamette Scene*, Oct. 1971, Apr. 1972, Apr. 1973, Apr. 1974.

10 Quote in *Collegian*, Sep. 6, 1973, Sep. 7, 1972, Sep. 6, Oct. 18, 1973, Feb. 21, Apr. 18, 1974; *Willamette Scene*, Jul. 1973.

11 This and the next paragraph are based on ibid. and: *Collegian*, Feb. 21, 1974, Apr. 17, Sep. 11, 1975; *Willamette Scene*, Jan. 1974, Mar. 1975, Sep. 1977, Sep. 1978; see also Robert Lisensky, President's Evaluation Statement, 1973-74—1977-78, Smith Papers, Box 21A, Willamette University Archives.

12 Committee for Institutional Change, Report to President Robert Lisensky, Feb. 7, 1974, AGSM Records, Box 2, Willamette University Archives; Willamette University Project Report: Faculty Development in an Era of Change, Jul. 4, 1978, AGSM Records, Box 1, Willamette University Archives.

13 The Special Committee to Consider a Graduate Center in Administration to the Board of Trustees, Memo: Proposal for the Establishment of a Graduate Center in Administration, (n.d.), Smith Papers, Box 29B, Willamette University Archives; Minutes of the Board of Trustees, Feb., Jun., 1965, ibid; see also, Geo. H. Atkinson Graduate School of Administration—The Development of GSA at Willamette University (n. d.), AGSM Records, Box 1, Willamette University Archives; Program for GSA Building, Jul. 26, 1973, ibid.

14 *Collegian*, Nov. 4, 1971; *Willamette Scene*, Jan. 1974; Proposal to the Trustees of the Seeley G. Mudd Fund, Aug. 15, 1968, Smith Papers, Box 29B, Willamette University Archives; The Graduate School of Administration at Willamette University, Jul. 18, 1973, AGSM Records, Box 1, Willamette University.

15 Memo on GSA Building Requirements, Aug. 15, 1973, AGSM Records, File Cabinet 7, Drawer 3, AGSM Archives; Memo GSA Building-Meeting with Architects, Oct. 2, 1973 , ibid.; Milo Harris to James Payne, Oct. 25, 1973, ibid.; George Atkinson to Robert Lisensky, Sep. 19, 1973, Smith Papers, Box 26B, Willamette University Archives; Robert Lisensky to George Atkinson, Oct. 8, 1973, ibid.; Milo Harris to Pres. Lisensky, May 3, 1974, ibid.; Minutes—GSA Policy Committee, Jul. 26, Aug. 3, 1973, AGSM Records, Box 1, Willamette University Archives; *Willamette Scene*, Apr. 1974; *Oregonian*, Feb. 21, 1974.

16 Quote in *Willamette Scene*, Fall, 1975; *Collegian*, Oct. 2, 1975.

17 *Willamette Scene*, Summer 1975; Robert Lisensky to To Whom It May Concern, Jun. 3, 1976, Smith Papers, Box 14A, Willamette University Archives.

18 Robert Lisensky, President's Evaluation Statement, 1973-74—1977-78, Smith Papers, Box, 21A, Willamette University Archives; *Willamette Scene*, Sep. 1978.

19 Minutes, Buildings and Grounds Committee, Board of Trustees, Jan. 6, 1977, Smith Papers, Box 26A, Willamette Archives; Request for Support of Phase II of Willamette's 3-Phase Renovation and Renewal Project (late 1977?), Smith Papers, Box 32A, ibid.; News Release of $150,000 grant from the Kresge Foundation, Aug. 25, 1977, ibid.; Report to Northwest Association of Schools and Colleges, 1980, ibid.; *Collegian*, Feb. 24, Sep. 16, 1977; *Willamette Scene*, Feb. 1977, Jul. 1978.

20 Quote in, *Willamette Scene*, Jul. 1978.

21 Quote in Martin, Soderstrom, Matteson, AIA Architects, Willamette University Campus Development Study, Jan. 1979, AGSM Records, Box 1, Willamette University Archives; *Collegian*, Oct. 4, 1979, Oct. 18, 1979; Robert Lisensky to Ralph Ellsworth, Jan. 14, Feb. 7, Apr. 1, 1977, Smith Papers, Box 5A, Willamette University Archives; Ralph Ellsworth, Report on the Willamette Library, Mar. 1977, ibid.

22 Robert Lisensky to Kendra O'Donnell, Sep. 28, 1979, Smith Papers, Box 26A, Willamette University Archives; *Collegian*, Oct. 11, 1979; Robert Lisensky to Pat Stockton, et al., Apr. 23, 1979, Smith Papers, Box 14B, Willamette University Archives; Robert Lisensky to Leo Daly, Jun 25, 1979, Smith Papers, Box 32A, ibid.; Ralph Ellsworth to Robert Lisensky, Nov. 2, 1979 and Lisensky to Ellsworth, Dec. 3, 1979, Smith Papers, Box 5A, ibid.; Patricia Stockton, Memo for the Record, Jun. 18, 1979, Smith Papers, Box 39B, ibid.

23 This and following paragraphs are based on Martin, Soderstrom, Matteson, AIA Architects, Willamette University Campus Development Study, Jan. 1979, AGSA Records, Box 1, Willamette University Archives (copy also available in Facilities Records, Willamette University); John Matteson to Robert Lisensky, Jul. 27, 1978, Facilities Records, Willamette University.

24 *Collegian*, Jan. 31, Feb. 28, 1980

25 Roger Fritz to Louis Menk, Aug. 14, 1969, Smith Papers, Box 2B, Willamette University Archives; Robert Fritz to G. Herbert Smith, Jan. 22, 1970, Smith Papers, Box 78A, ibid..; Robert Fritz to Stephen Bechtel, Jr., Nov. 13, 1970, Smith Papers, Box 2B, ibid.; Milo Harris, Memo to the File: Southern Pacific Proposal, Nov 13, 1974, Ibid.; George Rhoten to Oglesby Young, Jun. 20, 1975, ibid.; Milo Harris, Memo to the File: Trustee Property Acquisition Committee, Oct. 1, 1973, Smith Papers, Box 29B, ibid.; Copy of Deed from Willamette Trustees to Southern Pacific RR, Deed Book 33, Page 556—Marion County, Sep. 1, 1886, ibid.

26 The South Pacific Switch Track through the Willamette University Campus (n. d.), Smith Papers, Box 2B, Willamette University Archives.

27 *Collegian*, Oct. 4, 1979; *Willamette Scene*, Apr. 1979.

28 *Collegian*, Feb. 14, 1980.

8 The Early Hudson Years

The university began the 1980s with optimism that, with minor adjustments, it could ride out the short-term effects of inflation and a projected decline in the number of traditional college-age students. A new collegiate culture had developed through the 70s, and the experiences governed by tradition became overwhelmed by the "youth culture" of the larger society. The media-driven music, values, and interests of youth pervaded student life even in college. Long-revered campus events and rites of passage came under increased scrutiny and often fell by the wayside as students focused on more compelling interests. (At Willamette, the most notable victim of this change in student culture was the end of Freshman Glee, a spring rite since 1909.)

A faculty planning committee urged a strategy based on overall quality improvements to programs that would prove attractive to prospective students. As top priorities, they recommended a major revision of the undergraduate curriculum, ambitious facilities renovation plans, an active faculty development program, new presidential leadership, and a renewed commitment to Willamette's rich academic heritage.[1]

To fill the role of president, the board chose Jerry Hudson, a historian who held a Ph.D. in American history from Tulane, had taught at Pepperdine University, and had served as the president of Hamline University. He, too, expressed optimism about the university's potential. In an interview shortly after arriving on campus, he stated that Willamette "has all the essentials to be the premier small private liberal arts university in this region of the country. I was impressed by the faculty, by the endowment … there's no reason why an institution with the reputation it already enjoys in this area of the country could not be

President Jerry Hudson early in his tenure.
Facing page: Eaton Hall

Above: The innovative fume hood work stations for organic chemistry soon after installation in Collins Hall. **Right:** The renovated Collins Hall now had an entrance oriented toward the quad.

one of the class institutions in the nation."

As for his commitment to the development plans worked out under President Lisensky, Hudson expressed some initial hesitancy in fully embracing them. "Clearly there's been a great deal of planning. It may be exactly what's needed. It may need some modification. I'm not buying into the fact that every decision is already a predetermined one. That's not acceptable to me." Still, he went on to assure the Willamette community that "assuming for the moment the legitimacy of those plans that have been adopted, I'm committed to providing the resources necessary to improve our ability to offer a quality education." In fact, Hudson soon threw his considerable energies into the large-scale fundraising effort to pay for the major renovations of Collins and Eaton halls. He also assured the members of the university planning committee of his commitment to planning based on "the institution's mission, purpose, goals and priorities." He promised that the planning committee's "recommendations will be highly regarded and respected. It can assumed that the Committee's views will be reflected in budget preparation."[2]

The first facilities renovations undertaken in the early 1980s involved Collins Hall. Ironically, the justification for the work was the same as that used 40 years earlier in the original construction of Collins: the science equipment and laboratories were outdated for the demands of current scientific education. To modernize the science facility, university planners and the architect, Will Martin of the Portland firm of Martin, Soderstrom, Matteson (MSM), decided to gut the interior of the building and start over. They could do this because the post and beam internal structure meant that partitions were not load bearing, thus allowing for a complete rearrangement of rooms and laboratories. Much of the existing equipment was given away or junked. While the contractor carried out the renovations, instruction went on. The administration relocated temporarily the chemistry labs to mobile units, moved the biology labs to Matthews Hall basement, and put the earth science and physics labs in the Belknap Hall basement. Faculty offices and some science lecture rooms ended up in York House. Over time, science students attended lectures in classrooms scattered across the campus. After 15 months and $4.1 million, Willamette finally had its new science center.[3]

The Collins Science Center had at least two

noteworthy features. One was a first-of-a-kind-anywhere organic chemistry laboratory, which provided an open-type, supervisable fume hood work stations for each student. This apparatus helped alleviate the old problem of persistent chemical odors, which permeated the old Collins Hall. Another innovation, which grew in popularity over time, was an informal student/faculty meeting area, figuring prominently in the design for the second floor of the science center, called the "hearth." It apparently resulted from a collaboration of the project architect, Will Martin, and President Hudson. In fact, when—in the struggle to contain project costs—at least one administrator suggested deferring the hearth, Hudson responded, "I feel very strongly that it should be included." And so the hearth was kept in the renovation.[4]

While the Collins Hall renovation focused almost completely on the building's interior and attempted to retain, as the *Collegian* noted, "at least the Georgian flavor of Collins Hall," the exterior did not entirely escape alteration. In the apparent interest of energy efficiency, the renovation architect replaced the double hung, multi-light windows of Belluschi's original design with modern double-paned casement windows. This change markedly detracts from the stripped Georgian styling of Belluschi's tasteful but simple design of Collins Hall. Fortunately, the window alterations could be reversed easily in any future renovations to the building. Another exterior modification reoriented the main entrance of the Collins Science Center to the southeastern corner of the 1961 rear addition to the building. At that location, Martin designed a plain, modernist concrete ensemble, consisting of an angled, three-part triangular arch supported by four columns, resting on an open porch at the top of a flight of stairs. The redesigned entry, perhaps a whimsical reference to classical architecture, now looks to the quad rather than State Street.[5]

The next major renovation project occurred in Eaton Hall, phase two of the Willamette University improvement campaign. The dingy, worn out interior of stately Eaton Hall received a thorough makeover in the early 1980s. After removing the financial affairs and administrative offices from the building,

President Jerry Hudson checking out the renovations to Eaton Hall.

Eaton Hall soon after its renovation in 1982. The new entryway from the quad tastefully mirrors the original design of the building.

the project architect, Jon Weiner of MSM revised the space to create 14 new classrooms, 26 faculty offices, 6 seminar rooms, and a terraced lecture room. The administrative and financial aid offices were relocated to the Putnam University Center. The revised interior took on a distinctly modern ambiance with new stairways, light fixtures, furniture, carpets, walls, and ceilings, along with new mechanical and electrical systems. The guiding design approach to the renovation sought to recall rather than duplicate forms and details of the original interior. As President Hudson put it: "Our emphasis is on productivity, efficiency and economical maintenance. The changes in Eaton are not as pronounced as those in Collins. With Eaton we have a building some 70-odd years old. It's very solid, well-built and well used building that needs revitalization to allow us to continue in the same fashion." The contractor completed the project in less than five months, cutting eight months off the original schedule and saving a significant sum of money. The Eaton Hall renovation cost $1.7 million.[6]

The only external change to Eaton Hall arose from the prominent new main entryway facing the quadrangle. Weiner had to decide whether to make the entry a dramatic statement in the manner of the new Collins Hall entry or to craft a more restrained opening in keeping with the existing architectural style of the building. The design of the entry elicited much discussion among the faculty, many of whom preferred a simple, small entryway made of the same materials from which the building originally was constructed. They evidently felt that the Collins entry contrasted too much with Belluschi's stripped Georgian design. Professor William Braden of the English department eloquently made the point when he wrote to President Hudson, "I would like to register some opinions ... regarding the proposed work on Eaton Hall. ... I guess what I am concerned about is an apparent indifference at Willamette to the whole business of style. I could make a depressingly long list of examples of our tendency to make awkward or tasteless gestures, but I trust that point does not need making. Grace and style do not happen by accident, nor are they, in the short run, particularly efficient or practical. But they may be the most enduringly significant qualities of what a university like Willamette does, and I think they should be given lots more weight in our planning." Hoping to reassure those of the campus community concerned about the Eaton entry design, Hudson stated, "I share some of the views that you expressed and have had extensive discussions with the architects. I do not know what we will eventually do, but there is no question that some will dislike what is done. I do not expect the building to reflect totally my prejudices, nor those of anyone else on campus, but it will definitely be a building of which we can be proud."[7]

Ultimately, Weiner chose a conservative approach. His tasteful design crafted a two-story, slightly projecting, double-gable portico of brick and stone that carefully mimicked the large original triangular roof gable directly above it. The new entry structure had a rusticated stone belt course separating the first and second floors that aligned with the existing belt course of the building. The entryway faced the campus quadrangle with understated dignity and created an inviting opening into the strikingly new interior. The architect also carried out an extensive cleaning, repointing, and sealing of the exterior brick, stone, and mortar facade. After the contractor completed the project, Eaton housed the history, philosophy, English, sociology, and education departments.[8]

After finishing work on Eaton Hall in January 1982, the administration focused its energies on building a new library and completing the $18 million Capital Campaign, which was paying for the renovations of Collins, Eaton, and Waller halls as well as the replacement of the library. By the fall of 1982, only $7 million had been raised. As described above, architects had been selected while Lisensky still served as president, and Hudson continued with that arrangement. Ted Wofford served as the St. Louis firm's lead architect on the library project.[9]

Given all of the well-known shortcomings of the old library, professors and students made clear what they wanted in the new facility. In a report for the architect, the library committee stated that the planned library should provide "easy access to books to encourage independent, exploratory reading, ... an inviting reading and study environment, ... pleasant interiors free from noise and distractions, ... [and] facilities and equipment ... for the use of microforms, computer technology and other non book resources." Above all, the report emphasized, there needed to be adequate space for the collection with provisions for future growth. The committee consensus, based on a separate consultant's report, also recommended that non-print media be centralized outside the library.[10]

Although in February 1980 the board had approved the working drawings provided by Murphy, Downey, Wofford and Richmond for the new library, some on campus questioned its proposed siting and design. New to the scene, President Hudson listened to the critics and decided to take another look at the library plans. In September 1980, he asked Will Martin of MSM architects—the firm that had produced the campus development study of 1979—to review the placement and design of the library. In his subsequent analysis, Martin argued that the proposed location of the massive library west of Smith Auditorium and south of Doney Hall would disrupt "the scale, rhythm and pattern" of courtyards, openings and circulation among existing buildings. Moreover, he found the proposed siting would not make optimum use of the Millrace now that recent removal of the railroad tracks freed it from the confines of a linear channel.

Martin's design review also criticized certain elements of the library design related to the roof, entryway, and window treatments. He worried that Wofford's design "is the language of twentieth century magic and while entirely appropriate in other settings, it speaks of different values than the one-hundred plus years of Willamette University. If this form is to be introduced it must be situated with even more care so as not to overwhelm or degrade its more historic neighbors." In sum, Martin stated in his transmittal letter accompanying his review that "there are some pretty fundamental problems created by this building and its location. We hope that we have been clear-headed enough in our analysis that our comments will aid you in determining the course of the project."[11]

President Hudson faced a difficult situation: Library planning was well advanced, but Martin's review raised important questions concerning the siting and design of such an important campus building. Hudson was particularly struck by Martin's point that "the Willamette campus is comprised of individual, distinctive structures located more by fortune than long-range planning; none-the-less, there may be discerned a number of unifying characteristics which are essential to the harmony and coherence of the whole. This set of characteristics must be sensitively and skillfully addressed to express the individuality of the institution in this new landmark structure." After careful consideration of Martin's report, Hudson reluctantly asked the library architect and Martin to cooperate in better coordinating the library siting and design with the goals of the current campus plan devised in 1979. At that point, Hudson was not ready to change the initially adopted location for the library, but he signaled that he had an open mind about the issue. He also indicated that he would assume overall responsibility for planning the library building.[12]

Wofford and Martin discussed the library planning situation, and Wofford decided to rethink both the siting and design issues. While this review occurred, Willamette's librarian resigned and a new librarian needed to get acquainted with the project. The new planning process consumed most of 1981 and resulted in significant changes to the project. University officials and Wofford decided that the library would be built south of the millstream between Sparks Recreation Center and Putnam Center and that the entrance to the library would face the quad at an angle. At one point, the architect toyed with the idea of building the library over the millstream but gave that up for technical and cost reasons. President Hudson, showing a perceptive grasp of the spatial relationship involved, urged the architect to consider "the possibility of moving the library a bit more southward off of the mill race in order to allow pedestrian traffic on the south side of the mill race in front of the library. Naturally, it would not be desirable to line up Putnam, Sparks and the library in a line, but the library could be moved southward and still the south wall would be further north than either of the other two buildings." Wofford responded positively to Hudson's suggestions, noting that to relieve the sense of constriction in the library/millrace relationship, the library could be moved ten to fifteen feet south and five feet east. Wofford also suggested "widening the millrace at this point, [so that] its impact on the viewer within the library could be strengthened. Also by spreading the volume of water over a larger and shallower bed, the type of flow around rocks with riffles and sounds like those encountered in mountain streams … could be introduced." Hudson and the trustees embraced these ideas, and Wofford proceeded to refine them, working with the landscape architect who was then drafting a master plan for the university in the spring of 1982.[13]

By March 1982, Wofford had submitted new plans that tried to address criticisms of his previous efforts. While addressing the technical requirements inherent in a functional library, he especially sought to capture in a tangible form the existing architectural expression of the campus. He felt that the essence of the Northwest regional setting was its:

> *mild, moist climate, abundant water, and lush landscape. ... This is the striking physical quality of the Willamette University campus and has been paramount in our thinking regarding the library. Our early attempts to use exterior wood, sloping roofs and the nearby water drew strong negative response from some of the Board of Trustees because it did not reflect the 'Georgian' architecture of the campus. Even if the library program could be housed in a good Georgian building, ... we do not think it would be appropriate to the site or its surroundings, which are not truly 'Georgian'.*

He went on to say:

> *What we are attempting to do in the design of the library is to try to achieve optimum functional relationships in the interior and house this necessarily large block of space in a structure which blends with its neighbors without imitation or pretension, recognizes and reinforces human scale through the articulation of its masses and patterns of its fenestration, strengthens the much needed sense of entry and form for the overall campus and, by its transparency and relationship to the millrace, allows the lovely landscape to participate in and dominate the building and the user's experience of it.*[14]

As to the functional aspects of the library, Wofford sought to create good staff workflow patterns and easy collections access for the library user. He especially tried "to soften the effect of the stack massing without sacrificing continuity, capacity, or the north-south orientation which allows light and views to penetrate it." He also studied the use of alternative energy but had been unable to justify measures beyond passive energy principles such as insulation, a consistently tight building skin, and careful landscape screening.[15]

The university librarian, the library committee, and the architect continued to exchange information and ideas as the architect refined the building layout. One issue of continuing debate concerned whether the library building should be two or three stories. The architect held firm to a two-story design, asserting that "in our opinion, the additional cost in building skin and vertical circulation inherent in the three-story approach, is unwarranted. We do not see that the building would be more efficient from the standpoint of either staff or users." Over the course of the spring, the architect and the library committee continued to refine the interior layout and the role media resources would play in the library.[16]

By the fall of 1982, the library siting and exterior design issues had been largely resolved. The new site, east of Smith Auditorium and south of the Mill Stream, placed the building between Sparks and Putnam. This location was ratified in a recently completed campus master plan done by Walker and Macy, a Portland landscape architecture firm. The new campus development plan sought to guide future growth and change with a special emphasis on improving access and internal pedestrian circulation. Other considerations included the visual enhancement of open space, upgrading the millrace, removal of barriers that limited access by the handicapped, and improved parking access. Completed in July 1982, after six months of study, the plan represented the first thorough master plan for development in

The Mark O. Hatfield Library soon after construction.

Mark O. Hatfield Library

Wofford's exterior design for the Hatfield Library emphasizes transparent facades on the north and south to allow a visual link between the north and south sections of the campus. Solid walls of brick on the east and west sides give definition to new landscape spaces between existing buildings and provide a backdrop for the library forecourt. The architect uses red-brown brick to harmonize with the brickwork of adjacent structures. Expanses of glass and trim of bright metal serve to lighten the effect of the building's mass. Underneath the overhanging square roof plane, the side walls step back, reflecting the flow of the adjacent mill stream and suggesting the flow pattern of pedestrian circulation around the building. The only questionable exterior design element in an otherwise fine building comes from placing bricks vertically in the imposing brick cornice. The contrast between the mass of horizontal bricks in the body of the building and the thin strip of vertical bricks overhead in the cornice appears unnaturally jarring.[18]

the university's history. It presented a campus plan achievable through phased improvements. One of the earliest improvements completed was the reworking of the Mill Stream between Smith Auditorium and Putnam Center to create a widened and meandering flow for the stream, soon to be dubbed, "Hudson's Bay." President Hudson later remarked about the Mill Stream work, "I probably had more anxiety over that than any other project. With a building you can read a blueprint and not have many surprises. ... I had a few sleepless nights wondering what would happen when we stopped the flow of water to do the digging and then opened up that channel. I worried that the water would not flow and would become a stagnant pool but it turned out nicely. Every time I visit the campus, I see students enjoying the bay and its surroundings."[17]

Further refinements to the interior of the library continued during the winter of 1982-83. In the interest of economy, the architect reduced the overall area of the building by 10,000 square feet to approximately 53,000 square feet. He accomplished this reduction by deleting an auditorium and an after-hours study space and their supporting facilities, including a second elevator and restrooms. The estimated cost for the revised building plan stood at $4.9 million. Still, discussions continued during the spring of 1983 over the matter of an auditorium, after-hours study space, media facilities, and the special collections

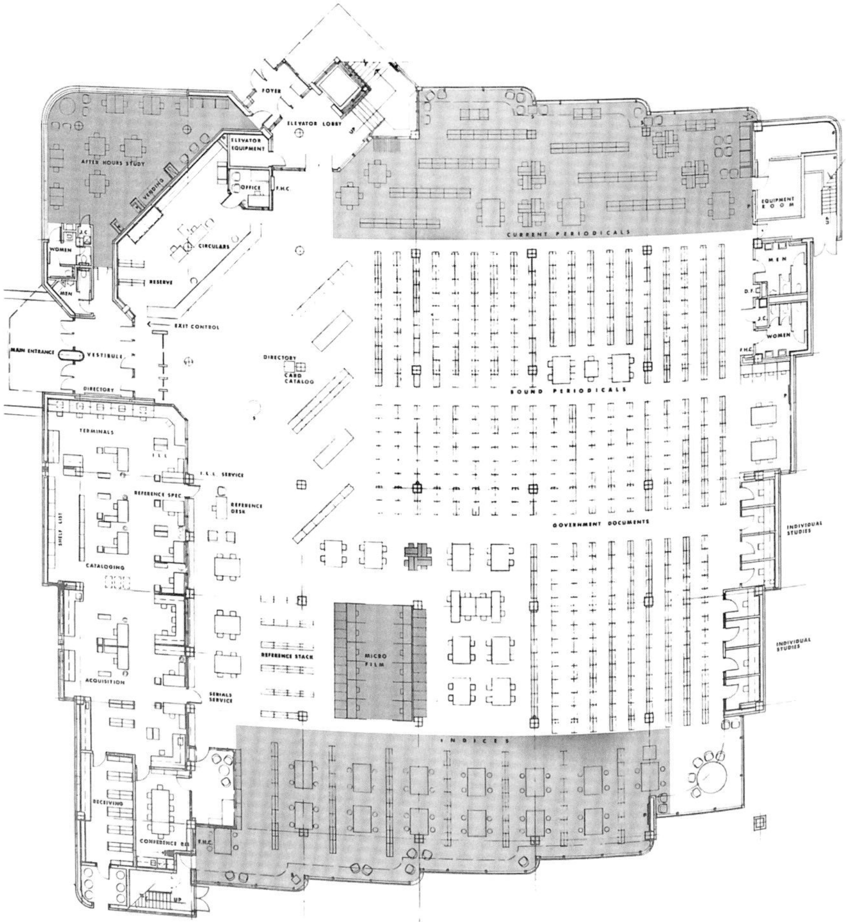

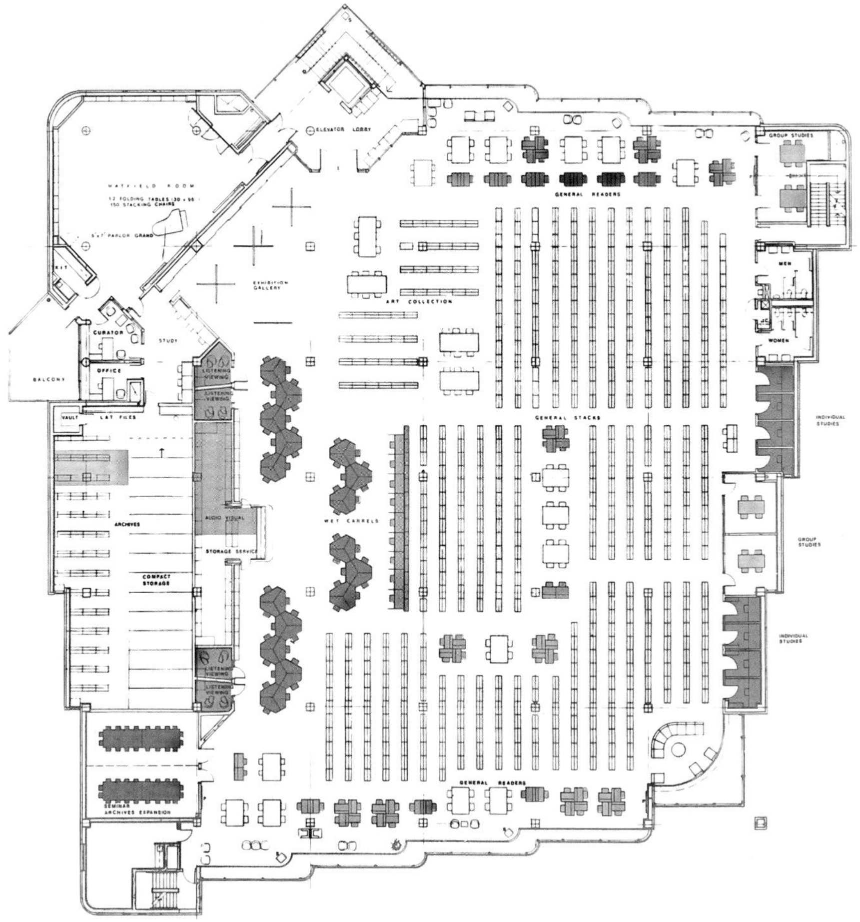

space. Finally, Wofford requested that the university hire an outside library expert to review the April 1983 plans and allay any lingering concerns of the library committee. That consultant, Andrew Eaton, Washington University director of libraries emeritus, judged the proposed library layout to be excellent, stating, "I am sure that your new library will be a functional and attractive addition to your campus."[19]

The revised plans that Eaton reviewed included both external and internal modifications from previous iterations. The main exterior change involved shifting the entry from the northwest corner to the center of the west elevation of the building. This represented a major reorientation of the library focus from addressing the quadrangle to an alignment that created a more coherent visual relationship with Sparks and Putnam centers. The change in orientation also related the ensemble of buildings more effectively with the reconfigured Mill stream. All were boxy, flat roofed, modernist structures that needed good sight lines between them to maintain the visual coherence of the southern portion of the campus. On the interior, the revised plan reviewed by Eaton included space for a 24-hour study room but no auditorium. At the time, Wofford also expressed himself "more comfortable with the tricky main floor relationships of reference tools and staff than I ever have been." With the exceptions of the final inclusion of a small auditorium and relocation of the special collections space for the Hatfield and university archives, the plans were set by the summer of 1983. The focus now shifted to fundraising for the library.[20]

Left: Floorplan of the Hatfield Library, first floor. **Right:** Floorplan of the Hatfield Library, second floor.

By the summer of 1983, Willamette was halfway through the $18 million capital campaign—"The Campaign for Willamette"—with almost $9 million raised. Renovations of Collins and Eaton halls had been completed and plans by the architectural firm of Settecase, Smith, Doss were being readied for a major overhaul of Lausanne Hall. By the time the administration broke ground for library construction, the cost for the building (which now had grown to 59,000 square feet), furnishings, and site development had risen to $6.5 million. Finding that sum proved very challenging. President Hudson had hoped to begin construction in August 1983, but large foundation grants were slow to come in. As part of the search for library funds, Hudson made a concerted effort to attract a major grant from the Olin Foundation (established in 1938). Money from this philanthropic organization was eagerly sought after by colleges and universities because an Olin grant paid for an entire building project. Such largess made Olin grants extremely competitive, especially since the foundation selected only one or two recipients a year. In fact, Willamette had made its first approach to the Olin Foundation in 1966, when it sought funds to replace Eaton with a new academic facility. Olin rejected this application, and the university tried again in 1977, when President Lisensky requested an Olin grant for a new library building. Again, the appeal also went nowhere. Undeterred by this poor track record, President Hudson renewed Willamette's request for an Olin grant to fund the proposed library and yet again came up empty-handed.[21]

The Board of Trustees and President Hudson, after the quest for an Olin grant seemed fruitless, took a new approach in the search for library funding. In a canny attempt to spur interest in the capital campaign and honor a distinguished former administrator/teacher and alumnus, they decided to name the library after Senator Mark O. Hatfield and house his papers, political memorabilia, and books in a portion of the building's second floor. The designation of the library as the depository for Hatfield's papers did help in attracting contributions, for as Hudson noted to Hatfield, "the presence of your papers gives historic significance and greater importance to the entire project and sets it apart for foundation funding." In fact, the largest gifts came from the Fred Meyer Trust ($1 million), the Murdock Charitable Trust ($1 million), the Kresge Foundation ($500,000), the Collins Foundation ($500,000), Grace Goudy ($745,000), and the Atkinson Foundation ($300,000).[22]

The decision to provide space in the library for the Hatfield archives and a performance/lecture venue entailed further redesign of the second floor and an expansion in overall building size to 63,000 square feet. Finally the dream of a new library became a reality with groundbreaking on April 13, 1985. President Hudson made it clear that as construction got underway, he would be in charge of the project: "Because it represents such a high institutional priority and because of my personal interest in the project, I intend to personally coordinate the over-all direction." As construction proceeded over a 16-month period toward a September 1986 completion date, attention focused on selecting and installing the latest in an automated, integrated library system. Orchestrated by Sandy Weronko, Willamette University librarian, this new technology was designed to computerize the card catalogue to achieve a fully automated circulation system. One of the benefits of the networked system was that it improved the research process, which depended not only on accessing the library collection but also being able to search other online databases and finding aids. Willamette became the first college library in the Pacific Northwest to achieve such a level of automation. It represented a groundbreaking

achievement. As Weronko put it, "I can't go to my colleagues and ask how *they* automated. *We* are the pioneers."[23]

At the library's dedication on September 4, 1986, Daniel Boorstin, Librarian of Congress, gave the main address, and other festivities marked the occasion. Attendees admired the library's expansive entry plaza and dramatic free-standing clock tower. Soaring 62 feet above its surroundings, the tower consisted of three components—an 18-ton concrete base; 49-foot steel, brick, and woven glass structure; and a copper roof and spire. Setting off the tower was a four-faced clock with carillon. Completed later (October 1989), the striking Mark and Antoinette Hatfield Fountain serves as the southern entrance to the library plaza and the final component of the library project. According to landscape architect Douglas Macy, the fountain was "intended as a modest yet important point of departure between the main parking lot and pedestrian core of campus and a focal point for pedestrians approaching and departing campus." The water feature consists of several large granite boulders (weighing up to 12 tons each) surrounded by a circular brick plaza base. Two bronze eagles, which represent peace, are making a nest atop the boulders and thus establishing their home on campus. Noted landscape architect Lawrence Halprin and sculptor Tom Hardy created the fountain and sculpture ensemble.[24]

The new library had an immediate, positive impact on the university. After a year of use, the facility had fully established itself as the intellectual heart of the university. Sandy Weronko noted that "this place makes people want to come to it. It is a very elegant building, but comfortable. It's not a monument. It lends itself to a variety of use that wasn't possible in the old library." Both faculty and students enjoyed the attractive reading and study space, especially the 24-hour room and private study carrels. On average during the first year of use, 1,000 people a day came into the library, compared with 150 a day in the old library. Circulation rocketed from 17,500 items in 1984-85 to almost 32,000 in 1986-87, the first year of the new library's operations. While some faculty lamented the loss of the traditional card catalogue, students rapidly embraced the new technology as represented by the computerized online catalogue.[25]

While President Hudson pursued library construction, he also pushed ahead with other campus

The Antoinette and Mark O. Hatfield Fountain that graces the entrance to campus near Putnam University Center. The fountain serves as a popular rendezvous point.

The architect's rendering of the Smullin renovation which incorporated Belluschi's library and Payne's Walton Hall.

Smullin Hall Renovation

While the end result of the rebuilding that incorporated the old library and Walton Hall provided much needed academic and administrative space, the exterior architectural details of the new structure are not entirely harmonious. A modernist opaque glass-and-metal grid center section awkwardly joined together the stripped Georgian brick sections on either end. In an attempt to visually unify the conjoined new and old elements, the architect Phillip Settecase moved the Georgian-styled cupola from the Belluschi part of the structure to the roof above the modern center section, which housed the main entryway to the building. Unfortunately, in its new location the cupola now seems out-of-scale and anachronistic above the modern glass façade of the center section. Moreover, the two-story projecting, plain brick portico, with its hint of the elements of a Palladian window, seems rather heavy-handed compared to the handling of the stripped Georgian detailing on either Belluschi's or Payne's older sections of the new structure. Still, the interior of the 53,000 square-feet of the new academic building—named after Smullin—fulfilled the goal of providing a functional home for five of the university's most rapidly growing departments.

improvements. He earmarked $900,000 in badly needed alterations to Lausanne Hall's interior. In the summer of 1985, the venerable old dormitory received new plumbing, heating and electrical systems; new windows and insulation; an upgraded fire alarm and sprinkling system; and new interior finishes. Hudson's biggest headache, however, involved finding proper space for a number of the university's thriving academic disciplines that suffered either inadequate or temporary quarters. Economics, political science, physiology, mathematics, and computer science all needed more classrooms and better faculty offices. As Hudson put it in one of his funding requests to the Olin Foundation seeking a $3.5 million grant to construct a 35,000 square-foot academic building, "The one significant academic building project that remains [after completing the new library] will be the home for the five academic departments that remain scattered around the undergraduate campus in less-than-desirable settings."[26]

Hudson was so desperate for the new academic space that he proposed that Waller Hall, beloved but needing structural upgrades, be torn down and replaced by a new building. Based on studies, he doubted that Waller could be renovated to meet the space requirements of the five academic departments requiring new accommodations. Once again, the Olin Foundation spurned Willamette's several requests for funding the proposed academic building. Hudson's final request to Olin presented a revised plan for a $3 million academic facility where the old library stacks had stood, which connected Walton Hall with the old library. The plan also included renovating and altering space in the old library by inserting a floor where the main reading room with its high ceiling had been. The loss of the main reading room in Belluschi's library was unfortunate. As art historian Roger Hull observed, "the break-up of the Belluschi reading room is one of Willamette's architectural tragedies. It was one of the most impressive academic spaces in the Northwest." The new, four-story structure would house offices and classrooms, while Walton Hall would continue to hold the foreign language departments. When Olin did not find this proposal attractive, President Hudson and the board sought alternative funding and construction occurred in 1987-88, after William Smullin, a Willamette alum ('29), donated $1.25 million toward the $3.1 million project.[27]

With the completion of Smullin Hall, Willamette could look back on a highly successful decade. By almost every measure, the university had achieved important accomplishments during the 1980s. Defying the projections that forecast falling enrollments and declining income, Willamette instead, over the course of the decade, increased its undergraduate enrollment from about 1,200 to over 1,500, while growing its endowment from approximately $35 million to $79 million. Willamette's operating budget remained balanced during the 1980s as well. In 1986, the university successfully completed its $22.6 million Campaign for Willamette, resulting in the renovation of two major academic buildings, construction of a new library, and significant improvements to campus landscaping. After completing the Campaign, President Hudson succeeded in raising the funds to convert the old library space and build a new structure for academic and administrative purposes. At the same time, Willamette's law school celebrated its 100th anniversary in 1983 with a growing program.[28]

Willamette also began, under President Hudson, to achieve national recognition for its academic quality in the 1980s. In 1983, a *U. S. News and World Report* survey cited Willamette as the best school of its type west of the Mississippi River. Additionally, in 1987, *U. S. News*, ranked the Atkinson Graduate School of Management as one of the five best regionally accredited business schools in the West and Midwest. The strength of Willamette's academic program and the school's increased recognition enabled it to increase enrollment and raise admission standards—a considerable feat in the face of the overall national decline in the number of high school students during the 1980s.[29]

Endnotes

1 University Planning Committee Report, Nov. 20, 1980, Smith Papers, Box 14B, Willamette University Archives.

2 *Collegian*, Sept. 11, 1980; Jerry Hudson to Members of the University Planning Committee, Oct., 1, 1980, Smith Papers, Box 14B, Willamette University Archives.

3 Frank Chlad to Dr. Robert Lisensky, Jul. 21, 1980, Smith Papers, Box 14 A, Willamette University Archives; Collins Science Renovation Budget Status Report, 12/15/82, ibid; *Collegian*, Sept. 11, 1980.

4 Collins Hall Memo for Dedication, nd. Smith Papers, Box 32A, Willamette University Archives; Summary of Cost Savings Effort for Collins Hall, Feb. 20, 1981, Facilities Records, Willamette University; Jerry Hudson to Dave Shawaker, Mar. 19, 1981, David Shawaker to Jerry Hudson, Mar. 29, 1981, May 13, 1981, ibid. (Hudson quote in May 13 correspondence is a handwritten note); Will Martin to Jerry Hudson, Feb. 27, 1981, Smith Papers, Box 52A, Willamette University Archives; *Collegian*, Sept. 4, 1981.

5 Hoffman Construction Co., Record of Construction Coordination, Collins Hall Renovation, Oct. 1, 1980, Facilities Records, Willamette University; Roger Hull to author, personal communication, Jun. 13, 2014.

6 Quote in *Willamette Scene*, Winter, 1982; John Matteson to Jerry Hudson, Jan. 26, 1982, Facilities Records, Willamette University; Jerry Hudson to Brian Hardin, Feb. 1, 1982, ibid.; Hoffman Construction Co., Record of Construction Coordination, Eaton Hall Renovation, Sept.- Dec. 1982, ibid.; Eaton Hall Renovation Budget Status Report, Nov. 11, 1983, ibid.; *Skyline*, vol. 14, no. 2 (Oct. 1983); *Collegian*, Sept. 17, 1981, Apr. 22, 1982, Sept. 16, 1982, Jan. 20, 1983.

7 Bill Braden to President Hudson, Mar. 1, 1982, Smith Papers, Box 26B, Willamette University Archives; Dean Berberet to Jerry Hudson, Jun. 24, 1982, ibid.; Jerry Hudson to Dean Berberet, Jun. 28, 1982, ibid.; Program Review Meeting, Eaton Hall, Mar. 9, 1982, ibid.

8 Jon Weiner to Jerry Hudson, Sept. 22, 1982, Smith Papers, Box 26B, Willamette University Archives; Hoffman Construction Co., Record of Construction Coordination, Eaton Hall Renovation, Oct.-Nov. 1982. Facilities Records, Willamette University; *Collegian*, Oct. 28, 1982; Jan. 20, 1983; *Willamette Scene*, Winter, 1982.

9 *Collegian*, Oct. 28, 1982.

10 Library Committee, Building Program Statement, Apr. 1980, 4, Smith Papers, Box 5A, Willamette University Archives.

11 Will Martin, Review and Analysis of Proposed Siting and Design Willamette University Library, Oct. 1980, Smith Papers, Box 39B, Willamette University Archives; Will Martin to Gerald Hudson, Oct. 13, 1980, ibid.

12 Pat Stockton to Jerry Hudson, Aug. and Sept. 10, 1980, memos related to library planning, ibid.

13 Ted Wofford to Jerry Hudson, Jan. 26, 1981, Smith Papers, Box 52B, Willamette University Archives; Jerry Hudson to Ted Wofford, Oct. 20, Dec. 31, 1981, Feb. 26, 1982 and Ted Wofford to Jerry Hudson, Nov. 25, 1981, ibid.; Ted Wofford to J. Douglas Macy, May 3, 1982, ibid.; Ted Wofford to Charles Weyant, May 3, 1982, ibid.

14 Ted Wofford to Charles Weyant, Mar. 15, 1982, Smith Papers, Box 39B, Willamette University Archives.

15 Ibid.

16 Charles Weyant to Ted Wofford, Mar. 22, 1982, ibid.; Ted Wofford to Charles Weyant, Mar. 26, 1982; Charles Weyant to Jerry Hudson, Apr. 5, May 12, Sep. 17, 1982, ibid.

17 Walker and Macy, Willamette Campus Development Plan, July 1982, Facilities Records, Willamette University; Ted Wofford to J. Douglas Macy, May 3, 1982, Smith Papers, Box 52B, University Archives; Ted Wofford to Charles Weyant, May 3, 1982, ibid.; *Willamette Scene*, Fall 1983; quote from an interview by Barbara Mahoney with Jerry Hudson, Aug. 2007, author's collections.

18 Ted Wofford to Jerry Hudson, Nov. 8, 1982, Smith Papers, Box 39B, Willamette University Archives.

19 Ted Wofford to Jerry Hudson, Feb. 18, 1983, Smith Papers, Box 39B, Willamette University Archives; Sam Hall to Library Committee, Feb. 25, 1983, ibid.; Andrew Eaton to Jerry Hudson, Apr. 11, 1983, ibid.; Andrew Eaton references, Apr. 11, 1983, ibid.

20 Ted Wofford to Jerry Hudson, Apr. 11, 1983, ibid.; Ted Wofford, May 4, 1983, Smith Papers, Box 52B, Willamette University Archives.

21 *Collegian*, Sept. 16, 1983; *Willamette Scene*, Spring 1985; G. F. Fredrickson to Jerry Hudson, Feb. 19, 1985 (Library Cost Estimate), Smith Papers, Box 39B, Willamette University Archives; G. Herbert Smith to Olin Foundation, Oct. 12, 1966, Smith Papers, Box 52B, Willamette University Archives; Robert Lisensky to Olin Foundation, Dec. 21, 1977, ibid.; Jerry Hudson to Olin Foundation, Jan. 19, 1981, Mar. 3, Apr. 22, May 2, Dec. 19, 1983, Aug. 13, Oct. 9, 1985, Oct. 28, 1986. President Smith and the board increased the Capital Campaign to $21 million in 1984, primarily to add to the endowment; *Collegian* Apr. 13, 1984.

22 Quote in Jerry Hudson to Mark O. Hatfield, Aug. 14, 1984, Smith Papers, Box 52A, Willamette University Archives; Ted Wofford to Jerry Hudson, Apr. 8, Jul. 26, 1985 (and attachments), Smith Papers, Box 52B, Willamette University Archives; Jerry Hudson to Charles Rooks, Nov. 15, 1984, ibid.; Fred Meyer Charitable Trust to Jerry Hudson, Jan. 15, 1985, ibid.; *Collegian*, Feb. 8, 1985.

23 Jerry Hudson to Sam Hall, Rosemary Hart, Brian Hardin, Jerry Whipple, Feb. 25, 1985, Smith Papers, Box 52A, Willamette University Archives; Sandy Weronko to Faculty and Administrators, Oct. 7, 1985, Smith Papers, Box 12B, Oct. 7, 1985; *Willamette Scene*, Summer 1985, Spring 1986; *Collegian*, Oct. 4, 1985.

24 Vic Gilliam to Jerry Hudson, Apr. 23, Jul. 10, 1986, Smith Papers, Box 52A, Willamette University Archives; quote in Doug Macy to Lawrence Halprin, Apr. 29, 1986, ibid.; Willamette University Historical Plantings, Memorial Site Features and Other Points of Interest, May 21, 2007, Facilities Records, Willamette University.

25 *Willamette Scene*, Fall, 1987.

26 Rosemary Hart to Lausanne Renovation Committee, Nov. 14, 1984, Smith Papers, Box 26B, Willamette University Archives; Jerry Hudson to David Chiappetta, Mar. 12, 1985, ibid.; Jerry Hudson to Jon Radmacher, May 29, 1986, ibid.; *Willamette Scene*, Spring, 1985; Jerry Hudson to Olin Foundation, Oct. 9, 1985, Smith Papers, Box 52B, Willamette University Archive.

27 Jerry Hudson to Olin Foundation, Aug. 13, Oct. 9, 1985, Oct. 28, 1986, Smith Papers, Box 52B, Willamette University Archives; *Collegian*, Oct 17, 31, 1986, May 8, 1987; *Willamette Scene*, Spring, 1987, Summer, 1988; Roger Hull, personal communication, Jun. 13, 2014.

28 Jerry Hudson to Olin Foundation, Oct. 28, 1986, Oct. 17, 1988, Oct. 27, 1989, Smith Papers, Box 52B, Willamette University Archives.

29 Ibid.

9

The Accomplishments of the Sesquicentennial Campaign

To extend the university's momentum into the 1990s, President Hudson led the university in a long-range planning process in 1988 that looked to 1992, the university's sesquicentennial. He posed the question, "What do we want Willamette to accomplish by its 150th birthday?" Hudson's and the Board of Trustees' answer was to announce a five-year $50 million campaign to increase the endowment, build and equip a $6 million science center, and renovate Waller Hall. Venerable Waller Hall, completed in 1867, had suffered two devastating fires in its lifetime, with major rebuilding after each conflagration. By the 1980s, it was in dire need of work to correct major structural deficiencies. The stairs and roof framing had begun to sag and the floors and main support trusses had deflected excessively. The building did not meet current code, especially for seismic loading. In short, the structure was unsafe.[1]

To deal with Waller Hall's problems, the board decided in May 1986 to spend $2.6 million for a thorough renovation. The project called for rebuilding the interior and adding a stylistically appropriate new south entrance facing the quad. While retaining and restoring the exterior, the architect Philip Settecase sought to correct deficiencies by replacing the existing wooden truss structural system with steel, which also freed up interior space above the second floor. To bring the building up to code, Settecase also replaced mechanical and electrical systems and installed an elevator. Another major repair required injecting cement and epoxy grout to fill the major void spaces between the inner bearing walls and outer brick veneer. The work plan also called for refinishing interior floors, wooden moldings, and the restoration of the stained glass windows. When completed, Waller's

Facing page: Waller Hall attic under renovation

Waller attic renovation in progress, creating the space that is now the President's offices directly below the cupola.

upper floors held alumni relations, development, and the president's office, while the second floor housed the chapel. As President Hudson put it, the work on Waller "allows us to preserve an invaluable part of our history and to rededicate the building to several of its original functions." The renovated Waller Hall was rededicated on October 20, 1989—the 122nd anniversary of the original dedication.[2]

While the $50 million Sesquicentennial Campaign focused chiefly on raising endowment funds for student scholarships, faculty and curriculum development, faculty chairs, and science and computer equipment, President Hudson also pushed for more academic and student facilities. His initial wish list for the 1990s included a centralized dining operation, another science building, and an addition to the law school.[3]

The administration had long known that its campus dining operations were costly and inefficient. In 1980, the administration had commissioned a food service study by the architectural firm Martin, Soderstrom, Matteson. The study found "food service at Willamette University has reached a critical stage. Rising costs and an inefficient, deteriorated food service system have collided with student expectations about food quality, variety and costs. The University and the food vendor, SAGA Food Service, are faced with the need to replace substantial amounts of kitchen equipment, to upgrade and streamline food preparation and serving, to reduce sources of waste and inefficiency and better meet the needs and expectations of students."

Based on their analysis, the architects recommended centralization of the university dining operations. They argued that a central facility, located in Putnam Center, would provide students with better quality, more choice, and less costly food. The university would be better able to utilize dining equipment, manage staffing and maintenance costs, and control utilities usage. Most importantly, having just one facility would improve the quality and freshness of the food. In addition, centralization would free up vacated residential food facilities for other student life and academic programs. Of the five food service alternatives considered, the architects estimated that a centralized Putnam Center dining facility would cost $2 million, while the other options ranged from $2.3 to 3.1 million.[4]

In spite of the obvious benefits of a centralized food service operations, many students were reluctant to give up the traditional living group/family-style eating arrangements. Fraternities feared the proposed change would erode their identities, while other skeptics doubted Putnam could be made over into an attractive dining facility. The mixed feelings on campus concerning such a radical change in dining arrangements, other pressing academic facilities renovations, and the need to build a new library, pushed the dining hall issue to the back of the line. By the late 1980s, the university maintained seven kitchens that served 14 dining rooms spread across campus in various living organizations and dormitories where students ate family style. Nearly a decade had passed; President Hudson decided to take up the food service question once again.[5]

In the spring of 1990, the university moved ahead with

its plan for central dining facilities with the two-fold benefits of improving the efficient delivery of quality meals, and creating an environment that would help to unify the student body and staff into a cohesive community. After interviewing three architectural firms, the President and board selected the noted Portland firm Zimmer Gunsul Frasca. Initially, the university wanted to expand and remodel Putnam Center to house a central dining operation and an improved environment for student life activities at a cost of not more than $4.5 million. As the architects tried to come up with a workable expansion plan, they soon realized it would be cheaper to build a new structure.

The decision concerning whether to build a new structure then led to the question of where it should be located. The best available site was between Lee and York houses on the south and Lausanne and Doney halls on the north. This location, however, required sensitive handling. The Mill Stream restricted the north side, while the area on the south required careful siting of any structure to maintain an unobstructed sightline from the Winter Street campus entrance to the central clock tower in the library plaza. The solution to making the proposed site work meant shifting the Mill Stream channel to the north by creating a slight curve or meander in it and designing the dining commons building with a narrow, linear footprint.[6]

Evett Ruffcorn, design partner at Zimmer Gunsul Frasca, had three architectural goals in mind in crafting the commons building. First, he wanted the structure to relate well to its immediate neighbors which reflected a variety of architectural styles—the Collegiate Gothic Lausanne and the modern Georgian Doney halls to the north and the Northwest/mid-century modern Lee and York houses to the south. As Ruffcorn stated, "I wanted the alumni to think the building was always there." Secondly, the commons would define a new campus quadrangle, encompassing

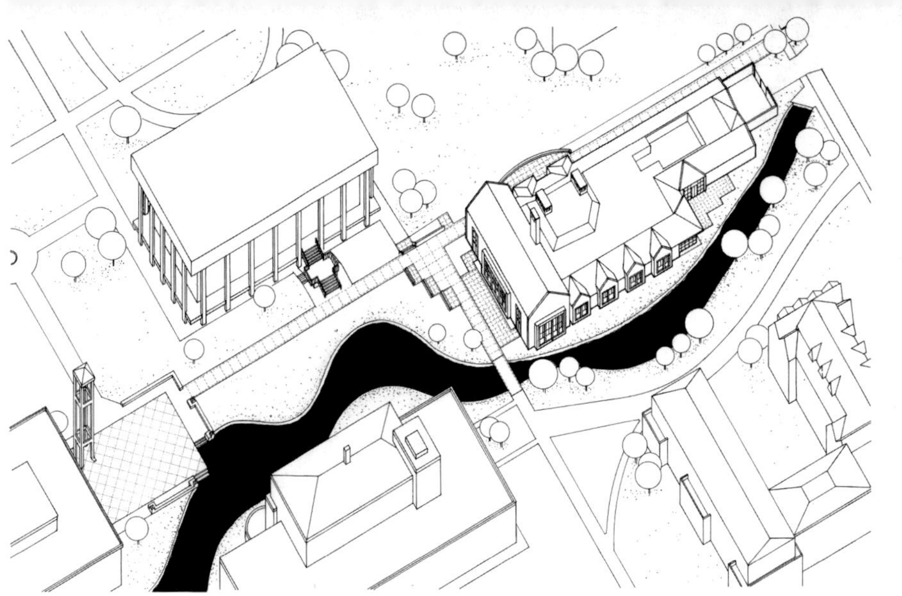

Architect's rendering showing the placement of Goudy Dining Commons. This inspired placement allowed the creation of a secondary quad, highlighted by the Mill Stream.

the back of Smith Auditorium, the front of the library, and the campus entry to Putnam Center. This goal required a building with massing that kept it low-key (as it related to its neighbors north and south), while still substantial enough to square off the quad (formed by large-scale structures). Finally, the building's form and scale had to indicate its function and draw students in with its warmth and airiness. Again, as Ruffcorn put it, "I wanted to create an inviting jewel box, a warm spot that offers sanctuary from the chilly, grey Oregon weather."[7]

To achieve his goals, Ruffcorn designed a single-story, brick veneer building with a long and narrow footprint. The building's north elevation, facing the Mill Stream, is broken up by five gabled bays with painted metal coping, each bay representing an interior eating space. The larger bay at the east end of the building contains the main dining room. The south facade has a modified hip roof over the main entry and a long brick wall, partially covered by a redwood trellis to break up the blank surface. The east facade has large windows under the dominant north-south facing roof gable. The west end of the building houses the service area with a walled driveway. The large windows on the east end of the building reveal a bright, wood-accented interior complete with a

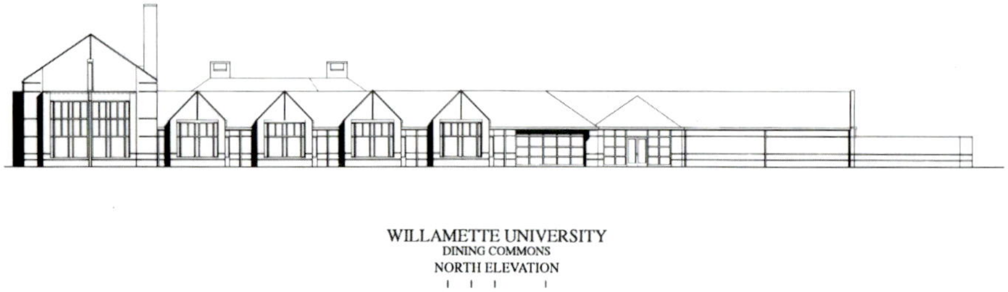

Above: Architect's elevation for the north of side of Goudy Commons and its realization. Note how the gables relate to the gabled roofline of Lausanne Hall just across the stream.

Right: The main dining hall in Goudy Commons bathed in light from three walls of glass. The East windows open to the secondary quad.

fireplace. Once inside, diners are invited to gather and greet in a spacious lobby area. Dining rooms are designed for flexibility, with five semi-private 75-seat dining bays and an outdoor dining terrace to provide a variety of eating environments in addition to the 300-seat main hall. In the serving area, diners can chose from a number of menu options available at separate stainless steel serving stations. After paying for their food selection, patrons can select from among the variety of seating areas to enjoy the level of dining intimacy they want. In all, the commons, named for Grace Goudy, a daughter of E. S. Collins and long-time benefactor of the university, was a hit with the campus community from the beginning. It even attracts diners from the larger Salem community. The 21,000 square-foot building cost almost $3 million to build and $1 million to furnish and equip.

Planning for renovating and enlarging the law school began in 1988. Although the existing law school building was only 21 years old, a growing enrollment and expanded public service legal programs had stretched the building to its limits. With an enrollment of 450, the law school had fifty percent more students than in 1967 when the building opened. The full- and part-time faculty had tripled over the years to accommodate the expanding number of students. As a result of this growth, the space for the law library, student facilities, and the Center for Dispute Resolution was woefully inadequate. The planned renovation of the existing building (46,552 square feet) and the proposed expansion (47,137 square feet) nearly doubled the size of the law school. The architect, Jon Weiner, of Soderstrom Architects, completed the plans for the $7 million law school expansion and renovation

in the spring of 1991, but unfortunately, all of the funds needed to pay for the project had not been raised by that time. With almost $4 million in hand, however, the board approved a bond measure, which provided interim financing until the rest could be raised from donors and foundations. With a large assist from the Collins Foundation and Richard and William Long, President Hudson secured the needed funds by 1995.[8]

By the time construction began, considerable effort had gone into scaling back the ideal project scope to fit the funds Hudson could realistically expect to raise for the expanded law school. To complicate matters, the architect estimated that inflation had increased costs by 15 percent over the four years of planning and initial design. With great effort by the architect and close consultation with the building committee (composed of administrator, faculty, and student representatives), the final plan achieved its objective—to enhance the quality of the legal education students received at Willamette.

The revitalized Collins Legal Center allowed for expanding the total library collection by 70 percent and greatly increased study spaces to serve a variety of student needs. Classrooms increased by 50 percent, offering computer and video capabilities. The architect designed most of the classrooms to serve smaller class sizes (18 to 60 students), based on a more interactive teaching style that had gained popularity in law schools. The layout of these flexible classrooms accommodates various arrangements up to 160 students, emphasizing good sightlines, acoustics, and comfortable seating. The moot court room also had instructional flexibility. The radically revamped and expanded library focused on making a high quality collection easily accessible to students. Law librarian Dick Breen explained, "By accessibility I mean things like good work space, adequate light, good acoustics, lots of seating, open long hours, and equipped with and for tools like computers." Because students spend so much time at the law school, the south addition contained many amenities, such as two large indoor lounge areas, lockers, a recreation room, and student activities and services facilities. Student input on the renovation was sought from the beginning of the project. As Wiener noted, "Students are the reason for

Above left: Interior view of a study area of the law library. **Above:** Amphitheater-style seating in one of the large lecture areas in the law school. **Below:** Student lounge area in the new south wing of the law school.

the school, of course. And not only do they pay a lot in tuition, they spend a great deal of time there as well." He continued, "The involvement of the faculty, students, and administration has been critical. I've never seen so much commitment and involvement. It's been an outstanding project to work on in this regard."[9]

The plan devised by Wiener and the building committee required that new construction and remodeling be carried out in two phases so that classes could continue during the work. The contractor built the additions in phase one, while the extensive remodeling occurred during the second phase. The law school temporarily moved its administrative and faculty offices and the Center for Dispute Resolution to the University House during the construction. Phase one ran from May 1991 to March 1992 and included the necessary demolition of the library building annex and construction of the new wings. Phase two, which took place from March to August 1992, focused on a floor by floor renovation of the existing building, while occupancy shifted to the new wings. The contractor made every effort to limit noise and disruptions during the construction and remodeling process. Even so, the noise could be deafening, especially when the demolition of concrete infrastructure or the erection of the steel frame for the south addition was underway. The contractor also had to take special precautions for fire, life, and safety requirements throughout the construction areas, since portions of the building were in use during work hours.

Clearly, the complexity and importance of the law school project demanded close supervision by the architect. As Wiener observed to President Hudson, "This is not an ordinary remodel; it is very complex. There are two different structural types at either end of the building. Each structural type has different details which adds complexity. The new construction connects to the existing building at two different points, creating a variety of circumstances. The ongoing operation of the school adds another layer of concerns. And, finally, the tight schedule leaves no room for error."[10]

Wiener's task required designing additions that would double the size of the existing law school while not overwhelming the character of the original building. The north addition, containing the law library, is about 6,000 square feet larger than the new southern section, which exclusively focuses on student activities. Wiener created jogs in his plan where the wings attach to the original building, allowing the two additions to be discernable yet compatible.

Willamette's sesquicentennial year, 1992, offered the opportunity to assess the state of the university and to measure the accomplishments of President Hudson's first 12 years. Hudson had begun his tenure in 1980 with a flurry of goals and objectives, covering all aspects of the university's academic program and physical plant. On the academic side of the ledger, his goals had been to raise tuition and faculty salaries and to increase faculty diversity. On the first two goals, Hudson could claim unequivocal success: Tuition had increased over 200 percent from $4,100 to $12,400, while salaries had increased, on average, over 100 percent. During that period, the CPI had gone up 80 percent. In the area of diversity, progress was more modest; more women had joined the faculty, but racial diversity still lagged. Overall, however, Hudson had grown the number of liberal arts faculty positions. To keep Willamette competitive, he increased student financial aid, especially for merit-based aid without cutting need-based support. Under Hudson, the college of liberal arts also established a business economics major, expanded the math/computer science program, and placed a greater emphasis on international

Law School Addition

Exterior shots and floorplan of the Law School addition. Wiener made nods in this design that honor the traditional Georgian design of the original building, while modernizing its sensibility. For example, the traditional Georgian cornice and balustrade of the original building are echoed, but not strictly duplicated, in Wiener's bolder, slightly flared cornice on the new additions. He applied a similar sensitive design treatment to the window arrangement on the new sections. The windows in the new wings, while varied in shape to accommodate the differing interior functions, are symmetrically placed on the facades and in proportion to the scale of the walls. Wiener also retained the overall sense of balance and proportion of the entire law school ensemble that is so important in the classical Georgian style by keeping the height and shape of the new additions in scale with the older center section. He further harmonized the new sections with the original portion by keeping the brick color and texture of the new sections identical to that of the existing building. In sum, Wiener's design for the new Truman Wesley Collins Legal Center nicely accommodates his modern Georgian additions to the traditional Georgian style of the original building. His work recalls but does not mimic the original features.[11]

Right: The exterior joining of the original Collins Legal Center to the south wing. **Bottom right:** Floorplan for the first floor of the expanded law school. **Below:** The south end of the law school addition.

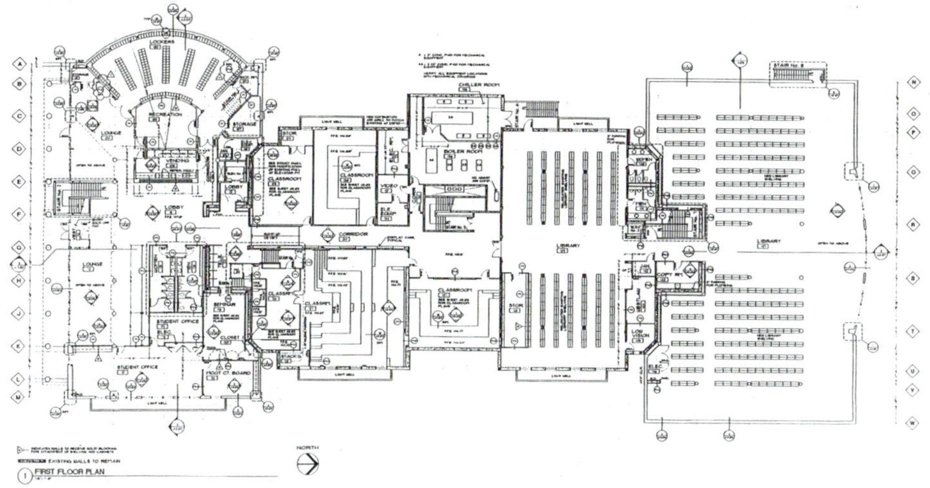

One of the campus cherry trees in full bloom on the bank of Hudson's Bay in the secondary quad.

The Growing Environment at Willamette

Despite being neglected in the early years of the university, the landscaping of the campus is now one of its stunning features. In addition to adding beauty, the trees and shrubs are also valued for providing shade to buildings, easing storm run-off and lessening erosion. The small specialized gardens and benches add outdoor study spots and places for quiet reflection. As of a survey done in May of 2015 (as part of her thesis), by student, Annette Marinello, there are 574 trees on campus, representing 112 different species.

A number of special trees were planted to honor individuals and important landmarks in Willamette history. The five sequoias were planted in 1942 (the centennial year of Willamette), the rose garden on the north border of the campus was established with 150 plants in 1992 in celebration of the sesquicentennial, and at the same time, a gift of 150 flowering cherry trees was received from Hishashi Heida (an honorary degree recipient and president of a Japanese television network). These major plantings plus the Martha Springer Garden and the intimate Japanese Garden add significantly to the beauty of the campus.

Willamette's relationship with the green environment continues to evolve. In 2008, the university purchased the 305-acre ecologically diverse Zena Forest ten miles west of campus. It is used in a number of ways, particularly by the sciences. On campus, best practices continue to be implemented, such as the swales used for rainwater capture around the newest building, Ford Hall. Formerly viewed as a beautification issue, the landscape at Willamette is an integral part of campus life providing pleasing outdoor living space, iconic symbols of the university, and a resource for biology and ecology studies.

Special thanks to Annette Marinello for her paper, Willamette University Campus Tree Map; A Resource for Education and Research. *Her interactive campus map can be found online with a Google search: Willamette University Campus Tree Map. Her thesis is available through the Hatfield Library at Willamette University.*

education with study-abroad programs. Hudson believed these changes made the university more attractive to prospective students.[12]

Hudson promised comprehensive facilities and landscape improvements. By 1992, much had been accomplished. Master plans for both buildings and landscaping had been completed early in his tenure. Specifically, Collins, Eaton, Waller, and Lausanne halls had been renovated, while a new library (Hatfield), dining commons (Goudy), and academic (Smullin) buildings were added to the campus. The law school was in the process of doubling in size. The Mill Stream was rerouted and turned into a pleasing focal point of campus, and a new bridge crossed it west of Smith Auditorium. Other noticeable visual improvements included removal of telephone poles and overhead electrical wires. Hudson had advanced these goals while maintaining a sound financial footing. He kept the annual operating budget in surplus through 1992, while tripling the endowment from $35 million in 1980 to $90 million in 1992. Solid finances meant that Hudson could offer more professional opportunities to the faculty, while increasing financial aid and improving facilities. Hudson believed, in its sesquicentennial year, that "Willamette should continue to be a small university built on a commitment to the liberal arts and engaged in career preparation and the enrichment of life of our students. It means we can take pride in each separate component of our university but acknowledge that all parts play a legitimate and vital role in making up the whole."[13]

Just as President Smith had invited a seasoned journalist to evaluate Willamette during its 125th anniversary, so, too, did President Hudson at the university's 150th birthday. The journalistic view from 1992 confirmed growth and development trends predicted in 1967. The emphasis on academic excellence as a small liberal arts university had not faltered, and Willamette's reputation for educational achievement reached well beyond Oregon. Over the previous 25 years, Willamette had achieved a larger, better paid faculty, more and better prepared students, and improved facilities. International study had emerged as a major opportunity not available in 1967. The beginnings of the relationship between Willamette and Tokyo International University started in the mid-1960s under President Smith and had strengthened over the years. In 1989, Tokyo International University opened a Salem campus across 12th Street from the Willamette campus with Willamette students occupying half the space in its dormitory, while Japanese students took courses at Willamette.

The journalist, Gregory Nokes, noted in his 1992 evaluation rather dramatic changes in the layout of the campus. Traditionally, the campus had oriented itself toward the State Capitol and the main entrance was from State Street. By 1992, the main entrance had moved to the south side anchored by a large parking lot and the Antoinette and Mark O. Hatfield Fountain. More importantly, the university buildings, through changes to their entrances, now opened to the quadrangle. In addition, a new, second quadrangle—surrounded by the library, student center, dining commons and Smith Auditorium—had taken shape. Willamette was halfway through its Sesquicentennial Campaign to raise $50 million that, if successful, would fund other additions to the physical plant.[14]

The final, primary goal in the Sesquicentennial Campaign was an additional science building. Collins Hall, built in 1941 and overhauled and expanded in 1962 and 1981, had again grown inadequate for current science instruction. The shortcomings only became more apparent with time as the number of science students and majors increased, faculty in biology and chemistry expanded, and instruction increasingly emphasized joint student/faculty research. Once again, in 1988, President Hudson applied for a grant from the Olin Foundation to construct a $4.9 million, 30,000 square-foot science research center that would provide more space for instruction and student/faculty research and better science equipment. As Hudson noted in his application, "A quality science education is an important part of a good liberal arts education. A truly liberating education must help today's students understand the increasingly scientific and technological world in which they live."[15]

By the time President Hudson applied to Olin for a grant, planning for the science building had advanced such that the science faculty were working with a Portland architectural firm to locate a site for the new structure and to develop a floor layout that would accomplish the science education program goals and identify equipment needs. Unfortunately, Olin was not yet ready to fund Willamette's building desires,

A view of Hudson's Bay from in front of Goudy Commons. The back of Fine Arts/Smith Auditorium is on the left, Putnam University Center is on the right, and the Hatfield Library is at the other end. The placement of the buildings, the water, and Jackson Plaza in front of the library create a pleasing secondary quadrangle. Jackson Plaza was named for Glenn Jackson, former Chair of the Oregon Highway Commission and friend of Senator Mark Hatfield.

The staircase inside the main entrance to Olin Science Center (off Winter Street) is a dramatic three-story space filled with light from the massive window bay.

continuing a twenty-year tradition of rejecting the university's overtures. Undaunted, Hudson continued his courtship of Olin, submitting three more grant requests for a science building. Finally, Olin acceded to Hudson's importuning and, in August 1994, signed a memorandum of agreement with the university to construct the new science building. An ecstatic President Hudson called the grant award "a monumental event and an exciting academic opportunity for our entire institution."

Hudson had doggedly pursued the Olin Foundation, in part, because he believed it would provide unimpeachable recognition of the university's academic quality and high standing among competing small liberal arts universities and colleges nationwide. Higher education institutions avidly sought the prestigious Olin grants. Hudson made this point in his winning application when he wrote,

> *Oregon and the Pacific Northwest are relatively poor in terms of the number of foundations and foundation assets elsewhere in the nation. An Olin Foundation grant to Willamette is solicited, therefore, for two reasons: 1) to fund this important project; and 2) to provide an endorsement of the University's quality that will prompt national foundations outside the Northwest to support Willamette and its [Sesquicentennial] Campaign.*

Certainly, Lawrence Milas, president of the F. W. Olin Foundation, seemed to confirm Hudson's view when, in announcing the grant on August 17, 1994, he stated, "Willamette University won the Foundation's support because of the excellence of its academic programs and the quality of its institutional management. Our grant will enable the sciences at Willamette to be at the cutting edge of undergraduate science education and to serve as a model for other liberal arts colleges throughout the country."[16]

By the time the agreement with Olin was reached, the size of the proposed building had reached 43,000 square feet and the total price tag for the building and equipment had increased to $7.1 million. As finalized, the Olin Science Center, designed by Jon Wiener of Soderstrom Architects of Portland, housed the biology and chemistry departments. It had 13 student and faculty research laboratories, 11 teaching labs, 13 faculty offices, 3 greenhouses, several classrooms, a computer study room, and the popular hearth areas where students and faculty could mingle informally. A renovated Collins Hall contains the physics, math, earth science, and computer science departments. Skybridges link the new building to Collins Hall on the second and third floors. One of the unique features of the science center is the state-of-the-art energy efficient HVAC system, which continually adjusts temperature and air pressure to the varying levels of building occupancy and the usage of the elaborate laboratory hood exhaust system. The building design places all offices and small research laboratories on the west side to take advantage of the view, while all of the large laboratories are located on the east side where the structural opening is bigger. The area in between

Olin Science Center

Wiener gave the Olin Science Center a contemporary design composed of brick veneer, Dryvit (a composite of rigid insulation and stucco plaster), and glass. The east exterior wall is mostly Dryvit. The west and south elevations are chiefly brick (lower three floors), while the north elevation is mostly Dryvit. The glazing is a standard double-pane glass with each window containing six panes set in a metal frame. The roof is flat and the flooring consists of concrete slabs, on grade at the ground level and on metal decking at the upper levels. The building nicely complements the adjacent collegiate Gothic Lausanne Hall to its south, continuing the brick on Lausanne – again showing Willamette's consistent effort to make the campus a cohesive whole. A distinctive aspect of the science center is its curved corner entrance, consisting of a large window area, brick plaza, and sculptural canopies. The ensemble creates an outdoor gathering place and a new entry to the main campus quad.

Architect's rendering showing Olin Science Center in relation to Lausanne Hall.

holds support spaces, customized rooms for technical instruments, and a hearth area for each department. At the science center's southwestern end, a dramatic three-story lobby and open stairway tie the separate floors together. When completed, the rectangular building covered over 44,000 square feet on four floors and measured 160 feet long and 82 feet wide.[17]

In making its grant for design and construction of the science center, the Olin Foundation retained considerable control over the entire project. The agreement with Willamette required the submittal, for approval by Olin, of all plans and specification, contractor bids and selection, construction change orders, and all equipment and furnishings necessary to complete the building. One clause of the agreement even stipulated that if the cost of constructing, equipping, and furnishing the building exceeded the grant amount, the university had to pay the excess out of its unrestricted funds; it could not use "funds received as a gift for this special purpose from any other person or corporation" to complete the project.

The new science center was solely Olin's gift, and they even had final approval of the building's name and any future changes to it. Interestingly, the process for construction of the science center was similar to that employed in putting up Eaton Hall, when in 1909, Abel Eaton had exercised total control over the erection of his building for Willamette and then handed the structure over to the university with the sole stipulation that Willamette had to have paid off all of its standing debt by that time.[18]

Work on the Olin Science Center began in April 1995 and proceeded smoothly until February 1996. On February 7 and 8, record rains led to the flooding of Mill Creek, which, in turn, caused the mill race flowing through campus to overflow its banks. The water flooded several campus buildings, including the first floor of the Olin project to the depth of two feet, seven inches. Significant damage occurred to drywall, casework, and mechanical systems. The contractor quickly arrived on the scene, built a levee to prevent additional flooding, pumped out the building, and made necessary repairs. Fortunately, insurance covered most of the damage.[19]

There was one structural casualty in the building of Olin. University House occupied the ground where the new science center would be placed. After careful study, President Hudson decided that the University House would be sold and moved off campus. Since the 1940s, the two-story Craftsman style house had served first as the president's home and later as offices for various university programs. The building was sold and relocated to 2340 State Street to be remodeled for low-income housing. While recognizing that the University House could not stand in the way of a badly-needed science center, art history professor Roger Hull nevertheless lamented the loss of "one of the last surviving residences from the era in which Willamette was surrounded by homes rather than institutions and traffic."[20]

While work went ahead on the Olin Science Center, the administration saw a need for additions and renovations to Putnam University Center and Sparks Recreation and Athletic Center. As stated previously, the Sesquicentennial Campaign was the main fundraising vehicle to carry out the extensive building and renovation plans begun in 1988. Initially, the campaign goal was set at $50 million to be reached in 1992, but new demands and early funding success led to extending the drive to 1995 with a new goal of $62 million. The campaign reached its new objective in February 1995, with $23 million raised for endowment, another $23 million for physical plant, and a final $16 million for financial aid and annual operations. Still, funding did not always arrive in synch with construction schedules, so the board had to devise an interim method of financing the building program. Taking advantage of the university's long-term financial strength, the board sold a $9.75 million bond issue in June 1991. The administration used the proceeds of Willamette's first public borrowing to temporarily finance construction of Goudy Commons, the Collins Legal Center, and the future renovation of Putnam University Center.[21]

Fortunately, alumni gifts paid for much of the addition to Sparks. The architectural firm of Settecase, Smith, Doss crafted a 10,500 square-foot addition, which their predecessor firm had originally designed in 1974. The addition included space for a new weight and fitness room, office space, two classrooms, new team locker rooms, a second-floor deck, an enlarged training room and an ADA-required elevator. Proceeds from a student benefit concert went toward new workout equipment. The whole campus community welcomed the improvements to Sparks. Athletic Director Bill Trenbeath noted that students especially were "anxious to have a first class fitness facility." The work on Sparks was completed in the summer of 1995.[22]

The renovations to Putnam University Center, largely paid out of the 1991 bond proceeds, included a 3,700 square-foot addition to the north side of the building, extensive renovation of the ground floor, and an upgrading of all major mechanical systems. The increased space allowed the enlargement of the Bistro (the popular student-run coffee house), the addition of a student convenience store, and a larger mail room and student lounge area. It also added to the bookstore's space. The renovation dramatically altered the south side of the building by demolishing the south entry stairs and the existing semi-circular driveway. The south lawn area was also regraded and a new south entry walkway added. The exterior changes resulted in the ground level rather than the second floor becoming the main entrance to the building on both the north and south sides. A major interior change involved removing the spiral staircase between the ground and second floors and replacing it with an elevator and U-shaped stairs.[23]

The Portland architectural firm of Zimmer Gunsul Frasca carried out the Putnam Center expansion in a very sensitive manner, carefully respecting the original architectural design. They achieved this by extending slightly outward the ground-level glass facade beneath the overhanging second-floor porch. This alteration kept the newly expanded area mostly within the building's original footprint, while adding 3,700 square feet of usable space. Anyone who did not know about the change, would assume that the building has always looked the way it does now. The contractor completed the work in August 1996 and the entire project cost $2.6 million.

Willamette had always had a few works of art that had been donated over the years, but in the early 1990s it accepted the gift of two major art collections. The receipt of the Sponenburgh and Paulus art collections forced the university to consider improving its storage and display of such items. In fact, a museum became a very real necessity. At the time of the gifts, professor and art historian Roger Hull observed, "What we need is a place where pieces in the Willamette collection could be displayed—a museum space—as well as an archives, some work space, study areas, and classroom space." He added that the proper housing and display "give(s) students a tremendous opportunity to study actual works of art, which is always better, when possible, than looking at slides." While the administration focused on the major projects for the law school and science center, Professor Hull kept alive the hope for a university art museum. In 1994, he presented a proposal to the university planning committee for just such a venue, but it would take a little more time to fulfill Hull's dream.[24]

In the eyes of one observer, it was Hudson's commitment to eventually establishing an art museum that would be one of "his major legacies to Willamette." With a $1.8 million grant from the Ford Family Foundation of Roseburg, Oregon, the university bought the US West building at 700 State Street for the Hallie Ford Museum of Art. Some supporters envisioned the museum as a "cultural resource for the entire Salem community," in addition to supporting the university's liberal arts curriculum. It would stage special traveling exhibits and display art from its permanent collections. In addition to the Sponenburgh and Paulus collections, the university had a significant collection of Native American art and artifacts, as well as important works by Constance Fowler and Carl Hall—two past Willamette art department professors.[25]

The university hired Jon Weiner of Soderstrom Architects to design a complete interior remodel with only minor exterior changes to the 1965 two-story International Style structure. The exterior of the building, designed by James Payne, is clad in marble

The exterior of the Hallie Ford Museum of Art on the corner of State and Cottage Streets.

The inviting lobby of the Hallie Ford Museum of Art creates a welcoming transition into the exhibit spaces.

and glass and has a brick garden wall along the front sidewalk of the building that creates an entry space apart from the busy street. Wiener's plans for the interior space of the 27,000 square-foot space created five separate galleries: The Carl Hall Gallery of Pacific Northwest and American Art; the Grand Ronde Gallery of Native American Art and Artifacts; a print study room and gallery; the Mark and Janeth Sponenburgh Gallery, which includes European, Asian and classical art; and the Henderson-Rubio Gallery, which is a changing exhibition area that presents a variety of short-term shows ranging from Northwest modernism to ancient art. The museum also contains an archive for research material related to the art collections; a classroom/seminar room; print, curatorial, and work rooms; and offices. Under the guidance of the director, John Olbrantz, the Hallie Ford has become a highly-regarded regional museum, launching a wide range of impressive exhibits.

Initially, to save money, the plans left the existing basement "as is" and two areas on the second floor unfinished. A large two-story indoor atrium brings light into the first floor galleries and allows for the display of large works of art. The openness of the floor plan permits the viewer to see the art in one place from several locations in other galleries and allows for easy movement among the display areas. An important component of the plans required insulation and a continuous Visqueen vapor barrier to achieve proper climate control for protection of the art collections from excessive moisture intrusion. The second floor also houses a 65-seat lecture hall. At the completion of the $2 million project, Hull believed that Wiener had "come up with a deft way of transforming a simple office interior into intriguing gallery spaces."[26]

While preliminary planning for the art museum got underway, the Board of Trustees, in May 1997, authorized the construction of the last major building project of President Hudson's tenure. They approved a new music facility estimated to cost $7.9 million. Since 1870, music education had been a formal part of Willamette; in that year the university established a school of music with the authority to confer a bachelor's degree in music. In 1880, the administration merged the music program into the Women's College and in 1887 housed it in the women's dormitory. In 1907, a donor bought, refurbished, and moved to the campus a Salem residence to use as a music building. In 1916, the board changed the operation of the music school, making it a part of the college of liberal arts and putting the staff on salary. (Until then, the head of the music school operated it on a contract basis, negotiating with the board to establish his salary and that of the music teachers based on a percentage of the tuition charged.) In 1941, the music school moved into the refurbished old medical school building. As the music program grew following World War II, the band and orchestra relocated into surplus military buildings moved onto campus for temporary use. Finally, these programs took up space in the Fine Arts Building constructed in 1955. In 1975, the entire music department moved into the Fine Arts Building, while the art department took over the old music department

building. By the 1990s, the music department, with over 300 students, badly needed a new facility. In particular, Smith Auditorium, designed chiefly to accommodate student assemblies and lectures, was acoustically lacking for the wide-ranging performance needs of the music department. In addition, the existing practice rooms and teaching studios were inadequate for both faculty and students.[27]

Initial planning for a new music facility began in 1996 after the music faculty analyzed current and projected needs to develop a preliminary program for the proposed music center. Then, architect Greg Baldwin of Zimmer Gunsul Frasca Partnership began serious design work in the winter of 1996 and early spring of 1997. The program called for a 500-seat concert hall, a rehearsal hall supporting both instrumental and choral uses, and soundproof individual practice rooms and studios. A computer classroom would offer new opportunities for music composition students. The plan also included a large lobby and gallery for the display of art. The architect coordinated closely with Wallace Long of the music department on the design. As usual for Willamette building projects, the architect struggled to keep within the budget.[28]

The spot chosen for the new music building promised several advantages to the campus but had a drawback as well. The music building was to be located on the existing site of the Bishop Memorial Health Center. This would put it between the playhouse on the east and the Fine Arts/Smith Auditorium on the west and the Mill Stream/Hatfield Library on the south, creating an eastern edge to the main quadrangle. In addition, a courtyard planned for the area between the Fine Arts building and the new music center would establish a sense of cohesion between the two structures. This connection was important because some music functions would remain in the Fine Arts Building. The courtyard also linked to the primary pedestrian corridor connecting the northern and southern parts of the campus, thus enhancing the overall unity of the campus. The university no longer needed to provide an infirmary, but regardless, the decision to place the new music center on the site occupied by the Bishop Memorial Health Center was not taken lightly. The administration consulted the Bishop family and named the new courtyard in the family's honor.[29]

The striking yet simple design of the 25,000 square-foot music center and the gracious way it relates to its surroundings make it a standout building on the campus. Greg Baldwin, the lead architect on the project, had very clear ideas about designing spaces for the arts. In the case of the music center, he believed that "music is the enrichment. Too much ornament would detract, just like a museum." Baldwin especially worried how the building would relate to its surroundings. It had to fulfill its internal purpose for making music and its external goal of welcoming and drawing an audience. Or as Baldwin phrased it, the building had to have the qualities of an "introvert and an extrovert at the same time."

A view of the quad facing southeast showing Rogers Music Center in relation to Fine Arts/Smith Auditorium.

Mary Stuart Rogers Music Center

The main section of the center's rectangular volume houses the concert and rehearsal halls. At the south end of the structure, the mass is reduced as a one-story linear section, containing the practice rooms and studios, extends toward the east behind the theater building. The building is clad in a warm-colored brick and has a long, ground floor, glass-walled lobby, which opens onto the courtyard. The upper portion of the brick facade is pierced with small, square glass-block openings that emit welcoming light at night. The hall's internal light also glows out from the narrow ribbon of glass bricks at the eave of the roof. The north facade has a two-story wall of windows that open up the rehearsal hall to the quad. This element made it possible to see the music being made and creates an attractive space for receptions, as well. The rehearsal hall's expansive glass wall also provides sound shaping; the glass panels are placed at precise angles, forming a series of three Vs above the three sets of double doors to achieve the desired acoustical result.

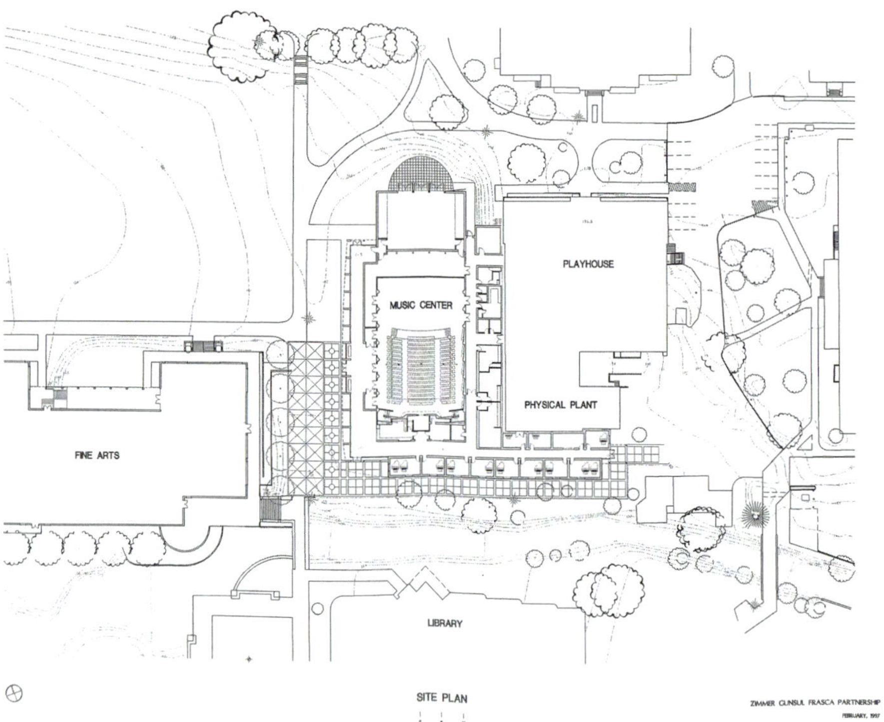

Above: The exterior of the Mary Stuart Rogers Music Center.
Left: The floorplan of the Mary Stuart Rogers Music Center shows not only how the concert hall (Hudson Hall) relates to the offices and practice rooms, it shows how the building itself relates to the Fine Arts building and the theater. The planners did a notable job of shoe-horning the building into a tight space. The building stands on its own, without it being overwhelmed by the mass of the Fine Arts building just a few feet away.

To achieve the maximum potential for good music-making, the building had to be opaque. That is, it had to keep music in and shut out external noise. Building proportions are critical in performance space, and the concert hall is the minimum size necessary to produce the needed volume of sound. The challenge for Baldwin was to scale the resulting box of 60 x 60 x 180 feet in harmony with its surroundings. Baldwin and his team, especially architect Peggy Tasker, accomplished this task by isolating the boxy concert and rehearsal halls inside a carefully scaled-down envelope, with its long, substantial face in context with Smith Auditorium across the way and best viewed from the southwestern edge of the campus. The inviting, transparent lobby is a convenient gathering space for patrons, while providing a visual transition between the concert hall and the outside. Overall, the building's clear, spare lines balance substance with intimacy and mass with accessibility to achieve the desired effect of harmony with its neighbors on the quad. "It's," as Baldwin observed, "a very quiet, reserved building."[30]

The most dramatic aspect of the building is its steeply pitched, 70-foot-high patterned copper-clad roof—which appears to float on the band of glass bricks. This is Baldwin's attempt to provide an appropriate scale to the building. He was afraid that with a flat roof the building would loom over the quadrangle and appear out of place with the surrounding buildings, all of which have sloped roofs. His approach to the music center roof also had acoustical advantages for the concert hall. The 45-degree pitched roof throws sound against the side walls into patterns which sustain reverberation. The rest of the acoustic treatment employed a number of devices to achieve first-class sound. For example, the walls around the seating area are battered to reflect sound upward to the diffusively shaped walls. The custom designed diffusing concrete masonry and millwork walls are made up of a number of wells, each with specifically designed depths. The sound is supposed to bounce out of the individual wells at slightly different times and result in a richer, livelier sound and an enhanced sense of spatial depth. To reduce the possibility of echoes, the inner walls of the concert hall (later named Hudson Hall) are slightly non-parallel, and the hardwood infill at the lower level of the walls, while primarily for acoustic purposes, also gives the room a feeling of warmth. Another active acoustic treatment is the computerized variable acoustic banners, which allow for control of the sound from a central podium as if the room itself were a musical instrument. As Baldwin described the acoustics, "Like an instrument, Hudson Hall can be tuned." The banners on the walls and fabric "clouds" between the catwalk and ceiling can be adjusted to accommodate a variety of performance groups, from choral to instrumental ensembles of varying size.

The interior design of Hudson Hall belies its basic shoebox shape.

The concert hall features fir wood as both an acoustical and design element. Baldwin remarked that he used fir wood because he "liked the way it ages." The fir-floored stage can accommodate up to 200 musicians. Considerable effort went into isolating the concert hall from exterior noise and fine-tuning the hall acoustically, especially to achieve clarity in the sound of the piano. A good measure of the music center's success in achieving a great sound is the main hall's maximum reverberation time, which at better than two seconds is considered excellent. The world-renowned firm of Kirkegaard and Associates served as the acoustical consultants on the project. The exhausting pursuit of acoustic excellence came at a high cost. While a typical office building might cost $75 a square foot, the music center ran to $300 a square foot.[31]

The Board of Trustees named the state-of-the-art

music center Rogers Hall in honor of Mary Stuart Rogers, whose foundation gave a major gift in support of the building. Several trustees and friends of the university provided gifts to name the concert hall after President Jerry Hudson. The construction of the Mary Stuart Rogers Music Center marked a fitting reminder of Hudson's commitment to the arts and higher education as expressed by the programs and facilities of Willamette University established under his leadership. When work began on the $8.7 million music center, art historian Roger Hull predicted it would be "a stunning addition to the campus," and so it is.[32]

In an interview near the end of his tenure at Willamette (he retired in July 1997), Hudson reflected on his accomplishments. While stating that "A commitment to academic excellence is essential," he was clearly "proud of the facilities" he built and of properly maintaining the entire physical plant. To remain competitive in the academic marketplace, he felt he could do no less: "Whether we would have been able to attract the students or have the quality program we have without putting investment in the physical plant is doubtful." Above all, Hudson wanted to be remembered as somebody on whose watch the institution became better. At least one knowledgeable observer believed he got the balance right. Former president of Whitman College (1975-88) Robert Skotheim observed:

> *When Jerry Hudson came to Willamette, he worked very hard to put Willamette on secure financial footing; he oversaw academic program improvements; he then went to work improving the facilities, and engaging in renovations and capital construction. All of this brought Willamette up-to-date, and at the same time returned the University to its historic place as a leading institution of higher education in the Pacific Northwest.*[33]

Endnotes

1 Quote in Jerry Hudson to Olin Foundation, Oct. 17, 1988 and Oct. 27, 1989, Smith Papers, Box 52B, Willamette University Archives; *Willamette Scene*, Winter, 1989.

2 *Willamette Scene*, Summer, 1988, Winter, 1989, Winter, 1990; Waller Hall Remodel File, Facilities Records, Willamette University.

3 *Willamette Scene*, Summer 1993.

4 John Matteson to Roy Ruffner, Aug. 13, Nov. 23, 1979, Smith Papers, Box 52A, Willamette University Archives; Martin, Soderstrom, Matteson AIA Architects, Willamette University Food Service Study, 1980, Facilities Records, Willamette University.

5 Martin, Soderstrom, Matteson AIA Architects, Willamette University Food Service Study, 1980, Facilities Records, Willamette University.

6 Brian Hardin to Facilities Committee, May 11, 1990, Facilities Records, Willamette University; Robert Packard to Brain Hardin, Jun. 20, Dec. 13, 21, 1990, May 7, 1991, ibid.; Zimmer Gunsul Frasca, Dining Commons, Willamette University, Design Development and Building Description, Mar. 5, 1991, ibid.; Douglas Macy to William Sobolewski, Aug 27, 1991, ibid.; Dames and Moore, Geotechnical Investigations, Proposed Dining Commons Building, Willamette University, Feb. 27, 1991, ibid.

7 Amy Milshtein, "Good Enough to Eat," *Contract Design* (June 1993).

8 Jerry Hudson to Jon Wiener, Mar. 7, 1988, Facilities Records, Willamette University; *Willamette Lawyer*, Spring, 1991; *Willamette Scene*, Fall/Winter, 1994; Richard Breen, Files and Correspondence Related to Law School Expansion, Binders A-F, Law School Records, Willamette University.

9 Jon Wiener to Jerry Hudson, Apr. 30, 1990, Jun. 12, 1990, Facilities Records, Willamette University; Jerry Hudson to Jon Wiener, May 29, 1990, ibid.; Jon Wiener to Brian Hardin, Aug. 2, Nov. 21, 1990, May 21, Sep. 5, 1991; quotes in *Willamette Lawyer*, Spring 1991.

10 The south addition had a steel framed structure, while the north addition was framed with reinforced concrete. *Willamette Lawyer*, Spring, Fall/Winter, 1991; Jon Wiener to Jerry Hudson, Oct. 22, 1991, Files and Correspondence related to Law School Expansion, Binders A-F, Law School Records, Willamette University;

Hoffman Construction Co., Renovation Schedule, Nov. 15, 1991, Facilities Records, Willamette University; Hoffman Construction Co. to City of Salem, Nov. 1, 1991, ibid.; Jon Wiener, Construction Specifications, Jul. 1, 1991, ibid.; Jon Wiener, Design Development, Nov. 28, 1990, ibid.

11 For the window layout, see Jon Wiener to Dick Breen, Oct. 29, 1991, Files and Correspondence Related to Law School Expansion, Binders A-F, Law School Records, Willamette University.

12 *Willamette Scene*, Winter, 1992.

13 Ibid.

14 Ibid, Spring, 1992.

15 Jerry Hudson to Olin Foundation, Oct. 17, 1988, Smith Papers, Box 52B, Willamette university Archives.

16 Jerry Hudson to Olin Foundation, Oct. 27, 1989, Sept. 14, 1990, quote in Sept. 17, 1991, Smith Papers, Box 52B, Willamette University Archives; For Future Generations: The Newsletter of the Sesquicentennial Campaign, Sept. 1994, Facilities Records, Willamette University; Memorandum of Agreement between F. W. Olin Foundation, Inc. and Willamette University, Aug. 20, 1994, ibid.

17 F. W. Olin Science Center, Celebrating Science, (n.d.), Facilities Records, Willamette Archives, Olin Science Building, Willamette University Campus, Baseline Building Description, (n.d.), ibid.

18 Memorandum of Agreement between F. W. Olin Foundation, Inc. and Willamette University, Aug. 20, 1994, Facilities Records, Willamette University.

19 Brian Hardin to Theodore F. Schultz, Feb. 26, 1996, Facilities Records, Willamette University.

20 *Willamette Scene*, Spring, 1995; quote in ibid., Spring, 1997; see also Jerry Hudson to Lewis Kanthack, Nov. 8, 1993, Facilities Records, Willamette University; Tom Stephens to Lewis Kanthack, Nov. 29, 1993, Feb. 11, 1994, ibid.

21 Willamette University, Annual Report, 1991-92, Willamette University Archives; *Willamette Scene*, Summer, 1993; Spring, 1994, 1995.

22 *Willamette Scene*, Spring, 1995.

23 Agreement between Willamette University and Zimmer Gunsul Frasca Architects, Putnam University Center Remodel, Dec. 6, 1994, rev. Mar. 15, 1995, Facilities Records, Willamette University; University Center Renovation Committee, Minutes, Nov. 2, 9, 16, 23, Dec. 7, 1994, Jan. 26-27,1995, ibid.

24 *Willamette Scene*, Spring 1994.

25 Ibid.

26 Ibid. Summer 1998; Jon Wiener, Art Museum Meeting notes, Apr. 10, Jun. 20, Aug 7, 1997, Facilities Records, Willamette University; Jon Wiener, Art Museum Specifications, Jun 20, 1997, ibid.; James Gainfort to Jon Wiener, Dec. 10, 1997, ibid.

27 *Willamette Scene*, Winter, 1994; Zimmer Gunsul Frasca Partnership, Willamette University Music Center, Program Summary, Dec. 1996, author's records.

28 Curtis Pence to Brian Hardin, May 7, 1997, Facilities Records, Willamette University; Bill Hutchinson to Wallace Long, May 21, 1997, ibid.; Zimmer Gunsul Frasca, Willamette U. Music Center Design Development Schedule, Feb. 21, 1997; *Willamette Scene*, Summer, 1997.

29 Program Summary, Dec. 1996.

30 Discussion of the design elements is based in part on the following: Amy Milshtein, "Willamette Rhapsody," *Contract* (n. d.); *Willamette Scene*, Spring, 1999; Randy Gragg, "The Big and the Small of ZGF," *Oregonian*, May 2, 1999, sec. E; Ron Cowan, "Willamette Debuts Music Hall," *Statesman Journal*, Mar. 7, 1999.

31 There is a lengthy correspondence concerning the acoustic refinement of the building in "Rogers Hall," Facilities Records, Willamette University.

32 Quote in *Willamette Scene*, Summer, 1997.

33 Ibid., Spring, 1997.

10

Moving into the New Millennium

President Jerry Hudson's achievements as president included more than campus improvements. In reviewing his accomplishments over 17 years as Willamette's president, Hudson proudly asserted, "I am a builder—I think building is important—but I would be disappointed if my legacy revolved around campus improvements. These were means only, and I was far more interested in the end that bricks and mortar would serve." He need not have worried, for his contributions to the university extended far beyond new or improved facilities. Throughout his tenure, he worked to attract and retain outstanding faculty, increased financial aid to create a diverse and intellectually strong student body, developed a strong international education program, and raised approximately $128 million to support his various initiatives. The theme that united all of Hudson's endeavors was, as he put it, a single-minded "pursuit of excellence." That was the charge that he would hand off to his successor, Lee Pelton. [1]

The new president arrived in time to oversee the completion of Rogers Music Center, Hudson's final building project. Fortunately for Willamette, Pelton brought with him a similar commitment to excellence. In his time at the university, Pelton would continue the broad themes of his predecessor, with special attention to improving the intellectual quality and diversity of the student body, achieving increased national recognition for Willamette, and continuing facilities enhancements. Pelton also recognized what the arts had to contribute to Willamette's educational experience.

The construction of the art museum and music center had reflected a major commitment at Willamette to the

Facing page: Oregon Civic Justice Center

Architect's digital rendering of the stylistically sympathetic addition to the art building.

teaching and performing arts as a key component of a liberal arts education. This might seem surprising, for in the late 1990s, fine arts majors amounted to only 10 percent of the college of liberal arts graduates. The emphasis on fine arts was a recognition, according to Lawrence Cress, dean of the College of Liberal Arts, that fine and performing arts "inform the lives of all students on a variety of levels in the classroom and beyond." While the arts maintained a relatively steady graduate rate, increasing numbers of students participated in music ensembles, theater productions, and studio arts, demonstrating "a pervasive curiosity about the creative process." In addition, the curriculum in the college of liberal arts sought to inspire and promote an interest in the arts. Faculty designed courses in various aspects of artistic creativity, promoting student discovery, exploration, and self-expression. To support the growing opportunities for pursuing creativity in the arts, the administration expanded the art building in 2002 and developed plans to renovate other performance and rehearsal spaces on campus, such as the theater and Smith Auditorium.[2]

The art department had long struggled to meet the needs of increasing demand for art classes. Between 1977, when the art department moved into the old 1905 medical school building, and 1997, the department had increased its majors by 40 percent and minors by 83 percent. During that time, the art building had not undergone a significant expansion. Finally, thanks to a $2 million gift from James F. Miller, a retired investment broker, Willamette remodeled the existing art building and built onto it a 6,604 square-foot addition. The new and renovated space (a total of 14,576 square feet) provided a painting studio, new classrooms with state-of-the-art projection equipment, student and faculty lounges, more offices, a student gallery, and a seminar room. In particular, the art building's spacious new annex created a well-lighted painting studio with floor-to-ceiling windows. As art professor Roger Hull observed at the beginning of the project, "By taking this historic building, renovating it and expanding it, we are preparing it for another century of use. The practicality of this is obvious, but the challenge is to remain sensitive to the historic nature of this building."[3]

The annex, as designed by Jon Wiener of Soderstrom Architects, accomplished the impressive feat of creating an addition that honored the original 1905 building, while quietly establishing its own presence. The new annex does this by maintaining the key style elements of the original: matching brick and masonry surfaces; using the same-sized wooden, double-hung windows; aligning the belt courses and cornices; and keeping the same roof pitches. The annex, moreover, defers to the original structure by being set back from it at the front elevation, having a slightly lower height, and connecting by means of a discreetly recessed glass atrium. The entire project, completed in the fall of 2003, cost $3.5 million. The overall success of the rejuvenated art building is reflected in the comment of art professor James Thompson that "students love the renovation, which gives us more space, more storage and safer, better ventilated environments. In painting, more students can work larger. In the printmaking lab, they can do different types of printmaking like photo-etching. ... Students can do digital imaging, video and web-based work. We also have all new photograph studios. ... It's really exciting."[4]

In the early 2000s, at the beginning of President Lee Pelton's administration, the university also undertook to renovate Baxter, Eaton, and Waller halls. The remodeling of these structures enhanced student recreation opportunities, expanded classroom space, and improved the structural integrity of a venerable building (Waller). The work on these buildings began in 2002, with the receipt of $2 million from the Montag family and $650,000 from the Collins Foundation to establish a 16,500 square-foot student recreation facility in the lower level of Baxter Hall. The renovation created a place for students to play pool, watch big-screen TV, play video games, do laundry, and have late-night snacks. It had comfortable furniture for socializing or studying. President Lee Pelton had recognized the need for improved student recreation facilities soon after his arrival in 1997, and the Montag Center filled this need. In planning for the center, administrators had sought input from various student organizations. As Jim Bauer, Dean of Residential Life during the planning phase stated, "There really isn't any aspect of the center that was not generated from the students' input." The center was planned to be open from 8:00 a.m. to 1:00 a.m. The exterior of the center also included a redevelopment of the landscape and other outdoors amenities. The university completed the project in 2002, and the students finally had a convenient space to mingle and relax, specifically designed for them.[5]

After Waller Hall, no building on campus had better symbolized the commitment over time to intellectual excellence than Eaton Hall. Since 1909, it had served as the center of numerous administrative offices and academic departments. When the administration began planning for changes to Eaton in the early 2000s, George McCowen, a history professor for over thirty years, remembered his early years in the building:

> *Eaton Hall today is both the same and very different from the summer of 1967 when I moved into an office there. It will be even more different, but still the same, with the addition of a fourth floor of modern classrooms and offices. In 1967, the building, in its semblance of Queen Anne architecture, presided like a dowager over the Willamette campus. On the first floor were located offices of the president of the University and the dean of the College of Liberal Arts, as well as the Registrar's Office, the business offices, the campus mailboxes and the campus telephone switchboard. In the '60s, Eaton Hall was truly the hub of the campus. ... In spite of its outmoded qualities and various inconveniences, the building had a spacious and inviting appearance with its high ceilings and many large windows with vistas of beautiful green lawns and the State Capitol. ... In the early '80s when the building was renovated, modern office and classrooms were built, some of which were designed for smaller classes. The halls,*

windows and high ceilings remained giving the building an air of spaciousness and dignity. The atmosphere in the building was now more subdued and studious.[6]

In 2003, the university carried out the first major renovation of Eaton since the early 1980s. This time the exterior remained unchanged, while the interior was renovated to take advantage of previously underutilized space. The project remodeled Eaton's fourth floor to create 9,000 square feet of faculty offices, modern classrooms outfitted with the latest media technology, multi-purpose meeting areas, and a storage room. The administration planned to relocate the departments of rhetoric and media studies and anthropology to the new space. This would bring a number of the humanities under one roof. The Salem architectural firm of Arbuckle and Costic designed and carried out the $2.5 million remodel, which also included some minor remodeling in Smullin Hall.[7]

The remodel of Eaton Hall presented a number of structural challenges related to such matters as seismic sufficiency, replacement of the roof, and location of mechanical systems. The university facilities committee also wanted to use sustainable design criteria (i.e., "green") in the project. To maintain the historic character of the roof structure, the architects kept the mechanical equipment inside the roof space and placed all of the mechanical and attic vents, as well as the fire access hatches, in such a way as to minimize their visual impact on the historic roof structure. Skylights, necessary to bring natural light into the remodeled areas, also were placed to reduce their visibility. Unfortunately, the Eaton Hall project considered, but opted not to restore the roof cupola and dunce's caps on the two turrets—all of which had been removed in 1966, supposedly to save on maintenance costs. Pressures to stay within the 2003 project budget apparently overruled considerations

Eaton Hall in a happier day with its cupola and turrets intact.

of historical integrity. Hopefully, these important, character-defining architectural elements can be restored at some future date, such as when the current roof must be replaced.[8]

In the summer and fall of 2005, the university carried out a renovation of Waller Hall. This $1.8 million project was carried out by Arbuckle Costic architects and mainly concentrated on exterior maintenance issues. Contractors repointed all of the masonry and replaced rotted window frames and casings, wood trims, fascia boards, roofing and gutters, and all flashings. In addition, the cupola was completely restored, giving it a new copper roof. All necessary wooden window replacements were in kind to meet historic preservation requirements. A seismic upgrade necessitated repairing floor diaphragms and wooden headers and stabilizing bricks. All exterior trim was repainted as well. As is often the case in rehabilitation work of this kind on a historic building, the contractor encountered unanticipated structural problems that required expensive and time-consuming fixes.[9]

By 2005, the law school once again was experiencing a spurt in growth. For three consecutive years, applications had increased 20 percent or more for an overall increase of 106 percent since 2002. During that time, the national increase for law schools was only 4.6 percent, but the College of Law's specialized programs had proved very attractive to prospective students. In addition, Willamette law students reported the best bar exam pass percentage in 25 years. While 85 percent of Willamette's graduates passed on the first try, the state average stood only at 74 percent. Donations to the law school also reached an all-time high in the early 2000s. Growing programs and enrollments required more space. With an eye to meeting that need, Willamette had purchased the 1912 Salem Carnegie Library building adjacent to the law school at the corner of State and Winter streets, in 2003. The university planned to renovate the building to house such programs as the Clinical Law Program, the Center for Law and Government, the Center for Dispute Resolution, the Center for Religion, Law and Democracy, the *Willamette Law Review*, and the Oregon Law Commission. Moving these programs would free up badly needed space in the main law school building.[10]

Unfortunately, after ceasing to serve as a library in 1972, the building had been modified internally and used for office space and other purposes. Willamette planned the renovation to recapture the building's original architectural distinction, while making it serve a new purpose as a part of the life of the law school. Since the programs to be located in the Carnegie building have substantial community outreach components and engage in similar or complementary activities, the architect, Jon Wiener (now of SRG Partnership), designed the interior to offer shared spaces. This design approach, he hoped, would encourage collaboration and collegiality among the various law programs housed in the building.[11]

The exterior renovation cleaned and repointed the bricks and cleaned the stone work. The project also replaced the roof, performed a seismic upgrade of the building, and repaired windows. The interior work removed non-historic alterations and restored crown moldings, hardwood floors, and other period details. Named the Oregon Civic Justice Center, the reborn library building created a civic space for the benefit of both the College of Law educational programs and the wider Salem community that used the legal services. The entire project, completed in September 2008, had a budget of $4.5 million.[12]

As President Pelton launched new academic initiatives and building projects that would help to win greater

The old Carnegie Library, now Willamette's Oregon Civic Justice Center.

Oregon Civic Justice Center

The former Carnegie Library is a handsome Beaux-Arts Style building with rich but understated architectural detail. The square, three-story, 14,350 square-foot building is faced with buff-colored brick with stone accents on the lintels and cornice. The front facade consists of a central projecting portico with a rigid metal awning, flanked by symmetrically placed, three-part, vertically divided windows on each level. Brick pilasters separate the windows and wrap around each corner. The sides of the building have a similar window-and-pilaster arrangement, although the side elevation windows are smaller than those on the front. This architectural gem, a significant part of Salem's cultural life in the first half of the twentieth century, is a fine example of historic preservation.

national recognition for Willamette, he realized that two other needs closer to home required action. It had been almost twenty years since the university had completed its last master plan, and relations with the Salem community also had been somewhat neglected. To remedy this situation, Pelton sought approval from the Board of Trustees to develop a new master plan that would facilitate future growth, while more actively sharing the university's unique resources with the larger surrounding community. As Pelton succinctly put it: "Philosophically, I believe colleges and universities cannot in the 21st century claim simply to be ivy-towered communities cut off from the society at large. Because universities and colleges have enormous human and capital resources, we have an obligation to share those resources with the community in which we reside." His establishment of the Willamette Academy, a program for first-generation college-bound students, is an example of this belief. In terms of the campus itself, he wanted the master plan to ensure that future buildings reflected the architectural heritage of the campus, to be flexible enough not to limit the needs of future generations, and to promote excellence.[13]

In the fall of 2002, the board selected the Portland architectural firm Zimmer Gunsal Frasca to develop the new master plan. As drafted, the key features of the plan called for establishing five residential commons to transform student housing, emphasizing an expanding the west side of the campus toward downtown Salem, restructuring of on-campus parking, and facilitating greater pedestrian access across university grounds. The plan was grounded in certain realities. Because a hospital complex on the south, the Capitol on the north, and a residential neighborhood to the east blocked development in those directions, expansion to the west remained the only feasible option. The master plan's ambitious call for a new performing arts center linking the Willamette and Salem communities and revamped campus parking reflected the resource challenges facing the university. Financing a performing arts center, even in partnership with the city, would require major financing, while relocating parking from the center to the periphery of the campus in either an above- or below-ground structure would be costly. Over the next decade, a difficult economy and other, more pressing priorities kept these two proposals in the master plan unfulfilled. Still, as Pelton noted at the outset, "the master plan is a living, organic document. It is a framework that provides direction based on principles. … It's not a plan that is written in stone. It will evolve over time as we develop new ideas."[14]

One part of the master plan that did move forward was the undergraduate residential program. With an $11 million gift from Tokyo International University of America, Willamette converted and enlarged Toyko International University's Kaneko Hall, which sits east of 12th Street at the end of the sky bridge, into Kaneko Commons. The expanded facilities include 500 beds, classroom and meeting space, and improved recreation amenities covering 160,000 square feet. This commons represents the first step in the new undergraduate residential concept, which ultimately envisioned five commons in total: freshman, three sophomore-to-senior commons, and a Greek system community. The idea envisions a vibrant 24/7 living environment with a live-in faculty mentor, faculty associates, and student preceptors to oversee academic programs, advising, community service, and student activities. Students are expected to play a large role in governing their living/learning environment, with a say in programming, budgeting, and enforcement of standards. "Our goal," explained College of Liberal Arts Dean Carol Long, "is to create residential communities that enhance student learning and increase the opportunities for intentional and reflective living." While residential commons is not a new concept to East Coast universities, Willamette hopes it will enrich its student's whole living and educational experience.[15]

During President Pelton's first five years at Willamette, the university had added substantially to its physical plant in ways that enhanced student academic and social life. The new buildings reaching completion included the Hallie Ford Museum of Art and the Mary Stuart Rogers Music Center. Eaton Hall was remodeled, the art building was expanded and refurbished, and Montag Center was created. In addition, the administration had received funding for the Kaneko Commons project. Fundraising efforts had secured a $19 million increase in endowed scholarship funds since 1998. Moreover, an 8 percent rise in minority student enrollment during that time meant greater educational diversity. Major investments were made in technology upgrades in both academic and student support operations. Pelton also made headway in his effort to advance Willamette's national reputation, as measured by recognition from the National Survey of Student Engagement prepared by Indiana University Center for Postsecondary Research and Planning and the *U. S. News and World Report* rankings. All of this progress came in spite of difficult regional economic circumstances.[16]

As awareness of global climate change grew, Willamette made a major commitment to adopt environmentally sustainable practices in its building and facilities operations. Part of a national movement among institutions of higher education, Willamette's efforts were especially noteworthy but not really new to the community. As far back as the 1980s, the university conducted energy audits of its buildings and implemented various conservation measures. After installing a computerized energy management system, the savings came to $470,000 in the first five years alone. Facilities crews bought environmentally safe paint and carpet in place of more toxic materials and proactively protected Mill Creek from polluted storm runoff. In addition, grounds crews began using natural applications to lawn and garden maintenance, using fewer pesticides and synthetic fertilizers. The Board of Trustees showed its support for sustainability in 2003 by endorsing green building practices for all new construction and renovations.

In November 2004, President Pelton established a 15-member, campus-wide sustainability council to push Willamette environmental actions wherever possible. One continuing example of such efforts was the campus food service's support of local farms and a focus on organic foods for its operations. By 2008, the university's environmental initiatives were showing good results. That year, Willamette's operations and maintenance administration won an award for reducing energy consumption and for recycling materials in renovation and construction projects for five campus buildings. During the same year, the National Wildlife Federation, after surveying 1,068 colleges and universities, declared that Willamette was the first in the nation for engagement in sustainable activities. The Federation noted that "Willamette is committed to energy efficiency and conservation, greener transportation, environmentally friendly landscaping practices, as well as to orienting personnel and faculty to the sustainability goals of the campus." Sustainability would be an important consideration in the design of the next major building erected on the campus.[17]

The planning for the new academic building, named Ford Hall in honor of its major donor, faced several challenges concerning location, sustainability, and programmatic objectives. The Board of Trustees had chosen the Portland firm of Hennebery Eddy Architects to design the 47,000 square-foot building. The architects proposed to honor the historic character of the building's surroundings and produce a long-lasting structure that would meet the teaching needs of five diverse but related departments. The chosen site at the northeastern corner of the campus has limited open space and sits amidst three historically significant buildings, each representing different architectural styles. To maximize space around the building for educationally-related outdoor activities and provide room for intersecting pathways, the end portion of the northwest wing of Baxter Hall was necessarily removed. This unfortunate amputation of part of Belluschi's building is a drawback to an otherwise successful effort to harmonize the modern architectural style of Ford Hall with its older, traditional style neighbors. The building is definitely of its own time, but it relates well to the others around it. Timothy Eddy, David Wark, and Doug Reimer, the lead architects on the project, accomplished this compatibility by careful use of massing, materials, color, and texture that reflect continuity but not rote emulation of style.[18]

In recognition of the university's strong commitment to sustainability, the architects wanted to create a 100-year building. They achieved this goal by using durable materials—brick, limestone, glass, and copper—and embedding sustainable design strategies throughout the building. These include easily accessible mechanical, electrical, and plumbing systems; operable windows; no interior bearing walls; and the use of recycled and energy-efficient materials wherever possible. One interesting example of the architects' commitment to sustainability was their use of all of the black walnut trees that had to be removed from the site. The trees were subsequently milled and the wood incorporated throughout the building in such elements as ventilation grilles, countertops, theater wall finishes, and ceiling slats. The south-facing portion of the roof contains a photovoltaic array, a technology first invented by two Willamette graduates working at Bell Labs, which provides renewable energy. The incorporation of a displacement ventilation system improves both thermal comfort and indoor air quality while saving energy.

The building design also allows for copious amounts of natural light from the north-facing clerestory and the large windows to flood the classrooms. The success of Hennebery Eddy's sustainability efforts is reflected in the fact that Ford Hall is certified LEED Gold, meets the 2030 Challenge for energy reduction, and received a first-ever 2030 Challenge Design Award.

The architects designed the interior of Ford Hall to accommodate the instructional needs of five departments, which include computer science, rhetoric, mathematics, digital art, and WITS (campus technical services). The instructional rooms are fitted out with the latest technology and emphasize flexible use, especially for small discussion classes. Picking up on the "hearth" concept that is a popular feature

Ford Hall at night.

Ford Hall

The reinforced, poured-in-place concrete, three-story modern structure is clad in warm-colored red brick with limestone details. It makes extensive use of glass with overhanging sunscreens, especially on the first floor, and employs copper extensively on the upper portions of the building's south and north elevations. The punched-out windows on the upper floors attempt to reflect the proportions of those on the south elevation of Eaton Hall. The set back, pitched roof made of copper recalls the pitched roofs prominently used on other campus buildings. The north side of the roof contains a glass skylight to bathe the interior with natural light. In keeping with the buildings around it, Ford Hall projects strength, but, because of its extensive use of glass, it also has an inviting transparency that breaks with the closed-off nature of so many older academic structures.

The glass writing walls in Ford Hall are the latest expression of the many hearth spaces found throughout Willamette's campus. There is also a glass wall to the right of the south entrance to serve as an outdoor whiteboard.

of Willamette's science buildings, the architects maximized the number of areas given over to informal gatherings, making them intellectual bridges between the classrooms and offices. Put another way, the "hearth" can be thought of as a third space apart from classrooms and dorm rooms in which students can live and learn. Glass walls at hearth spaces and seminar rooms invite creativity and sharing of ideas as informal marker boards and projection surfaces. Other elements emphasizing openness are the broad corridors that bisect each floor and the high ceilings throughout. In short, the interior space of Ford Hall is designed to promote collaboration for both personal and group interaction between students and faculty. After two years of use, Associate Dean Don Negri summed up the campus-wide opinion that Ford Hall's second floor "is the best example of exceptional educational design. Faculty and students love it ... and fill the space throughout day and night." Based on the success of the second floor hearth space, the first floor soon was remodeled to incorporate its key learning elements.[19]

While initial planning for Ford Hall got underway, President Pelton asked for an update of the existing university master plan. In 2007, the university hired Hennebery Eddy Architects to reexamine the 2002 plan with the goal of taking into account recent changes such as new buildings, land acquisitions, and proposed capital projects, while providing a fresh look at the overall campus. As the authors of the plan stated, "The Master Plan is both aspirational and practical. It is aspirational in that it increases defined open space on campus by over 150 percent and provides for potential expansion building square footage by 30 percent within the well-defined boundaries of the core campus. The path to this ambitious vision is outlined in practical, pragmatic steps." They went on to note, "The challenge to this master plan is to unify the University community within its expanded boundaries, but at the same time, to reach beyond those bounds to engage downtown Salem. This challenge is to be met in a manner that is flexible, yet is clearly supportive of Willamette University's long-range plan."[20]

The new master plan places a special emphasis on better defining campus open spaces, such as quads and other green areas. It notes that the green spaces south of the Mill Stream continued to lack "the clarity and campus qualities that the original campus offers." In this area, the plan proposes new housing commons and academic buildings. It also places more emphasis "on State Street, as currently the most prominent edge of campus, with the North Lawn, Waller Hall and Eaton Hall. The Art Building, Collins Science Center, and Smullin Hall also have a major presence on State Street. Recently the remodeling of the former Carnegie library into the Oregon Civic Justice Center and the addition of Ford Hall reinforces the State Street presence of the campus." It should also be noted that Willamette's presence on State Street extends farther west toward downtown Salem with the Hallie Ford Museum at the corner of State and Cottage Streets. Above all, the revised master plan encourages closing Winter Street and developing new green space at that locale to unify the campus. The intersection of Winter Street and Bellevue would become the new main entry to campus. Finally, the plan authors urge "further development of the Mill Race east and west of the center of campus [because] it will greatly enhance the already strong Spine [i.e. the Mill Race] to tie all the open spaces together on campus and beyond." The total plan aspires to "improve the facilities and quality of the campus for many years to come."[21]

Throughout much of its history, Willamette's landscape development occurred more as the result of opportunistic happenstance than from purposeful professional planning. Until the last half of the twentieth century, the university administration and Board of Trustees never felt they had the money to indulge in beautifying the campus grounds for their own sake. Plantings and lawn care in the early days resulted from the efforts of interested faculty, students, and alumni. In the early and middle years of the university's history, the 18-acre campus with an athletic field in its center did not offer much opportunity for grand landscape improvements. The situation began to change with the removal of Sweetland Field and the creation of a central quadrangle between Eaton Hall and Smith Auditorium in the 1950s. Next, the addition of over 30 acres through urban renewal and other property acquisitions in the 1960s and later began to present opportunities to rethink the campus layout. The long-sought removal of the Southern Pacific railroad tracks in 1980 also opened up new possibilities for greater landscape development. Willamette's first modern master plan in 1982 reflected the recognition of new possibilities and pointed the way to thoughtful improvements in grounds, pedestrian pathways, and utility placement and the reworked path of the Mill Stream through campus.

Along with an evolving interest in the campus landscaping, the university added a number of mini-gardens. In 1988, a team of faculty, students and staff developed the Martha Springer Botanical Garden. Located behind Sparks Recreation Center on the old railroad right-of-way, and named in honor of a long-time professor of biology, the planting consists of raised beds containing a variety of plant life. Some portion of the plan included a layout that suggested a garden sprout theme, such as plants used for medicine, each identified with a tag listing the plant's name, family, geographic origin, and other pertinent information. Other sections of the garden include vegetable plants, a rock garden, and numerous native plants. Another hidden campus garden, the Japanese Garden, was planted by the late Professor Germaine Fuller and art department students. It is located behind the Art Building, and offers a quiet, restful place to sit and enjoy attractive arrangements of plants and rocks. In commemoration of Willamette's 150th anniversary, the administration established a rose garden of 150 roses. Future graduating classes are allowed to add a rose bush to the collection so the garden will continue to grow.[22]

On the north side of Collins Hall, students from the class of 1942 planted a grove of giant Sequoias to commemorate the university's 100th birthday. They placed the trees in a specific formation so that when viewed from the center of the planting looking upward, the tops of the trees form the silhouette of a five-pointed star. Nicknamed the Star Trees, the

One of the benches to be found in the peaceful Martha Springer Botanical Garden. The garden is an exceptional addition to the campus, and beautifully enhances an otherwise awkward space.

university started an annual holiday tradition in 1997 by lighting the trees during the month of December. In 1992, as part of the landscape setting, Willamette installed a cast bronze sculpture, *Town and Gown*, located north of Waller and Eaton halls. It is the work of noted sculptor Mark Sponenburgh, who described it as a piece "created to strike a balance in keeping with the neo-classical character of the architecture of the campus and of the state Capitol. The broad planes in the sculpture—two townspeople and two academics—are intended to interrelate figure representation and nineteenth century period-style costume. To me it is fitting and fortunate that a salute to the oldest University in the West be celebrated in enduring sculpture form." Over time, many individual memorial features, such as trees, benches, sidewalk engravings, plaques, and flowering shrubs have been added to the campus. All of the plantings and furnishings accumulated over the years have helped to give the Willamette campus the special character and ambiance it exhibits.[23]

In the period between 1970 and 2010, Willamette carefully navigated the cross-currents of threatening demographics and challenging finances. It achieved national recognition for its academic programs, which emphasized the strengths of the liberal arts in a small university setting. In 2010, Willamette could boast of a student /faculty ratio of 10:1 and continuing commitment to close student/faculty research and learning opportunities. With strong leadership from its administration and Board of Trustees, Willamette maintained a balanced operating budget while raising the funds necessary to expand its facilities in support of its academic programs and enriched student life.

The approach of thoughtful renovation coupled with

sensitively designed new construction reflected national trends in collegiate building plans and designs. After flirting with eclectic, hard-edged modernism in the design of Putnam and Sparks centers and Atkinson School of Management in the 1970s, architects working at Willamette after 1980 generally employed a softer, more restrained modernist approach—one that showed respect for the existing traditional architectural styles on the historic campus.

Willamette never had the space or the funds to engage in extravagant or vanity building and landscape projects. Instead, it built sensibly and deliberately, stressing the lasting qualities of good architecture and planning. Recognizing the historical and architectural importance of Waller, Eaton, and Collins halls, as well as the telephone company and Carnegie buildings, Presidents Hudson and Pelton chose to sensitively renovate rather than raze them. New construction, such as the addition to the art building, Goudy Commons, and Rogers and Ford halls, took their design cues from the existing buildings. The university architects repeated the use of long-lasting materials, such as brick, copper, and stone masonry, and they paid careful attention to massing and siting, surface detail and broken roof lines, and sensitive integration of buildings within the landscape. Again, during recent times, Willamette—following the historic form of American campuses—continued planning its future growth in grounds and facilities so as to reach out and engage the broader Salem community.

For over 170 years, Willamette University's buildings and landscape have provided a harmonious, attractive, and supportive setting for the university's educational mission. For the years to come, the challenge would be to continue supporting that educational mission with new or refreshed buildings and grounds that respected the past but also looked to the future.

Town and Gown is located to the north of Eaton and Waller Halls.

Endnotes

1 Jerry Hudson, *The State of the University, 1980-1997* (Salem, OR, Willamette University, May 1997), 5, 6.

2 *Willamette Scene*, Summer, 1999.

3 Ibid., Summer, 2002.

4 Ibid., Fall, 2003, quote in ibid., Spring, 2005; Edward Allis to Jon Carder, Oct. 18, 2001, Art Building Renovation and Expansion, Facilities Records, Willamette University; Soderstom Architects, Art Building Renovation and Expansion, ibid.

5 *Willamette Scene*, Winter 2001, Winter 2002.

6 Ibid., Fall, 2003.

7 Ibid., Spring, 2004; Edward Allis to Brian Hardin, Apr. 1, 2002, Eaton Hall Renovation, Facilities Records, Willamette University; Lee Pelton to Brian Hardin, May 17, 2002, ibid; Alan Costic to Nick Allis, Jul. 2, 2002, ibid.; Committee on University Facilities, Minutes, Aug. 15, 2002, ibid.; Edward Allis to Don Negri, Sep. 23, 2002, ibid.; Edward Allis to Jeffrey Eisenbarth, Dec. 31, 2002, ibid.; Edward Allis to Linda Lombard, Feb. 18, 2003, ibid.; Don Negri to Lee Pelton, Jan. 31. 2003, ibid.; Fact Sheet: Eaton Remodel, Apr. 22, 2003, ibid.; Edward Allis to Jon Carder, Apr. 14, 2003. Ibid.; Final Decision of Historic Landmarks Commission, May 6, 2003, ibid.; Edward Allis to Jeffrey Eisnebarth, May 21, Jun. 30, 2003; Kim Arbuckle to Nick Allis, Aug. 12, 2003, ibid.; Nick Allis to Kim Arbuckle, Aug. 18, 2003, ibid.; Edward Allis to Jeffrey Eisenbarth, Dec. 31, 2003, ibid.

8 Ibid.

9 *Willamette Scene*, Fall 2005; Richard Rothweiler to Thomas Neil, Jul. 12, Aug. 2, 2004, Waller Hall Renovation, Facilities Records, Willamette University; Richard Rothweilter to Marjorie Mattson, May 12, 2004[5?], ibid.; Richard Rothweiler to Dave Pratt, May 18, 2005, ibid.; Final Decision of the Urban Planning Administrator, Review of in-kind historic window replacement, May 24, 2005, ibid.; Marjorie Mattson to Richard Rothweiler, Apr. 21, 2005, ibid.; Amy McFeeters-Krone to Marjorie and Dave Pratt, Apr. 15, 2005, ibid.; Arbuckle Costic Architects, Field Observation Report, June. 13, 2005, ibid.; Gary Grimm to Waller info Committee, Jun. 8, 2005, ibid.; BMGP Engineers to Jan Gardner, Jul. 11, Aug. 4, Sep. 22, Nov. 30, 2005, ibid.; Jan Gardner to BMPG Engineers, Jul. 26,2005, ibid.; Jeff Perrin to Jan Gardner, Oct. 13, 2005, ibid.; Jan Gardner to Richard Rothweiler, Jun. 23, 24, 2005, ibid.; Change Orders for Waller Hall Façade Renovation, Jun. 23, 2005, Feb. 27, 2006, ibid.; Final Billing for Waller Renovation, Mar. 24, 2006, ibid.

10 *Willamette Scene*, Fall 2005.

11 Jon Wiener to Jan Gardner, Nov. 15, 2006, Carnegie Building Renovation, Facilities Records, Willamette University; Carnegie Building Program Statement, Nov. 27, 2006, ibid.; Carnegie Building, Revised Program Statement, Feb. 21, 2007, ibid.; Jon Wiener to Jan Gardner, May 25, 2007, ibid.; Dick Breen to Jon Wiener, Jul. 24, 2007, ibid.; Interim Report: Oregon Civil Justice Center, Dec. 18, 2007, ibid.

12 Ibid.

13 *Willamette Scene*, Fall, 2002.

14 Ibid.; *Willamette Scene*, Fall, 2005.

15 Ibid., Fall 2003; quote in ibid., Fall 2005.

16 Ibid., Spring 2004.

17 Ibid., Spring 2007; quote in, ibid., Winter 2008. A good summary of the university's sustainability accomplishments can be found in Hennebery Eddy Architects, Willamette University Campus Facilities Master Plan, Feb. 8, 2009.

18 Ibid., Spring 2007; Timothy Eddy to Jeffrey Eisenbarth, Dec. 4, 2006, Ford Hall , Facilities Records, Willamette University; Hennebery Eddy Architects, Academic Building Program, May 11, 2007, ibid.; http://www.henneberyeddy.com, accessed May 28, 2014; William Willingham, Interview with David Wark, May 28, 2014; William Willingham, Interview with Timothy Eddy, May 30, 2014.

19 Don Negri, personal communication, Jun. 21, 2014.

20 Quotes in Hennebery Eddy, Campus Facilities Master Plan, 8, 19.

21 Quotes in Ibid., 26.

22 *Willamette Scene*, Summer 1991, Spring 1992.

23 Quote in *Willamet*te Scene, Spring 1992.

Epilogue

Fundamentally, campus architecture exists to assist the college or university's mission of furthering knowledge through teaching, research, and community service. To accomplish this, as architectural writer Richard Dober has written, "Campus design has to ennoble the past, enhance the present, and provide for the future by balancing continuity and change. Campus architecture implements these objectives through specific projects. … Good solutions must meet functional needs on a well-selected site, with creative responses to aesthetics and budget, and gain endorsement among those affected by the design." He goes on to argue, "The best designs are not imposed from the top but surface from consensus and participatory planning" and that there is no "single model or process for encapsulating higher education physically." According to Dober, however, the best conceptualization of campus architecture, whether "the search for and expression of diversity and distinctiveness, or a reaffirmation or reinterpretation of design continuity" comes "through collegial efforts." How does Willamette's architecture and landscape development measure up according to these standards?[1]

Until Pietro Belluschi entered the scene, Willamette's architecture was eclectic in style, largely following the fashions of a particular era. Hence, Waller Hall exhibited its period's taste for the Classical Revival, Eaton Hall represented a late Victorian attachment to the Richardsonian Romanesque, while Lausanne Hall embraced the early twentieth century fascination with Collegiate Gothic. The 1923 gymnasium embodied the clean lines of Waller Hall without its grace and tasteful detailing. All of these early campus buildings established a preference for structures of modest

Facing page: Woodcut of Waller Hall by Constance Fowler, who taught art at Willamette 1935-1947

scale, sloped roof lines, and simple materials—primarily brick exteriors with stone and wood stylistic embellishments. Willamette's early development reflected the typical evolution of the American collegiate campus as a cluster of disparate buildings built over time on open grounds. In the early twentieth century, those colleges and universities with ambitious plans for expansion and the cash to match created and carried out visually unified grand master plans based on specific architectural styles, often Collegiate Gothic or Georgian, for buildings and accompanying landscape. While nursing the desire for such schemes, Willamette, at the time, lacked the funds to achieve such a goal.

Belluschi, with his 1937 Willamette library, established a new paradigm that, with some variation in the 1970s and 1980s, has dominated Willamette's campus architecture ever since. His execution of a stripped or modern Georgian style, exhibiting clarity of design, attention to detail, rightness of proportions, and simplicity of materials set a high mark for succeeding architects. Belluschi's subsequent designs for a science building and a men's dormitory demonstrated that, in the hands of a master, the stripped Georgian form could be applied equally well to buildings with varying educational functions. His successor in shaping Willamette's postwar architectural development, James Payne, closely adhered to Belluschi's paradigm or framework in designing the auditorium/fine arts building, women's dormitory, health center, and a classroom building. Only in the late 1960s and 1970s did Payne and his partner, Phillip Settecase, break from the contextualism of the buildings grouped around the main quad. Payne's university center, physical education and recreation center, and graduate school building, located across the Mill Stream and on new land south of the original campus, employ a more expressionist modernism, marked by flat roofs, exteriors formed of exposed concrete and expanses of plate glass, and boxy proportions.

The important campus buildings that followed from the 1980s to the early 2000s attempted to relate to the best of the earlier designs, emphasizing a desire to return to contextualizing Willamette's later campus architecture. Taking design cues from the older buildings located in the immediate vicinity of the newly planned structures, architects such as Jon Weiner, Greg Baldwin, Evett Ruffcorn, and Tim Eddy carefully crafted new expressions of existing styles. In particular, they paid homage to roof lines, scale, proportions, traditional detailing of doors and windows, and texture and color to create an impression of the buildings being emulated. This design execution, at its best, is not eclectic but represents borrowings specific to the originals. Standouts in the application of contextualism are Goudy Commons, Olin Science Center, and Rogers and Ford halls. For example, Goudy's mass and exterior finish harmonize with its modernist companions (the library and the university center) to the east and south, while its roof line echoes that of its neighbors to the north and east (Lausanne and Smith Auditorium). For their part, Rogers and Ford halls pick up on key design cues of the existing structures that surround them, while expressing some of the best ideas of contemporary architecture. These recent buildings find something new to say about the older paradigm of campus architecture. The design relationship within Willamette's contexualized campus architecture is also achieved by careful attention to siting, visual connections, and circulation patterns. These factors are apparent especially in the secondary quad formed by the library, dining commons, auditorium, and university center. In addition, the design of campus buildings such as Olin Science Center and Ford Hall that creates open, transition spaces to facilitate creative thinking through proximity and conversation is spreading to public and private colleges and universities nationwide.[2]

Because Willamette's leaders insisted on building well by using good materials and workmanship, over time the university has been able to renovate its building interiors in response to the changing needs of teaching and research. In particular, Collins and Waller halls exemplify the lasting qualities of the older buildings on campus. As the teaching and research demands of the sciences changed, Collins Hall received additions in the 1960s and complete renovations in 1981 and 1996. To accommodate new classroom configurations and faculty office arrangements, Eaton Hall underwent interior updating and modification in 1983 and 2003. In the rehabilitation and reuse of both Waller Hall and the Carnegie Library building, the administration applied the principles of historic preservation, making those buildings able to support new academic purposes for the twenty-first century while remaining true to their original designs. Waller Hall represents the ultimate in survivability, undergoing necessary rebuilding after two fires and receiving various renovations over time to enable it to carry out almost every aspect of teaching and administrative work called for at a small liberal arts university.

Willamette University began in 1842 with one wooden building—called the Oregon Institute—on 60 acres of land. Over the remainder of the nineteenth century, while the university still consisted of one main building—now brick—its land base had shrunk to 19 acres. University trustees sold off land to keep the school afloat during hard times. Through most of those early years, University Hall (later called Waller Hall) was the university, as well as the location of the Willamette Academy, which offered the equivalent of a high school education. In fact, in its earliest years, Willamette taught the primary grades to the children of early pioneers before public education became widespread. Willamette's origins as a one-building institution of higher education was not unusual, as that was how most denominational nineteenth-century colleges and universities started.

Before construction of the Medical School and Eaton Hall, built respectively in 1905 and 1909, the campus consisted of a few wooden structures in addition to University Hall, such as the women's dormitory in a house moved to the campus in 1880, a gymnasium erected in 1895, and the Kimball School of Theology built in 1907. As improving finances allowed university officials to gradually add new buildings between 1920 and 1960, the 19-acre campus became increasingly crowded. In order to accommodate planned future growth, university presidents and trustees gradually increased the campus through purchase and urban renewal until the main campus reached over 50 acres. The university has continued to make small, strategic purchases of land and now owns 61 acres comprising the main campus, probably sufficient to support the academic programs for its current student body size.

Until the 1980s, the landscape of the campus was always a secondary concern. In the early years, insufficient funds prevented thoughts of beautification, and the campus had a rather unkempt appearance; livestock grazed on the grounds to keep the grass under control. From time to time, the university received gifts of trees and shrubbery, and alumni occasionally took an interest in adding flowering plants to the grounds. Over time, some faculty who had an interest in horticulture attempted to give the areas around buildings a more attractive look. Willamette's seeming indifference to the look of its campus was out of step with Eastern collegiate landscape trends, especially in the early part of the twentieth century, as some wealthier institutions of higher education developed elaborate master plans that integrated buildings and grounds.

Willamette became serious about the condition and appearance of its landscape as more land was added, the railroad tracks were removed, and the Mill Stream was seen as a malleable feature rather than a channelized barrier. Finally, in the early 1980s, Willamette commissioned a master plan to better integrate the buildings and landscape into a well-considered whole. Architects then designed subsequent buildings to take into account siting considerations, visual relationships, circulation patterns, and the proximity of the Mill Stream. Campus architecture truly came to embrace buildings and landscape in a holistic sense. By the end of the twentieth century, Willamette began applying sustainable environmental practices to better care for its landscape and buildings. These practices became a tangible demonstration of the environmental values taught in its course—instruction by example.

Willamette's campus architecture—both built and natural environment—and its employment of sustainable building and grounds maintenance practices carries on the tradition Thomas Jefferson had in mind with his plan for the University of Virginia ("an academical village"). It was his hope that by surrounding and exposing students to inspiring campus architecture, the lived educational experience would plant the seeds of a greater appreciation for good design and environmental awareness, along with the larger educational message of the institution.

In a very general sense, architecture is a social art rather than a personal one, a reflection of a society and its values rather than just a medium of individual taste. This study demonstrates that over time, Willamette has constructed buildings that have served well their specific academic functions and have been capable of renewal to keep up with changing pedagogy and technology. The best and most functional of its collegiate buildings, moreover, are not imposed from above but have been those that were conceived through carefully worked out programs derived by a collegial process that included all institutional stakeholders: donors, trustees, administrators, faculty, and students. Examples include the science facilities, university library, law school, Goudy Commons, and Rogers and Ford halls. Above all, Willamette is thankfully devoid of grand, out-of-context projects that only vaguely relate to campus history and the visual character of the immediate setting. Taken as a whole, Willamette campus architecture does evoke a strong sense of place worthy of respect, one that furthers the institution's historic educational mission.[3]

To ensure the continued vitality and viability of Willamette's campus architecture, the university developed in the first decade of the twenty-first century two master plans that embrace the design goals of contextualized place making and place marking for all future development. This approach will allow future buildings and landscape to continue supporting Willamette's educational mission and sense of place. In addition, just as the university uses master plans, it should also develop a management plan to identify and maintain the character-defining features of its architecturally and historically significant buildings and landscape. This will enable the university to address the issues of change and continuity surrounding campus architecture as it moves forward in time, for a campus is never really completed.

Endnotes

1 Dober, *Campus Architecture*, 166.

2 Alexandrea Lange, "Designed to Inspire," in *Education Life* (*New York Times*, Aug. 7, 2016), 12-15. Rosemary H. Camazzi, "Under One Roof," in *Oregon Quarterly* (Spring, 2013), 18-19.

3 The idea of architecture as a social art is developed in Witold Rybczykski, *How Architecture Works: A Humanist's Toolkit* (New York, Farrar, Straus and Giroux, 2013).

APPENDIX A

Table of Buildings

To effectively tell and interpret the story of Willamette University's built and landscape environment, I focused on the buildings and grounds encompassed by the 18 acres of the campus during much of the nineteenth and twentieth centuries, as well as the land added by direct purchase or gift and urban renewal in the 1950s and 1960s. These lands and the buildings contained therein constitute the heart of the historic Willamette University. Subsequently, the university has bought parcels of land to the west and east of the campus, some of which contained existing buildings. Most notable of these are Hazeldorf, used for student housing, the University Services Annex, and the building formerly housing the School of Education. Other structures, not currently in use, such as the old Salem YWCA are included in these additions to Willamette's land holdings. In one a case, a new building, University Apartments, was constructed in 1995 on the western extension of the campus. For any disappointment arising from not including these additional structures or other properties, I extend my apologies.

BUILDING	YEAR BUILT	ARCHITECT	MATERIALS	RENOVATIONS/ ADDITIONS	STYLE
Waller Hall	1867		Masonry/Wood	1890, 1921, 1989, 2005	Classical/Greek Revival
Medical School/ Art Building	1905	Walter Pugh/ Jan Weiner (add.)	Masonry/Wood	1941, 2003	Neo Classical Revival
Eaton Hall	1909	John Tourtellotte	Masonry/Wood	1982, 2003	Richardsonian Romanesque
Lausanne Hall	1920	Fred Legg	Masonry/Wood	1985, 1996	Collegiate Gothic
Gymnasium/Playhouse	1923	A. E. Doyle	Masonry/Wood	1974, 1979	Georgian
Library/Walton Hall/ Smullin Hall	1937/ 1965/ 1988	Pietro Belluschi/ James Payne/ Phillip Settecase	Masonry/Concrete/ Glass		Stripped Georgian/ Post Modern
Collins Hall	1941	Pietro Belluschi	Masonry/Concrete	1962, 1981, 1996	Stripped Georgian
Baxter Hall	1948	Pietro Belluschi	Masonry/Concrete	2002	Stripped Georgian
McCullough Stadium	1951	Pittsburgh-Des Moines Steel Co.	Concrete/Steel	1992, 1994	Athletic Facility
Doney Hall	1955	James Payne	Masonry/Concrete	1995	Stripped Georgian

Smith Auditorium	1955	James Payne	Masonry/Concrete		Stripped Georgian
Lee/York Houses	1960	James Payne	Masonry/ Stucco	1994	Mid-Century Modern
Mathews/Belknap Halls	1961	James Payne	Masonry/Concrete Block	1990, 2001	Modernist
Pi Beta Phi	1963	James Payne	Wood	1963	Suburban Contemporary
Shepard House	1963	James Payne	Wood	2001	Suburban Contemporary
WISH House	1965	James Payne	Wood	1995	Suburban Traditional
Alpha Chi Omega House	1967	James Payne	Wood	2001	Suburban Contemporary
Delta Gamma House	1967	James Payne	Wood		Suburban, Colonial Revival
Truman Collins Legal Center	1967	James Payne/ Jon Weiner (add.)	Masonry/Concrete	1992	Traditional Georgian
Putnam University Center	1970	James Payne/ Phillip Settecase	Masonry/Concrete/ Glass	1995	Expressionist Modernism
Sparks Center	1974	James Payne/ Phillip Settecase	Masonry/Concrete	1994	Modernist
Seely G. Mudd Building	1975	James Payne/ Phillip Settecase	Masonry/Concrete	1994, 1999	Expressionist Modernism
Hatfield Library	1986	Ted Wofford	Masonry/Concrete/ Glass		Contemporary Modernist
Goudy Commons	1992	Zimmer/Gunsul/Frasca (Evett Ruffcorn)	Masonry/Concrete		Contemporary/ Traditional
F. W. Olin Building	1996	Jon Weiner	Masonry/ Steel/Dryvit		Contemporary Modernist
Rogers Music Center	1998	Zimmer/Gunsul/Frasca (Greg Baldwin)	Masonry/Steel Reinforced Block		Contemporary Modernist
Ford Hall	2012	Hennebery/Eddy	Masonry/Concrete		Contemporary Modernist
Gatke Hall*	1902	James K. Taylor	Masonry	1938	Beaux Arts Classicism
Oregon Civil Justice Center*	1912	George M. Post/ Jon Weiner (renov.)	Masonry	2008	Beaux Arts Classicism
Thetford Lodge*	1947	Pietro Belluschi	Wood/ Glass	1963	Northwest Regional
Hallie Ford Museum*	1964	James Payne/ Jon Weiner (renov.)	Concrete/ Steel/ Stone	1998	International
YWCA*	1954	Pietro Belluschi	Concrete/Masonry		International

** Not part of Willamette University when built*

APPENDIX B

List of Illustrations

Chapter I

Chapter II

Chapter III

Chapter IV

Chapter V

Chapter VI

APPENDIX C

Heads of the Oregon Institute and Presidents of Willamette University

Oregon Institute Period

1. 1844 Chloe Clark Willson
2. 1847-1848 Joseph Smith
3. 1848-1849 James H. Wilbur, D.D.
4. 1850 Nehemiah Doane
5. 1850-1853 F.S. Hoyt, D.D.

After Incorporation

1. 1853-1860 Francis S. Hoyt, D.D.
2. 1860-1865 Thomas Milton Gatch, Ph.D.
3. 1865-1866 Leonard J. Powell (interim)
4. 1866-1867 Joseph Henry Wythe, M.D., D.D.
5. 1867-1868 Luther T. Woodward (interim), A.M.
6. 1868-1870 Nelson Rounds, D.D.
7. 1870-1879 Thomas Milton Gatch, Ph.D.
8. 1879-1880 Charles E. Lambert, A.M.
9. 1880-1891 Thomas Van Scoy, A.M. D.D.
10. 1891-1893 George Whitaker, A.M., D.D.
11. 1893-1902 Willis Chatman Hawley, A.M., LL.B.
12. 1902-1908 John Hamline Coleman, D.D.
13. 1908-1914 Fletcher Homan, A.M., S.T.B.
14. 1914-1915 George Henry Alden (interim), Ph.D.
15. 1915-1934 Carl Gregg Doney, Ph.D., LL.D.
16. 1934-1941 Bruce Richard Baxter
17. 1941-1942 Carl Sumner Knopf
18. 1942-1969 G. Herbert Smith
19. 1969-1973 Roger J. Fritz
20. 1972-1973 James Corson (interim)
21. 1973-1980 Robert Lisensky
22. 1980-1997 Jerry E. Hudson
23. 1997-1998 Bryan Johnston (interim)
24. 1998-2011 M. Lee Pelton
25. 2011-present Stephen Thorsett

Photo Credits

Unless otherwise noted, all images are from the Willamette University Archives.
Contemporary images are provided by Willamette's staff photographer, Frank Miller.

Chapter 1

The Tanner engraving of Jefferson's Academical Village is courtesy of University of Virginia library.

The two nineteenth-century township (General Land Office) maps were provided by the Bureau of Land Management.

Chapter 3

The master plan for Reed College is courtesy of the Reed College library.

The 1905 Bird's-eye is from the Library of Congress.

Chapter 4

The map of Willamette University and the civic plaza is from the Library of Congress.

The campus map is from the Multnomah County Library digital archives of *The Oregonian*.

The photo of Pietro Belluschi is courtesy of Tony Belluschi.

Chapter 5

The photo Meis Van der Rohe's Crown Hall is courtesy of Joe Biggott.

Chapter 6

Photos of Thetford Lodge are courtesy of Ross Stout.

Chapter 9

Photos of the Law School addition are from Soderstrom Architects, courtesy of Dan Danielson.

The view of the quad showing the relationship of Rogers Hall to Smith is by Bill Willingham.

Chapter 10

Photos of Ford Hall were provided by Michael Mathers.

The photo of the Civic Justice Center is by Bill Willingham.

Index

About the Author

William Willingham received his Ph. D. in Early American History from Northwestern University and has taught and practiced history broadly. His research and publications are in the field of early American history, water resources development, architectural history, historic preservation, and family and community history. His major publications include *Waterpower in the Wilderness: A History of the Bonneville Lock and Dam* (1987), *The Classic Houses of Portland, Oregon, 1850-1950* (co-author, 1999), *Starting Over: Community Building on the Eastern Oregon Frontier* (2005), *Two Centuries of Experience in Water Resources Management: A Dutch-U.S. Retrospective* (co-author and editor, 2014), *Grit and Ink: An Oregon Family's Adventures in Newspapering, 1908-2018* (2018).